Ideas that shape politics

Ideas are the essence of politics: the means of debate, the inspiration for organisation, and the reason for conflict. This book interprets the most prominent of them to provide students with a handbook of political thinking in the late twentieth century. In a series of original essays distinguished writers analyse particular ideas according to their capacity to motivate and justify political action.

Ideas that shape politics will be essential reading for all students of politics as well as for all thoughtful citizens who care about politics.

Michael Foley is Professor of International Politics at the University of Wales, Aberystwyth.

Dedicated to the memory of Aaron Wildavsky (1930–1993)

Ideas that shape politics

edited by Michael Foley

Manchester University Press
Manchester and New York

Distributed exclusively in the USA and Canada by St Martin's Press

Published by Manchester University Press
Oxford Road, Manchester M13 9NR, UK
and Room 400, 175 Fifth Avenue,
New York, NY 10010, USA

Distributed exclusively in the USA and Canada
by St. Martin's Press, Inc.,
175 Fifth Avenue, New York, NY 10010, USA

British Library Cataloguing-in-Publication Data
A catalogue record for this book is available from the British Library

Library of Congress Cataloging-in-Publication Data
Ideas that shape politics / edited by Michael Foley.
    p. cm.
   ISBN 0–7190–3824–3. — ISBN 0–7190–3825–1 (pbk.)
   1. Political science—Philosophy. 2. Ideology. I. Foley,
Michael, 1948– .
JA74.I24 1994
320.5—dc20   94–16672
                          CIP

ISBN 0 7190 3824 3 *hardback*
ISBN 0 7190 3825 1 *paperback*

Photoset in Linotron Ehrhardt
by Northern Phototypesetting Co. Ltd., Bolton

Printed in Great Britain
by Redwood Books, Trowbridge

Contents

Contributors

Rt. Hon. Paddy Ashdown is Member of Parliament for Yeovil and Leader of the Liberal Democrat Party

Nazih Ayubi is a Reader in Politics at the University of Exeter

Richard Bellamy is Professor of Politics at the University of East Anglia

Sarah Benton, previously Political Editor for the *New Statesman and Society* and researcher for the Institute of Public Policy Research, is now a freelance journalist

Peter Calvert is Professor of Comparative and International Politics at the University of Southampton

Paul Cammack is a Senior Lecturer in Government at the University of Manchester

Terrell Carver is a Reader in Political Theory at the University of Bristol

Stephen Chan is Director of the United Kingdom London Centre of International Relations

Stuart Croft is a Senior Lecturer in Security Studies at the University of Birmingham

Andrew Dobson is Professor of Politics at the University of Keele

Michael Foley is Professor of International Politics at the University of Wales, Aberystwyth

Michael Freeman is a Senior Lecturer in Political Theory at the University of Essex. He is also Deputy Director of the Human Rights Centre at the University of Essex

Bryan Gould was Labour Member of Parliament for Dagenham at the time of writing

Eric Herring is a Lecturer in Politics at the University of Bristol

Alan James is Professor of International Relations at the University of Keele

Brigid Laffan is Jean Monnet Professor of European Politics at University College, Dublin

Philip Norton is Professor of Politics at the University of Hull

Philip Payton is Director of the Institute of Cornish Studies
Joel Peters is a Lecturer in Politics at the University of Reading
James Piscatori is Professor of International Politics at the University of Wales, Aberystwyth
Rachel Walker is a Lecturer in Russian Politics at the University of Essex
Aaron Wildavsky was, until his death in 1993, Professor of Political and Public Policy at the University of California, Berkeley
Paul Wilkinson is Professor of International Relations at the University of St Andrews
David Willetts is Conservative Member of Parliament for Havant

Acknowledgements

Editing a book with so many contributions required a team effort. I was given invaluable assistance in the drafting and redrafting of letters and contributions by Donna Griffin, Doreen Hamer and Elaine Lowe. I am also indebted to all those at Manchester University Press who helped to bring order and organisation to the creative processes of the project's participants. Pauline Leng, Jane Hammond Foster, Anne Hegerty and Elaine White are all owed a debt of gratitude. Particular thanks go to Richard Purslow and Celia Ashcroft who provided a great deal of encouragement, guidance and active support from the time of the book's inception to its completion. Finally, I must give due recognition to the team of contributors. Each had different pressures, and yet each approached the task in hand with a spirit of open enquiry and collaborative understanding. To those who were prepared to share their thoughts so lucidly and concisely, and to the many families and friends who supported them in doing so, my thanks.

Aaron Wildavsky was too unwell to finish the contribution on egalitarianism. He asked me to draw together the various pieces of material he planned to use for the essay. Any deficiencies in organisation or style, therefore, should be attributed to the editor. The substance, on the other hand, is the genuine article. It has the stamp of originality and insight that always characterised the work of the late Aaron Wildavsky.

Michael Foley

Michael Foley

Introduction

Anyone who is following a course of study in politics, or who may simply be interested in the forces that shape the contemporary world, is confronted by a bewildering array of terms that are used to denote the existence of distinct arrangements of political thought. Such terms are used substantively by participants and analysts alike. They are deployed as active ingredients in the organisation and classification of political conflict. The conditions and effect of their usage amount to the force of ideas in action – ideas that make sense of experiences; arouse and direct social consciousness; provide objectives to be sought; and prompt action in their pursuit.

This book is concerned with ideas that are closely implicated in political argument, understanding and action. It is about ideas that can draw disparate thoughts, experiences and impulses together, and transform them into positions of political engagement – each with their own political properties and each providing a distinctive contribution to the organisation of political dispute. Such ideas are used consciously and intuitively, by participants and analysts alike, as substantive deployments of meaning. They constitute the active ingredients in the organisation of experience and in the interplay of political positions.

It is very common for the existence of argument to be acknowledged. It is very uncommon for the ideas, concepts and beliefs that inform and structure such debate to be drawn together and subjected to rigorous enquiry and appraisal. It is true that a profusion of studies has examined the origins and historical development of ideas, together with their systematisation into ideologies. It is also true that the study of political issues and action and the development of political movements is an established genre of political enquiry. Far less common are attempts to link political ideas and action together on a broad and contemporary front in such a way as to provide a grasp of both their mutual and multiple relationships at any given time in different parts of the world.

This collection of interpretive essays is an attempt to correct the imbalance and to give emphasis to the actual usage and ramifications of ideas in contemporary politics, rather than on their evolutionary development, or their compositional integrity, or their intrinsic normative value. The objective is to examine those ideas that have shaped politics over the second half of the twentieth century and which will condition the issues, agendas and political responses of the next century. The main concern, therefore, is with those currents of political thought that have been instrumental in motivating and justifying political action.

Although the book is absorbed with ideas, it is not preoccupied with surveying the nature and content of ideologies, or with making speculative expositions on the meaning of ideology and what is, or is not, an ideology. The study is not primarily concerned with politics at a high level of abstraction. This is not to say that political philosophy is of secondary importance. The systematic analysis of concepts, the evaluation of their relationships with one another and with political circumstances in general, and the provision of moral and ethical judgements are of profound and fundamental significance to the understanding of politics. Nevertheless, political philosophy is a beast of heavy burden. Its chief benefit lies in the slow accumulation of logical and moral argument to establish valuable, but generalised, claims to 'truth'. The same characteristic is present in empirical political theory, the main objective of which is to produce causal and explanatory accounts of politics. Again, the emphasis is on the use of specific knowledge to arrive at integrated generalisations – i.e. explanatory laws capable of relating one set of phenomena with another set in a coherent and systematic way.

Both political philosophy and political theory are rightly devoted to clarification through the long term project of rigorous generalisation. Apart from being necessarily slow in development and always highly contentious in outcome, the working methods of political philosophy and theory are not particularly well equipped to capture the speed, agility and nuance which characterise the usage of ideas in a rapidly changing political environment. The purpose of this study is to match the style of enquiry to the diverse and open textured deployment of ideas in their contemporary milieu of social drives, political movements and contemporary issues. This is not to eschew the techniques and disciplines of political philosophy or to deny its purpose or influence. On the contrary, it is inevitable that philosophy will have had an inherent influence upon the contributions to this book. By the same token, it is safe to assume that many of the insights afforded by the contributors will provide further new materials for the various projects of political philosophy and theory. Notwithstanding the indispensability of general theory, therefore, this set of essays is primarily concerned with the working properties of political ideas in action. The assignment is to illuminate and to elucidate the present usage of ideas even if this should be at the expense of universal propositions.

Any attempt to compile a review of this type raises a host of arguments and objections concerning the subjects selected for appraisal. It can be claimed that some political ideas are not truly 'political' or even 'ideas'. There will be controversy surrounding the priority some ideas have over others. Questions will also be raised over the extent to which the selected ideas can be regarded as separate and autonomous, or merely permutations or derivatives of others. It can be argued, for example, that some ideas are not substantive so much as instrumental in nature; that some ideas are really just expressions of temperament and experience; that some are misnomers in that they represent a reaction against ideas; and that others are in essence really issues rather than ideas.

It is not possible to provide a comprehensive answer to such anticipated objections partly because of space, but mostly because the choice is inevitably a matter of judgement. The subjects have been chosen on the basis of a number of criteria. One is the extensive effect that the usage of an idea may have had upon political consciousness – transferring what may have been an idea originally confined to a particular region or people into one of global importance. Time as well as space is also a consideration. The meaning and significance of democracy, for example, has undergone considerable change even since 1945. Given the recent interest in the 'new democracy' and in 'democratic renewal', for example, the idea of democracy warrants consideration on grounds of value, world importance and historical development. Another consideration is currency – i.e. the sheer volume of references to an idea in the mass of political exchanges. Solidity was also taken into account. Paradoxical though this may apear in a study of ideas, solidity was a useful criterion in distinguishing those ideas that could relate to mass consciousness and could be translated to organisational form. Reason, rights, property and even justice, for example, might be elemental motivating ideas, but because they are so diffuse in character and normally lack the focus to be self-sufficient sources of political movement, such ideas remain either contextual in nature, or component in form as parts of larger and more defined aggregates of position.

It can be argued that not all the ideas selected for consideration are of equal status and that some are far more important than others. This is irrefutable. Indeed, relative importance is to some extent reflected in the space devoted to each subject. Nevertheless, the effectiveness of the review does not hinge upon the proposition that all the ideas must have a comparable ranking in an imaginary order of merit. The purpose is to describe and analyse the distinctive properties and special character of each idea. Every contribution will provide an account of the origins and usage of each idea, together with an appraisal of its immediate consequences and its ramifications for the future. Each contributor possessed an uninhibited mandate to draw attention to dimensions that are normally overlooked; to bring to light new perspectives that are only just beginning to be recognised; and to correct common and persistent misconceptions. The overall objective is to give the reader a thorough grounding in the contemporary meaning of each idea, the manner of its development in political life and its contribution to the plurality of political perspectives, motivations and allegiances in the post-Cold War world.

In contrast to other exercises of this kind, the emphasis is on depth rather than on breadth. The ideas are studied at length, in which their ethical, explanatory and social significance are given careful consideration. The intention is that they will not only inform readers and provide them with a fuller understanding of the meaning, usages and public resonance of political ideas, but will encourage further study and reflection.

That there is much to think about is a controlling premise of this volume. Recent events have heralded the end of ideological politics and have prompted the allegation that the progression of history has reached its point of culmination (Fukuyama, 1992). Organised ideological politics may well have suffered and it is true that, in the process, some ideas and movements might be said to have run into dead-ends. Nevertheless, history continues apace with a renewed licentiousness of political thinking and activity released from old conformities and attachments. In essence, there appears to be no lack of political ideas to fill the 'thought vacuum'. Quite the reverse. Given the abandonment of Soviet communism, and the end of the static bipolarisation of ideas that accompanied the Cold War, it seems likely that the hegemony of Western liberal democracy will underwrite a profusion of ideas. They will vary from liberal democratic revision or refinement to forms of outright opposition to what the West represents, especially to those lying outside the Western tradition. They will also be prompted by an unease, both inside and outside the West, over whether the precepts of Western political theory can 'capture the principal properties of our present political predicament' (Dunn, 1993, p. 123), let alone help us to understand the future.

If it is true, as Richard Dawkins (1989, pp. 189–201, 329–31) has suggested, that ideas in modern culture possess the properties of viruses, particularly in their capacity to spread very rapidly by compulsive replication, it is important to know the identity and significance of those ideas which – whether we realise it or not – are currently shaping politics in the world. Our intellectual and political health may depend upon it.

References

Dawkins, R. (1989), *The Selfish Gene*, new edition, Oxford University Press

Dunn, J. (1993), *Western Political Theory in the Face of the Future*, Cambridge University Press

Fukuyama, F. (1992), *The End of History and the Last Man*, Harmondsworth, Penguin

Liberalism

The political debates of the 1990s bear a disarming resemblance to those of the 1980s. Now, as then, there is a sense that liberalism has achieved something of a pyrrhic victory. The decline of socialist parties in Western democracies coupled with the collapse of the former Eastern bloc has been championed by a number of commentators as marking the ultimate triumph of liberal economic and political principles. Like the liberal radicals of the early nineteenth century, they have characterised this victory of the liberal ethos as part cause and part effect of changes in the nature of society and the economy associated with new technologies and work practices and a related transformation of the world market. However, this success has not been without its costs. Even more than at the turn of the last century, there are lingering doubts that far from reinvigorating and replenishing the moral, social and economic capital of Western states, liberalism may have somehow depleted it. In particular, the liberal concern with the individual has been blamed for promoting a culture of self-interested and increasingly vacuous consumerism, in which private gain frequently fails to redound to the public good. As a result, many contemporary liberal political thinkers have ended up emulating the project of those liberals at the turn of the last century who sought to construct a more community minded version of liberalism.

This chapter documents the trajectory of post-war liberalism traced above. It should be noted that the term liberalism is used here to describe a set of ideas rather than a party doctrine. From this broader perspective, new right conservatives, social democrats and democratic socialists can all be seen as offering different interpretations of the liberal language of rights, freedom and equality. As we shall see, the post-war social democratic consensus of the 1950s and 1960s, no less than the new right critique of the 1970s and 1980s and the current wave of communitarianism, are for the most part best viewed as offering contrasting versions of liberal ideas. In an important respect, therefore, the mainstream political arguments of the last fifty years have been within liberalism, rather than between liberals and those offering profoundly different social ideals that challenge at a fundamental level the legitimacy of liberal institutions such as constitutional democracy and the market. As John Dunn (1979, p. 28) has remarked, even liberalism's staunchest critics 'are fundamentally undecided as to whether they have come to destroy liberalism or to fulfill it'. This observation raises the question, provocatively posed by Francis Fukuyama (1989, p. 3) and discussed in the conclusion, of whether this century has witnessed 'the total exhaustion of viable systemic alternatives to Western liberalism'.

The post-war liberal consensus

The defeat of fascism and the onset of the Cold War produced particularly in Britain and the United States a broad body of theorising dedicated to contrasting the ideas and practices of Western liberal democracies with the supposedly totalitarian regimes of left and right. Amongst the most prominent of these theorists were J. L. Talmon, Karl Popper, Isaiah Berlin and F. A. Hayek. In spite of a wide degree of disagreement on matters of policy and to some extent on philosophical issues as well, it is possible to identify a number of common themes. These thinkers all argued that whereas totalitarian doctrines are ideological, utopian, historicist and holistic, liberalism is empirical, pluralist and individualist. It aims not at the construction of an ideal state but at a form of government which allows for a diversity of human values and interests. In place of what they viewed as the totalitarian's fanatical desire to rebuild society anew on the basis of some abstract schema, they advocated piecemeal reform and adaptation in the light of the revealed preferences of individuals. The prime virtue of the liberal state lay in its being neutral between rival views of the good life, rather than in its promotion of any particular notion of the good. They portrayed the liberal conceptions of the market, democracy and justice as essentially procedural devices for letting people holding different moral and material priorities and preferences live peaceably and profitably together. Until recently, most post-war liberals have continued to hold this view of the underlying rationale of liberalism.

During the 1950s and 1960s, the plausibility and apparent success of this project was sustained by the belief of a number of political scientists that in all developed industrial societies in the West ideological conflict had given way to a general consensus around the values and practices of the liberal democratic state. According to this analysis, all groups accepted that a mixed economy, a competitive party system and a degree of state welfare provided the appropriate institutional framework for individuals to pursue their various interests and values. Disagreements were over the details. A new school of pluralist political theory argued that democratic politics was consequently no longer an arena of ideological or class conflict, but a mechanism whereby all legitimate groups could promote their concerns and have their opinions heard. Such a politics was entirely process orientated and uninterested in substantive results. The system maintained its legitimacy by satisfying competing groups through marginal and incremental adjustments rather than in upholding any set of core values.

This liberal democratic consensus was not built around a shared sense of the common good, therefore, so much as the belief that liberal institutions provided the best means whereby individuals could pursue their own good in their own way without unduly interfering with others. According to this view, there can be no social good distinct from the preferences of individuals. Nevertheless, this represents a vision of the good society of sorts, albeit one that does not rest on strong beliefs as to what the good life for human beings consists in. As such, it requires some justification.

Post-war liberals thinkers have tended to articulate and justify this social vision in two main ways. The first is the utilitarian view, which defends liberal principles on the grounds that they maximise the general welfare. According to this argument, leaving citizens alone to pursue their preferred way of life increases the sum of human happiness because, even if individuals occasionally make mistakes, in the long run people choose better for themselves than anyone else could. Utilitarianism accords with modern liberal morality in treating all preferences equally, be they for beer or books. Maximising overall happiness does not involve judging people's values, but merely aggregating them in order to ensure as many people as possible get what they want. To a great degree, the post-war consensus can be regarded as implicitly endorsing this form of liberal utilitarianism. For, as the reaction of the late 1970s and 1980s was to show, it was largely sustained by the growing prosperity of the post-war period. Even those institutions, such as nationalised industries and the welfare state, which appeared to reflect a superficially collective spirit, were accepted on the liberal utilitarian grounds that they were efficient and popular means for securing the greatest happiness of the greatest number by ensuring full employment and a healthier population. Only rarely were they seen as expressing the mutal obligations we owe to fellow citizens sharing a common life.

Utilitarianism, however, can clash with liberalism. For a start, utilitarian calculations can be highly intolerant of the interests of minorities. If a large majority abhors the activities of a particular minority, such as homosexuals, then the balance of preferences will favour suppression. Even if the pain caused by this policy to each of the suppressed individuals is very great and the satisfaction felt by each member of the majority far smaller, the collective happiness of the oppressors may well outweigh the pain of the oppressed. Secondly, and just as important, in aggregating our preferences, utilitarianism requires individuals to put the happiness of the collectivity above their own. In so doing, it fails to respect the distinctiveness and frequently incompatible nature of different people's desires.

During the 1960s and 1970s such concerns were increasingly voiced by both the left and the right. The left pointed to the continued oppression of significant minorities in Western societies, a point brought to the fore by the black civil rights movement in the United States. The Vietnam War, which was largely prosecuted by the liberal establishment of the Democratic Party, also raised these issues. Utilitarian arguments loomed large both in justifying intervention on the grounds that it was necessary to prevent the ultimate horror of Soviet hegemony, and in defending bombing atrocities because they supposedly saved more lives (especially American ones) at the end of the day. Coupled to these criticisms were doubts about how well markets and the democratic procedures of existing liberal states responded to the interests of all sections of society. Pluralists were attacked for ignoring the blatant inequalities of influence and bargaining power between groups and individuals. Such discrepancies arose not only from the fact that some interests are by their nature better organised and more organisable than others, but also from the existing inequitable distribution of wealth and power within society. Rather than reflecting the people's conscious allegiance, the liberal consensus was the product of the apathy of the powerless. The right, in contrast, whilst sharing some of these worries, mainly questioned the legitimacy of the welfare system. Adopting a parallel argument about utilitarianism's tendency to use some individuals as a means to the happiness of all, they claimed that taxation for state welfare programmes coerced individuals into diverting funds from themselves and their families to support complete strangers to whom they had no ties or obligations.

Increasingly, therefore, liberals have turned to a second type of argument to ground their views, namely rights-based theories. As indicated, this language of rights can be employed in different ways by egalitarians and libertarians. Whereas the former are concerned to extend to all individuals the social, economic and political rights necessary to enable them to live an autonomous life according to their chosen ideals, the latter believe that a market economy, protecting private property rights and allowing individual choices to determine the share of resources, offers the only plausible embodiment of liberalism. What rights-based liberals of both camps have in common, however, is the belief that a distinction needs to be made between the framework of rights and liberties regulating social interaction and the particular ends people may choose to pursue within that framework. Both groups, in other words, agree with the post-war liberal project of creating a neutral state which simply serves to allow individuals to pursue their own conceptions of the good on a fair and equitable basis.

We shall turn to the libertarians in the next section, concentrating here on the liberal egalitarian theory of John Rawls. Rawls's *A Theory of Justice* is probably the most influential work of political philosophy written in English since the war. Although published in 1971, its arguments were progressively elaborated in articles dating from 1958. Rawls's book represents a return to political philosophising in a grand manner, that seeks to justify the basic principles of a legitimate social order. However, unlike most political philosophers of the past, he defines justice in terms of fairness rather than goodness or truth. He claims to divorce his principles of justice from controversial ethical, epistemological or metaphysical doctrines, in order to ensure their neutrality between differing conceptions of the good. He is particularly sensitive to the left critique of utilitarianism in this respect. As such, his book constitutes an attempt to defend and extend the liberal democratic consensus as a fair system of social co-operation.

Rawls uses the classical liberal device of the social contract to arrive at two principles of justice which he believes will serve to regulate the relations between individuals in modern societies. He asks us to imagine what principles we would choose if we were in a hypothetical situation in which we do not know either who we are or what the circumstances of our society might be. In what he calls the 'original position', we do not know if we are intelligent or stupid, ugly or handsome, poor or rich, black or white, hardworking or lazy and so on. Nor are we aware of whether the society into which we might be placed will be wealthy or not, what racial and religious mix it will contain, or where we come in the social hierarchy. All we have at our disposal are certain general facts about human psychology and political economy. As a result, we have no strongly held beliefs or opinions about how society ought to be run. Rather, we possess what Rawls calls a 'thin theory of the good', consisting of a number of 'primary goods', such as certain rights and liberties, powers and opportunities, income and wealth,, and the sources of self-respect. These goods are primary because Rawls assumes they are means to a wide range of ends which it is rational for all individuals, regardless of their values or aspirations, to want to maximise. Instead of having a particular interest in securing those goods necessary for us to realise a specific set of goals, therefore, Rawls endows us with a generalised interest in being able to secure the goods needed for whatever particular goals we may happen to have or acquire. He then asks which principles of justice it would be rational to select to govern the society into which you and your children and your children's children, etc., will then be catapulted from behind this 'veil of ignorance'.

Rawls believes that this thought experiment, which he elaborates in great detail, will produce a theory of justice that everyone will accept as legitimate because it is untainted by any preconceptions about the worth or lack of it of particular beliefs or ways of life. Faced with the radical uncertainty of the 'original position', most of us will adopt what he calls a 'maximin' strategy that forces us, metaphorically speaking, to put ourselves in the shoes of those less fortunate than ourselves. In other words, we will fear the worst. We will tend to worry that we could be an ugly, poor, untalented member of some oppressed minority group, rather than gambling on the possibility that we might be a rich, hugely gifted and attractive member of the ruling elite. Consequently, we will be drawn into a degree of mutual aid and tolerance that shows an equal concern and respect for all people, regardless of their tastes, opinions or circumstances.

Rawls claims this line of reasoning would lead us to choose the following two principles:

First Principle
Each person is to have an equal right to the most extensive total system of equal basic liberties compatible with a similar system for all.

Second Principle
Social and economic inequalities are to be arranged so that they are both:
    (a) to the greatest benefit of the least advantaged

(b) attached to offices and positions open to all under conditions of fair equality
    of opportunity.   (1971, p. 302)

Participants in the 'original position' also agree on a 'lexical order' for the
application of the Principles, according to which the First takes precedence over
the Second and in the Second Principle (b) has priority over (a).

Rawls is somewhat vague about the precise practical implications of his theory.
However, he appears to favour some form of property-owning constitutional
democracy, which he believes to be compatible with both welfare capitalism and a
'liberal socialist' regime consisting of self-managing workers' co-operatives
operating within a market system (1971, pp. 279–80). Moreover, he contends
that all established liberal democracies can be regarded as 'nearly just' societies
that sufficiently approximate to his ideal to command our allegiance most of the
time, even if civil disobedience rather than revolution might be justified in
particular circumstances in order to reform them.

In spite of this catholicity, Rawls's book has attracted a torrent of criticism.
Many commentators have pointed out problems with Rawls's derivation of his
two principles. They have remarked on the impossibility of abstracting individuals from any historical and social contexts, or of finding criteria of rationality
and justification in morals which are not relative to particular ethical perspectives. For some critics, Rawls only arrives at his liberal-democratic consensus by endowing the members of the original position with the characteristics
typical of idealised liberal citizens. Others have argued that had he taken his 'thin
theory of the good' and the principles of pure instrumental rationality seriously,
they would not have suported the particular index of primary goods which he
requires for his proposed theory of justice. Either these cyphers are too thin to be
able to conceive of any conception of justice, or, if they can, then it is because
Rawls has endowed them with certain culturally specific attitudes and modes of
reasoning.

Communitarian writers have developed these sorts of criticism in order to call
into question the whole Rawlsian project. They point out that we only acquire the
capacity for judgement through living in real societies embodying those conceptions of the good which give our lives their particular purpose, meaning and
character. They contend that Rawls's appeal to abstract principles jeopardises
our attachment to the social practices and values which make us moral agents in
the first place. His models of rational choice are claimed to make highly
unrealistic assumptions about the availability of information, the coherence of
people's different needs and aspirations, and their capacity for calculation. It is
doubtful whether many people, outside certain special situations such as shop-
ping or stock-broking, could or should aspire to them in any case, for to do so
would be to destroy the genuine moral bonds of community and to replace them
with the inherently unstable ties of reciprocal self-interest. Taking this criticism
further, social theorists remark that within pluralistic and differentiated societies
the categories of universalistic ethics invoked by Rawls break down. Individuals

and groups formulate and justify their demands in a particularistic and con-strained manner. They point out that Rawls can only achieve his consensus by ignoring the divergent historical identities and social and economic inequalities that in the real world mould and limit moral and political decisions. From this perspective, his theory is simply irrelevant. These criticisms essentially boil down to the question of what, once the 'veil of ignorance' is lifted and we find ourselves as particular people operating in concrete circumstances, could possibly motivate or enable us to adopt Rawls's arguments? Rawls has taken these sorts of criticism very seriously indeed, and in a series of articles that have recently been reworked into a book he has progressively developed his theory in order to meet them. We return to these arguments in the final section.

Other critics have concentrated on inadequacies they believe arise with the principles themselves, particularly the second. A number have argued that the individualistic bias of Rawls's account of social justice ignores the importance to people of collective goods, such as peace, a clean environment and the like, which cannot be distributed in an individualisable manner. Similarly, Rawls's concern simply to maximise the amount of primary goods available to the least well-off also ignores both the differential capacity and desire of particular individuals to take advantage of these resources. Some, such as the disabled, may need more than others to attain comparable levels of satisfaction; others, such as environ-mentalists, may not want to maximise access to all these goods at all. For parallel reasons, Marxist and feminist critics have attacked the division between state and civil society, private and public, implied by Rawls's lexical ordering and separa-tion of the two principles. They argue that he underestimates the extent to which the equal freedoms of the first require a more substantial degree of social and economic empowerment than he appears to concede with the second. However, although Rawls has done precious little himself to answer these sorts of criticism, his theory has a radical potential that ought to allow him to. For example, even if Rawls fails to do so himself, gender and class distinctions should be raised in the original position, precisely because we do not know who we might be. Similarly, one would expect his hypothetical choosers to be as concerned with discrimina-tion and oppression arising from how goods are produced as with inequalities in the distribution of existing social resources. Such reasoning seems called for by Rawls's wish to tackle the fairness of the basic institutions of society and to ensure that they provide a just system of social co-operation whereby individuals can pursue their divergent goals on an equitable basis. However, if Rawls's theory can be suitably rethought to accommodate these essentially left-wing concerns, others have wished to challenge his whole approach to the liberal project and have regarded it as essentially misguided.

The new right

Although the new right only came to prominence in the late 1970s and 1980s, when their ideas were taken up by the conservative administrations of Mrs Thatcher in Britain and Ronald Reagan in the United States, their views are neither that novel nor that conducive to many aspects of conventional right-wing thought. To a large degree new right thinking is an attempt to update the classical liberal tradition of John Locke, Adam Smith and Herbert Spencer to modern conditions. Moreover, new right advocacy of a free market, a limited state and possessive individualism is often in tension with conservative ideas of authority, paternalism, and social and moral unity.

During the 1940s, 1950s and 1960s there was a hard core of thinkers gathered around bodies such as the Mont Pelerin Society, the Institute of Economic Affairs, and the Virginia School of Public Choice which opposed the post-war linking of liberalism with social democracy. However, they had been largely ignored as holding anachronistic and eccentric views. For example, when F. A. Hayek, one of the most prominent members of this group, published *The Constitution of Liberty* in 1960, one reviewer simply commented that 'it does not seem possible any longer to state the case for *laissez-faire* in a manner that is at once logically consistent and socially relevant' (G. L. Arnold quoted in Arblaster, 1984, p. 340). Milton Friedman's *Capitalism and Freedom* (1962) and James Buchanan and Gordon Tullock's *The Calculus of Consent* (1962) also failed to generate much attention at the time. During the 1970s, however, everything changed and these ideas began to gain currency. Hayek, Friedman and Buchanan, for instance, were all to be awarded the Nobel prize for economics.

This transformation in their fortunes arose from the apparent exhaustion of the post-1945 capitalist boom with the oil crisis of 1973. The massive rise in oil prices not only threw the economic and political basis of the old liberal consensus into question, but seemingly lent substance to the ideals of the new right. On the one hand, Keynesian economic policies were attacked as inappropriate in these new conditions. The chief evidence of this redundancy was said to be the simultaneous acceleration of inflation combined with a steep rise of unemployment during the 1970s, which appeared to undermine the basic Keynesian assumption that the two would not occur together (i.e. 'Phillips curve'). On the other hand, the pluralist political system began to break down as governments found themselves squeezed between either raising taxation or enforcing wage restraint and cutting public services, resulting in widespread confrontation with state employees and other workers. The system was accused of placing excessive demands on the state to provide services it no longer had the funds to finance.

The new right built on these perceived weaknesses to promote its own case for the free market and the limited state. In defending the first, they argue that markets are both more efficient and more compatible with individual liberty than any degree of state planning could be. An economy is an enormously complex system, bringing together at a global level those responsible for cultivating or extracting natural resources, with manufacturers and entrepreneurs, sellers and consumers. The new right theorists, especially Hayek, have argued that it would be impossible for any single agency, such as a state, to co-ordinate all these operations in a manner that is as responsive to innovation, individual choice and all the multifarious factors of supply and demand as the market with its pricing mechanism. Indeed, to attempt to do so would not merely be highly inefficient but necessarily totalitarian as well. For the only way to reduce the volume of data to humanly manageable proportions would be for the social planner to bring all human activity into line with a single moral and practical vision that constrains the scope for experimentation and difference. Otherwise, conflicts would continually spring up between competing priorities and projects. The market, in contrast, reconciles a plurality of different activities and goals in a spontaneous fashion that automatically responds to those that prove most effective and desirable.

The state, therefore, must be severely limited in its operations, merely providing those public goods (such as education) and guarding against certain externalities (such as pollution) where market incentives are absent. The public choice school, in particular, has backed up this argument with a severe critique of pluralist democracy. It disputes the pluralist view of the democratic state as a benign and independent agency that responds to the demands of citizens in a disinterested manner. Instead, it portrays the state as staffed by self-serving bureaucrats and politicians, concerned solely to increase their own power and privileges. Such groups, it contends, only respond to those organised interests, such as trade unions, strong enough to strengthen or weaken their hold on office. Throughout the 1950s and 1960s, its adherents argue, a ratchet effect was in operation whereby these internal and external pressures led to the state becoming grossly over-extended and placing an excessive burden on the economy, whilst ignoring the wishes of the majority of individual taxpayers. They recommend the privatisation of most existing state run services. They claim that the introduction of market incentives into the public sector is the only means of ensuring that people get the services they want and that they are delivered in a cost-effective manner.

This advocacy of the market and attack on the state goes together with a critique of welfare provision. The very idea of social justice is held to be incoherent. The new right maintains that the complex division of labour involved in the creation of any product makes it impossible to ascertain how much is due to the effort or contribution of any particular individual. Such decisions have to be left to the invisible hand of the market. They acknowledge that many who reap large rewards are not particularly talented, hardworking or worthy individuals but simply lucky, just as those who fail to succeed are often upright, conscientious but unfortunately do not have the qualities the market wants at that time. However, whilst the plight of the latter is regrettable it cannot be rectified. Any standards of social justice that the state might choose to impose would be likely to be even more abitrary. Moreover, such interference with the free choices and preferences of individuals in the disposition of their goods gradually substitutes a planned economy for the market, with all its attendant difficulties. In fact, though relative inequalities may increase in a market society, the surplus of the rich is used in experimenting with new products and leads to advances in the economy as a whole. Through a 'trickle down' effect, the living standards of even the poorest increase with the general prosperity of society as a whole. Most people are far better off than they would be under a planned system. Finally, the pursuit of social justice produces a concentration of power in the hands of government officials that provides a constant temptation to corruption and ultimately undermines individual freedom. At most, the state should provide a safety-net for the destitute who have no hope of fending for themselves. Other than that, its role should be restricted to the upholding of contracts and the prevention of all direct attempts by others, such as force, fraud and theft, deliberately to invade an individual's liberty.

Like earlier post-war liberals, new right theorists often seem to base their case on some form of utilitarianism. New right policies, they contend, simply make people better off. However, we have already noted the unsatisfactory nature of these arguments. Not surprisingly, recent theorists have sought a rights-based defence of their position. The most famous account of this nature is Robert Nozick's *Anarchy, State and Utopia* (1974), which appeared just three years after Rawls's book. Adopting the thesis of John Locke, he contends that individuals have rights in their bodies and the products of their labour. He argues that any attempt to redistribute resources, or to intervene in the economy, involves an illegitimate attempt to use people to further some social purpose with which they may not agree. Taxation for any purpose beyond that required for the minimal state is on a par with forced labour, therefore, coercing us to work for the benefit of others. The distributions of the market, in contrast, reflect the unplanned results of free exchanges between individuals. So long as nobody is intentionally and physically coerced into exchanging goods or selling his or her labour to another, and there are no legal barriers discriminating against who can apply for jobs or what can be sold, then the liberal criteria of liberty and equality have been satisfied and the market system can be judged as fair. Market distributions are just, not because the best or most deserving persons are rewarded, but simply because they respect individual rights. He sums up his principle of justice in the following parody of Marx: 'From each as they choose, to each as they are chosen.' On this view, governments have no legitimate grounds for interfering with what he calls capitalistic acts between consenting adults.

Nozick's theory contains an important critique of Rawls, whom he accuses of attempting to impose a particular distributive pattern upon society, rather than accepting the unplanned but free results of market exchanges as they have evolved over time. Whilst he is right to point to a gap in Rawls's argument between how people are expected to reason within the constraints of his theory and how they think in practice, his own arguments are similarly wanting. He admits, for example, that in the past there have been numerous injustices and usurpations, such as the forceable seizure of native peoples' lands by white settlers in America and Australasia, so that the existing distribution of property cannot be characterised as the historical product of numerous free transferrals. Yet he has no satisfactory answer as to how this situation might be rectified. Nor does he explain why people have the rights he attributes to them and not others, such as rights to health and food. In common with other theorists of the new right, he assumes an extremely narrow account of liberty which allows him to treat the market in highly unrealistic terms as a 'powerless' mechanism of co-ordination, in which all consumers and producers meet on an equal basis. As a result, the extremely uneven life chances of different social groups and classes conveniently disappear, as does any appreciation of the whole complex of oligopolistic, corporate and monopolistic structures that shape the modern economy. So too, of course, does the obligation to do anything about them. Like the rest of the new right, he adopts a 'slippery slope' argument that falsely conflates all government intervention and redistribution with steps along the road to Stalinist-style state planning. The possibility, argued for by Rawls, that such measures can be seen as part of a stable democratic settlement providing the background conditions that enable individuals to choose in an autonomous fashion, is dismissed out of hand. Yet even the minimalist individualism of the new right cannot operate in a moral and social vacuum. It is the neglect of this context that has led a number of commentators to fear that the liberalism of contemporary societies risks undermining itself.

The end of history . . . or of liberalism?

With the collapse of the former Soviet bloc, it is once again fashionable to talk of the end of ideology and the unabashed victory of liberal values. Francis Fukuyama (1989, pp. 3, 4, 15) has gone so far as to argue that we are witnessing 'not just the end of the Cold War, or the passing of a period of postwar history, but the end of history as such: that is the end point of mankind's ideological evolution and the universalisation of Western liberal democracy as the final form of human government'. He associates this triumph with the 'omnipresence of Western consumerist culture' from New York to Beijing, Moscow, Rangoon and Tehran. The remaining sources of tension within or between states, most particularly those deriving from ethnic and racial tensions, do not, he claims, 'arise from liberalism as such as from the fact that the liberalism in question is incomplete.'

Others, such as Alasdair MacIntyre (1981), Michael Sandel (1982) and Charles Taylor (1985) have been less optimistic. They have pointed to the various ways that liberalism itself generates conflicts. According to these political philosophers, the liberal's conception of the individual as a self-absorbed chooser and consumer creates a moral void which actually encourages people to find a more stable identity in fundamentalist religion and atavistic ethnic ties. Moreover, liberalism provides no adequate principles and language to confront or mediate the resulting clashes of convictions. Rather, liberals' commitment to neutrality between conceptions of the good, their view of rival moralities as but the expression of differing preferences, and their insistence on rights discourse as the dominant political vocabulary, have all combined to create an adversarial and litigious political climate. The abortion debate and the Salman Rushdie affair, for instance, both reveal this feature of contemporary liberal politics and the inadequacy of modern liberal attempts to justify toleration on the grounds of procedural correctness rather than the substance of the views expressed.

Almost worse for some critics, however, is the anomic atomism of those who remain within the liberal fold. In spite of the apparent liberal reliance on the invisible hand to derive public benefits from the selfish pursuits of egoistic individuals, the successful operation of this mechanism assumes that all recognise at the very least the collective good of the market itself and abide by those norms, such as fair dealing, intrinsic to its functioning. However, modern day capitalists have consistently failed to display the rectitude inculcated by the muscular Christianity of their nineteenth century forebears. The championing of Victorian values by Mrs Thatcher, for example, seemed at best anachronistic, at worst cynical.

The current moral deficit of liberalism has often seemed to go hand in hand with a democratic deficit. Fukuyama assumes an automatic compatibility between liberalism and democracy. However, the market economy systematically reproduces massive assymetries of power and resources which frequently clash and subvert the democratic aspiration to greater equality and justice. Moreover, the predominantly instrumental and 'economic' view of democracy of the pluralists and public choice theorists leads to a denial of those intrinsic qualities of the democratic process that make political discussion a means for building a genuine consensus on liberal principles. The new right has attempted to sidestep these issues by denying that the democratic understanding of a free and equal society represents a valid interpretation of the liberal ideal. In contrast, those theorists, such as Rawls, who subscribe to a more democratic vision of liberalism have tended to avoid confronting the growing clash between the demands of the private economy as liberals have traditionally conceived it, and the welfare programmes required by their egalitarian version of liberal principles. Rather than proposing radical reforms of liberal institutions, they have progressively disengaged from politics altogether and turned political philosophy into an increasingly academic and utopian affair.

Contemporary liberalism stands charged with destroying the distinctive cultural environment that gave liberal principles their value and meaning. A number of political thinkers now stress the need to think of liberalism not in rights-based and procedural terms, but as a particular kind of community dedicated to promoting the common good of individual autonomy through the collective provision of worthwhile opportunities – especially a distinctively 'liberal' education. However, much of the inspiration for the contemporary liberal communitarians comes from the pre-modern world, particularly ancient Greece. The plausibility of the politics of the common good in the complex, pluralist and large scale societies of the postmodern world remains highly dubious. In most states, a homogeneous national political culture could only be achieved today at the unacceptable cost of a high degree of ethnic cleansing.

Moreover, creating the conditions of autonomous agency risks being not only highly paternalistic, and so paradoxically illiberal, but unrealistic as well. The enhanced specialisation and functional differentiation of modern societies greatly increases our dependence on unknown and uncontrollable structures and persons, thereby constraining our possibilities for autonomous thought and action in the first place. Indeed, the classic liberals' belief, naively espoused by the new right, that liberalism and capitalism go together, has been severely challenged by the rise of successful capitalist economies in the non-individualist and authoritarian cultures of South-East Asia. The prospects increasingly are that history will spell the end of liberalism rather than the other way round.

References

Arblaster, A. (1984), *The Rise and Decline of Western Liberalism*, Oxford, Blackwell

Buchanan, J. and Tullock, G. (1962), *The Calculus of Consent*, Ann Arbor, University of Michigan Press

Dunn, J. (1979), *Western Political Thought in the Face of the Future*, Cambridge University Press

Friedman, M. (1962), *Capitalism and Freedom*, University of Chicago Press

Fukuyama, F. (1989), 'The End of History?', *The National Interest*, 16, pp. 3–18

Hayek, F. A. (1960), *The Constitution of Liberty*, London, Routledge and Kegan Paul

MacIntyre, A. (1981), *After Virtue*, London, Duckworth

Nozick, R. (1974), *Anarchy, State and Utopia*, Oxford, Blackwell

Rawls, J. (1971), *A Theory of Justice*, Oxford, Clarendon Press

— (1993), *Political Liberalism*, New York, Columbia University Press

Sandel, M. (1982), *Liberalism and the Limits of Justice*, Cambridge University Press

Taylor, C. (1985), 'Atomism', in *idem, Philosophical Papers: 2*, Cambridge University Press

Further Reading

Bellamy, R. (1992), *Liberalism and Modern Society*, Cambridge, Polity

Gray, J. (1993), *Post-Liberalism*, London, Routledge

King, D. (1987), *The New Right*, Basingstoke, Macmillan

Sandell, M. (ed.) (1986), *Liberalism and its Critics*, Oxford, Blackwell

Social democracy

The meaning of social democracy – in Britain at any rate – has been hotly contested, not least amongst those who either lay claim to or scornfully reject the label. In recent times, the issue of terminology – as between 'socialism', 'democratic socialism', and 'social democracy' – has become for those who regard themselves as broadly on the left a matter of lively, not to say, bitter debate. It has become entwined in difficult questions of party identity, of loyalty and defection, of ideological purity as opposed to electoral pragmatism. In earlier times, and in other countries, these terms have largely been treated as interchangeable. In Britain, however, the establishment in the 1980s of the Social Democratic Party, principally by former leading members of the Labour Party, meant that the term 'social democracy' became invested with a party significance. Both supporters and opponents of the SDP used the term as a means of distinguishing themselves from each other. This conflict has tended to distort any sensible debate in this country about the proper meaning of social democracy – a debate which has not been similarly afflicted in most other countries. The question of whether the British Labour Party wishes to describe itself as a social democratic party has, however, also been influenced by other – and often conflicting – factors.

Many Labour Party activists regard themselves as and call themselves socialists, despite the fact that the Labour Party (as its name indicates) has never been an explicitly socialist party. Indeed, many of its critics, especially on the left, would attack the party on precisely the ground that it has never developed much in the way of ideology, preferring to embrace a sort of 'Labourism' which has rarely ventured much beyond a fairly ill-defined support for working-class interests. Nor have Labour Party 'socialists' been deterred by the fact that the term 'socialism' was claimed as their own by the communist or state socialist regimes of Eastern Europe. This confusion of terminology was, of course, eagerly exploited by those on the right, who seized upon the possibility of persuading voters that it was proper to tar the Labour Party with the Eastern European brush. The consequence of these confusions has been that the mainstream left in Britain has found itself too often embroiled in unproductive disputes about terminology, rather than looking at the more important issues of substance.

It is nevertheless possible to set aside differences and distractions and to identify and describe a body of political thought which is recognisably social democratic or 'socialist' in the sense in which that term is used in a Western democracy. Henceforward in this chapter the terms 'socialist' and 'social democratic' are used interchangeably. Perhaps the safest way of staking out, in preliminary form, the political territory occupied by social democracy is to describe it as that range of opinion represented by the major parties of the left in most European countries – the Labour Party in Britain, the SPD in Germany, and the Socialist Party in France.

Origins

In Britain, as in other countries, modern social democracy has developed from a rich mix of cultural, religious and ethical influences, as well as from the more obvious political and economic doctrines. Much early political doctrine which today we would recognise as having something to do with socialism arose from a basic assertion of fundamental rights on the part of ordinary people against those who wielded power at their expense. The Levellers, and later the Chartists, were motivated by a belief in the need to stand up for the downtrodden – a sort of egalitarianism which, like Thomas Paine's concern for the 'rights of man', has been at the heart of much social democratic thinking. In Britain, in particular, ethical and religious considerations have played a major part in the development of social democracy. The challenge to the established church represented by Methodism, the Christian injunction to 'love thy neighbour', a sense of 'noblesse oblige' on the part of the privileged, have all made their contributions. The result of this has been that British socialism has always been heavily imbued with altruism. And this despite Oscar Wilde's assertion that the great virtue of socialism was that it made altruism unnecessary and despite the fact that in practice left-wing politics in this country have always been pitched deliberately, if not always very precisely, at the self-interest of the working class.

Continental socialists were much influenced by the Marxist theories of 'scientific socialism', which attempted to lay down with the precision of scientific laws the way in which a socialist economy and society should be planned. But in Britain what is often called 'utopian socialism' has generally been the preferred model. Altruistic socialists like Robert Owen and C. R. Ashbee attempted to create communities living according to the ideals of self-help and mutual support. William Morris provided an aesthetic and anti-materialist dimension to socialist beliefs, and the Guild Socialists attempted a sort of 'home-grown', decentralised socialism in which people took control of their own working lives. In more recent times, social democracy has been much concerned with using the political power acquired through the universal franchise and political democracy in order to manage the economy in the interests of ordinary people. Keynesian economics offered the prospect of full employment and emphasised the responsibility of government to intervene in the management of the economy. The trade union movement provided organisation in the workplace to offset the power of the employer and make the wage bargain more equitable. William Beveridge provided a blueprint for the welfare state, in which the power of government could be deployed on behalf of the community to protect the vulnerable.

Community, contract and government

Many of these diverse beliefs, aims and attitudes are still reflected in today's social democracy. It is possible, as a consequence, to identify a number of characteristics of modern social democratic thought. Many of those who describe themselves as social democrats will subscribe to some, but not necessarily all, of these attitudes.

Common to most on the left is the belief that the underdog in society should be supported and protected. That protection should, it is believed, be provided by the community, which should recognise the rights of all citizens not only to a share in the benefits which are generated by the fact of living in society but also to a say in how that sharing out is to be done. The community, through its major agencies like the government, has a responsibility to allocate scarce resources equitably and to provide reasonable life chances to all citizens. This core belief and attitude points us, I think, to the distinctive feature of the social democratic position. What distinguishes social democrats from those holding other political views is the response they make to one of the central questions in politics – what to do about the natural tendency in any society for power to be concentrated in a few hands. Power will always be unequally distributed in every society. People will always be differently endowed with strength, intelligence, even luck. Those who exploit those advantages to acquire power will then use that power to entrench their advantage. Society will be organised to suit their interests and to perpetuate their power and privilege.

The response to this phenomenon is at the heart of politics. The paternalist right (represented in modern British politics by the old pre-Thatcherite Tory Party) acknowledges the inevitability of the unequal distribution of power. It goes further and welcomes that imbalance as a valuable force for continuity and stability. A sense of hierarchy is thought to be essential to the orderly functioning of society. It emphasises the importance of an acceptance by the disadvantaged of their lot in life and the corresponding obligation of the privileged to use their power in a more or less enlightened and paternalist fashion.

The new free market right (represented today by the Thatcherite Tory Party) also welcomes inequality, but it goes further than the old paternalist right in identifying its advantages. According to this view, inequality is the essential precondition for progress. It is the prospect of securing a differential advantage which prompts the forceful and able to strive. It is that striving – that drive for individual self-aggrandisement – which produces social advance and which in the end benefits even the disadvantaged, on the principle that a rising tide lifts the small boats as well as the larger craft.

The centrist attitude (represented, perhaps, by the modern Liberal Party and to some extent by the philosopher John Rawls) recognises that power will be unequally distributed in society and accepts that social advance may to some extent be dependent on this phenomenon. The extent of the the imbalance must however, according to this view, be restrained and its effects mitigated, for fear that it will otherwise create such a sense of injustice as to threaten social cohesion. Accordingly, everyone must be guaranteed equality of opportunity, and the least advantaged must gain an absolute benefit from the permitted inequality, so that the inequality which inevitably arises thereafter will be more acceptable to those who find themselves disadvantaged.

Only the socialist or social democrat regards the concentration of power in the hands of employer or landlord, bureaucrat or aristocrat as damaging in principle and as something which must be restrained and counteracted from the outset. Social democracy could be said to be the attempt to put in place a structure of rules, mechanisms and institutions which will have the effect of breaking up concentrations of power and restoring and redistributing power to those who have lost it. That attempt will be partly a matter of trying to equalise power in the first place, by equipping everyone in society with broadly equal legal and political rights, broadly equal rights to information and equal economic power in the market place, in the hope that the way in which society and the economy then operate will lead to a broadly equal distribution of power. To the extent that that hope is inevitably disappointed, the social democrat or socialist will then provide redistributive mechanisms, like the tax and benefit system and the provision of public services, with a view to making the outcome more equitable. Social democrats believe that this effort is worthwhile, not only because it benefits those individuals who would otherwise feel that they had lost out, but also because society as a whole will be better off and will function more cohesively if everyone feels that they are getting a fair deal and are able to make their contribution to the best of their ability.

According to this view, a sort of social contract is struck between each individual and the rest of society. Society organises itself so as to provide to the individual the sort of support which the individual acting alone could not hope to obtain. The individual is thereby enabled to realise his or her potential and, as a consequence, is able to reward society with a more valuable individual contribution than would otherwise be possible. If the prospect of individual advance is so important, as the defenders of inequality maintain, why not extend it to everyone so that society as a whole benefits? This view is often attacked on the ground that the equality that is aimed at necessarily means that everyone is reduced to the lowest common denominator and that individual effort and enterprise will be stifled. The answer to that was provided by R. H. Tawney.

Equality, he said, does not mean that 'all . . . perform identical functions' (1964, p. 168). It is not necessary, in other words, to be the same, in order to be equal. Each individual will use his or her equal power to make the best of his or her talents and energies – but naturally in very different ways. A related criticism is that a price is incurred for this degree of equality, i.e. a restraint upon the freedom of the individual. It is certainly true that the excessive power of a few individuals to exploit their advantage in power to the disadvantage of others would have to be limited. But the social democrat would respond by saying that freedom is maximised when it is equalised. The freedom that matters is the freedom of each individual to make choices about his or her life. That freedom is enlarged by providing to each individual – and not just to a few – an equal share of power.

Democracy and government

It is this view about society and the individual that leads social democrats to attach importance to the role of government. Modern social democracy no longer asserts that the state can or should do everything. That smacks too much of the state socialism, 'democratic centralism' and centrally planned economies of the communist regimes of Eastern Europe. But the national government remains the primary instrument of the organised community. There are of course other agencies – local government, quangos, supranational bodies and others – which exist to serve the community's interests, but it is the national state government which, for the time being at any rate, is the most powerful expression of the community's wishes. Social democrats believe that good government matters. We can each of us as individuals lead better and more fulfilled lives, and live in a society which functions better and more cohesively, if government in the widest sense does those things which no individual, however talented, powerful or lucky, can do alone. Yet this belief in the importance of government has suffered considerable setbacks over recent years, which have contributed to a significant loss of self-confidence on the part of social democrats in general.

In Britain, that loss of confidence began with what was perceived as the comparative failure of interventionist policies to produce an economic perform-ance to match that of other more successful countries. That was compounded by the impact of the oil price shock in the early 1970s, and the perceived inability in those circumstances of Keynesian demand management to rescue the economy from 'stagflation'. By 1976, James Callaghan – the Labour prime minister – was telling a Labour Conference that 'you can't spend your way out of a recession', thereby apparently conceding that government was no longer able to manage the economy so as to achieve, for example, full employment (quoted in Callaghan, 1987, p. 426). Once this concession had been made on economic management, it was difficult to make the case for government in other, less important, areas. If it was right and unavoidable that markets should decide the fate of the economy, how could social democrats resist the claims of marketeers that the market should decide other matters as well?

The 1980s were a difficult period for social democracy. Classical economics – the view that government could and should do no more than establish discipline (and that even this task would be better contracted out to bankers) – together with privatisation, deregulation, free markets, all became the order of the day. The left found itself unable to resist the onward march of market forces, particularly on the international scene. It is only recently, as disenchantment with deregulation and *laissez-faire* has grown, that some first signs of returning self-confidence on the left have become apparent.

It seems likely that social democracy may now enjoy a period of renewed relevance and fashionability. Many of the old ideological disputes, about – for instance – the role of markets or the ownership of property, have been settled if not resolved. The virtual demise of communism has opened up the way for democratic socialism or social democracy as the major alternative to *laissez-faire*, free market policies. The virtues of community responsibility and collective action, as an important concomitant of individual freedom, are now more apparent. There may be valuable political and electoral rewards to those who are ready to breathe new life into the social democratic ideal.

References
Callaghan, J. (1987), Speech to the Labour Party Conference, 28 September 1976, quoted in J. Callaghan, *Time and Chance*, London, Collins
Tawney, R. H. (1964), *Equality*, 5th edition, London, Allen and Unwin

Further Reading
Crosland, C. A. R. (1964), *The Future of Socialism*, rev. edition, London, Jonathan Cape
Gould, B. (1989), *A Future for Socialism*, London, Jonathan Cape
Hattersley, R. (1987), *Choose Freedom: The Future for Democratic Socialism*, London, Michael Joseph

Communism

Communism has a history, and some version of that history is invoked whenever the term is used. In the words of Karl Marx (1852, section I), probably the most famous communist of all: 'Tradition from all the dead generations weighs like a nightmare on the brain of the living.' In the case of communism the nightmare is more than usually vivid. But in order to grasp this lurid clarity we must examine carefully the tradition that the dead generations have left behind. This is because when the term is used in the present, the dead are made to walk among us. Rightly we must turn first to the earliest dead, as their work exposes numerous conceptual associations and contradictions that have fuelled subsequent political debate. Indeed the full texture of those debates, and the full irony of modern political practice, will not be visible unless we spend some time examining the origins and development of communist theory and politics (Seery, 1990).

Like all political terms communism arose in the context of debate, although this seems to have begun so long ago that our guesses as to the nature of these discussions are more speculative than documented. The evidence, for 'Western' thought, is that the debate was about 'possession' or 'property', defined as the use or control of material resources. This could, of course, include people, in so far as slavery was practised, formally or informally. Whilst we cannot know what the 'original' form of property was, it is widely assumed to have been a system of shared use that was rule-governed and normatively enforced. Through archaeology we have access to material artefacts, but in pre-literate cultures we do not have access to ideas, so we can have little knowledge of property relations in the earliest societies. With literate cultures, such as that of ancient Greece, we begin to have texts, and the evidence there suggests debate.

Plato

If the 'original' or 'early' form of possession was shared use within a community, no concept would be needed to describe it at all, as descriptions demarcate with respect to an alternative, something which the thing in question is not. A network of conceptual assumptions, perhaps rules and precedents, would be sufficient for practicalities, without an overall descriptive word or phrase. The political use of communism in the 'Western' tradition begins with Plato in his text *The Republic* (ca. 380–360 BC), at which point an alternative to shared use within a community was already clear. That alternative was 'private property' or 'individual ownership'.

'Private property' or 'individual ownership' of material resources creates problems. Clearly it was an idea which disrupted traditional arrangements, which were most probably those of shared use. That 'sharing' was, of course, not necessarily amongst all individuals, nor amongst those who did the sharing was it necessarily equal in respect of use. Indeed the notions of 'all' and 'equality' may not have been operative, as community boundaries may not have been fixed, nor had standards of interpersonal comparison necessarily become available. Notions of the 'individual' as an agent or personality apart from the requirements or traditions of community life most probably developed within communities. The idea that communities formed from pre-existing 'individuated individuals' (Marx's ironic phrase) seems most improbable, though it must be said that various parables and theories have suggested that this has been in some sense the case (1857, section I).

A notion of individuality, and of interests apart from or perhaps even at odds with community traditions and requirements, creates a debate. Arguably it also creates politics in its modern form as an activity for managing the interaction of self-conscious and self-interested individuals in such a way that some order within the group is, or at least could be, preserved. Obviously politics can also be pushed to the point where communities are radically reformed or even destroyed, as notions of what this 'order' should be, and who should be responsible for it, come to differ.

The Republic is informed by Plato's revulsion at a constant conjunction of political interest in Athenian society. This conjunction was of individual ownership of resources, political control of the institutions of authority, and military might. We know this as political corruption, and it usually takes the form of 'corrupt military dictators' who use the army to run the state, and then use this overwhelming advantage to secure material possessions for themselves, their families and their associates.

In Plato's view, military might and institutions of authority are necessary for any community to exist, though his first discussion of the 'ideal community', where 'justice' or 'order' has been achieved, reduces these requirements to a minimum. This is because his 'first community' produces no surplus or luxury goods, only basic necessities. There is no need for 'private property' or 'individual ownership' in any significant sense, as there is literally nothing to own individually that is not already available in the community.

Within that first community, individuals co-operate to produce physical necessities and to enjoy leisure time. Though by definition they consume as individuals, they do not, as it were, pause to 'own' what they consume, nor to stockpile 'property' in order to provide things they might need later. Plato argued that the temptation for outsiders to attack such a community would be minimal, as there would be no 'desirable' luxuries to steal, though some minimal defence against enslavement and sheer vandalism might be required.

This first community is based on a system of 'sharing' or 'communal' – as opposed to 'individual' – ownership, and it also represents what we might describe as a subsistence or near-subsistence society. For that reason the 'audience' in Plato's fictive 'dialogue' rejects this community as 'fit only for pigs'. The audience wants surplus production, the production of luxuries, and with that requirement Plato manoeuvres his discussion closer to the realm of practical politics for his day and ours (*The Republic*, ii. 372A–374E).

Communism is, in the first instance, a proposal to reject a system of property relations in which individuals are allowed to use, control and 'own' resources – i.e. a system in which these individuals can expect an organised and forceful guarantee of their 'property' rights, and in which these 'individual' rights have a priority such that community requirements, or the requirements of other individuals in the community, are not necessarily met, or met in full. Thus, a communal system of shared use presumes the community-direction of resources as a priority and the assignment of goods to individuals as a 'share' that may be consumed or controlled individually, but not held individually in defiance of community decisions.

How the community is constituted, and how distributive decisions are reached, are of course further questions. These distributive decisions, including the distribution of obligations or other requirements to work as well as to consume, could flow from traditional practices or from decision-making bodies. The decision-maker could be one individual alone or the whole group following a rule of consensus or some other mechanism of choice. What is crucial is that there is, on the one hand, no guarantee of individual rights to resources that the community must enforce, irrespective of the needs of other members. On the other hand, there is no danger to individuals that they will be abandoned to the exercise of their own rights in securing material goods without recourse to resources held collectively by the community.

Plato's discussion develops to encompass a 'luxurious' state, in which the temptation to combine political, military and private interests is introduced and sharply escalates. To prevent the rule of corrupt, powerful and self-interested men (women were not rulers in Greece), he proposes that rulers should have a lengthy education and training to give them skills in abstract reasoning and knowledge of human affairs. This otherworldly perspective was designed to be devoid of material self-interest, and to provide a balance in the character and emotions of the rulers. To keep them up to this mark he also proposes that they be forbidden family life and private property, so there would be no temptation for them to manipulate politics to their own advantage (ii. 375A–iv. 434D).

In a surprising move Plato also argues for the admission of women to the ranks of rulers, though whether they are admitted on terms of precise equality with men, or whether the terms of rulership are themselves conceived in a masculine mode, are questions on which the text is ambiguous at best (iv. 445B–v. 457A; Coole, 1993). Within this 'guardian class' there are also military leaders, presumably subject to the same or similar strictures. The economic and social arrangements of the rest of society are left undiscussed, but as luxury production is envisaged, it seems reasonable to assume that the individual incentive to material accumulation would require a system of private property in order to function.

In this way, Plato's novel proposal that rulers should be forced to practise communism simultaneously enriched and confused the concept as he moved from his first 'ideal' society to his second one. Much of the context outside and even inside the text has been lost, as selective attention, beginning with his pupil and critic Aristotle, has made Plato's recommendations notoriously imprecise. The non-luxurious or 'primitive' community, in which communism is instituted for all, has been rejected on the terms ('city of pigs') given by the Platonic 'audience', which are not necessarily those of the author. Plato's own characterisation of the luxurious community as suffering from 'inflammation' has also been played down by later commentators. The introduction of women into political life as potential rulers has pleased no one, though for many different reasons, nor has the requirement that rulers be absolute because they are specially educated and trained. Those against absolute rulers are seldom open about the intellectual or practical prerequisites of rulership, and those in favour of absolute rulers have uniformly appealed to criteria other than education to justify such sweeping authority (which is usually derived from birth or divine intervention or both).

The Platonic state has been criticised as too unified, on grounds that it is defined and maintained through the exercise of political and military authority by a self-selecting caste, thus neglecting the varied forms of institutions and interests that arise in a polity. And it has been dismissed as unduly divisive because it separates ordinary inhabitants quite markedly from any exercise of citizenship in choosing or influencing rulers, and because it institutes quite separate lifestyles and property systems for rulers, on the one hand, and subjects, on the other. The legacy of Platonic communism has been an enduring disjunction between the ideals of share-and-share alike in a community framework and a system of elite rule through unquestionable and ascetic authorities. It cannot be said that there has been any Platonic practice in politics, though one contemporary criticism of Plato was that he had borrowed the communal institutions and military training from the practice of nearby Sparta (of which little is independently known). That in itself was enough to condemn *The Republic* in classical Athens.

Thomas More

There is a decidedly more modern flavour to Thomas More's communism,
outlined in his *Utopia* of 1516. This is because the context of political debate is
again set in a communist alternative to a system of individual property rights, but
with the addition of a concept of economic class moved well into the foreground.
Again, like Plato, More shielded himself behind various narrative and dialogical
devices, so that it is more than usually difficult to attribute to him an authorial
view. However, within that framework it is clear that the appearance in England
of 'vagabonds' or landless labourers was perceived as a problem, and in the eyes
of some, as a consequence of moving from a communal system of mutual
obligation (at least in theory) within feudal or quasi-feudal society to a system of
individualised ownership of land and other resources in a commercial economy.
Within that system it became possible to sever the link between persons or
households and their means of livelihood (usually land). The commercial advantage in doing so was defended, or at least tolerated, within the prevailing legal
relations. More seems to emphasise the futility of draconian penalties for theft,
when theft seems to be the only alternative to starvation (book I). The discussion
presumes that this problem is a by-product of individual rights to property and an
economics of greed, and no exculpatory defence of individualistic commercialism is even attempted.

More's communist alternative is first and foremost a 'utopia', a word he
coined, meaning 'nowhere', and its institutions and values are recounted in the
genre of travellers' tales or 'tall stories'. Nonetheless Utopia is no city of gold or
land of luxury, so it is in a sense closer to Plato's non-luxurious or 'primitive'
community. Though Utopian society is rationalistic in the way that principles and
ideals are uniformly instantiated, the values of the community rest on seniority
and practical experience, a sexual division of labour, and considerable emphasis
on religion. Whilst learning is venerated and scholarship merits time off from
physical tasks, rulership is normally exercised through the male heads of households, with delegated representatives of those heads meeting at successively
higher levels. A similar pattern is used to organise a priesthood. Agricultural and
city-based pursuits are carefully rotated, money is unknown, and gold and other
luxuries openly mocked.

As More's imaginary community produces and distributes necessities, and as
all houses are permanently unlocked and periodically reallocated, there is nothing material that is private and exclusive. Sexual relationships are punished
outside marriage, and the population is kept regionally mixed and numerically in
balance through a system of exchange amongst cities and colonial foundations.
As a consequence, individual incentive to accumulation does not exist, and
leisure time is individually consumed as planned production proceeds through a
schedule of rotated activities and tasks. The young and sick are lovingly cared for
and any miscreants are punished with forced labour as community slaves. Men
and women undergo military training, but the community also uses superfluous

'wealth' such as gold to hire mercenaries. Wars, however, are fought only in self-defence or for other morally justified reasons. Surprisingly, More's Utopians are not Christians, though some undergo conversion as morally the Gospel teachings conform to their values. The sting in More's implied critique is that, unlike contemporary Christians, Utopians are tolerant of religious diversity (book II).

Intriguingly More chose to discuss the very issues that Plato seems to ignore, namely the day-to-day life of ordinary folk in the community, the detail of their arrangements, and the structuring of their values. In effect it improves considerably on Plato's sketchy 'city of pigs' and redeems it for discussion. But there is, of course, a price. The attractions of competitive individual accumulation and the materially innovative consequences of commercial incentives are completely foregone by the population as a whole. Perhaps in theory communal values could favour and encourage individual innovation for community rather than for private gain, but More chose to exemplify austerity, stasis and asceticism in his communist society. Whether the limitation of production to what is merely necessary represents the most desirable use of human resources is a question that he does not choose to debate, arguing that luxury generates corruption. Hence, he presumes that the association between conflicting interests, perhaps played out as class or at least mass action, and the achievement of material 'progress' in society as a whole, is an unbreakable one. Because More's communist society generates no individually held surpluses in material goods, it prevents social problems arising from want and penury, on the one hand, and greed and temptation, on the other. Accordingly the authority structure has little to do politically, and needs only a consistent application of a commonsensical and rational code to sustain the community.

The challenge of commercial society

This line of argument – that communist society is non-luxurious – became difficult to sustain as commercialism and industrialisation took hold in European society. The potential for the production of new goods, and for increased productivity in turning out familiar ones, overtook the old idea of austerity and made it look monastic. The diagnosis of the problem – known by the time of the eighteenth century as the 'social question' – remained very similar: how to prevent the poverty and worklessness engendered by commercial economies. The presumption was that this had happened because those economies severed links between labourers and the raw materials of their livelihood, in order to institute and guarantee rights to 'private property'. Confusingly, answers to the 'social question' were denominated 'socialism' as well as 'communism', sometimes interchangeably, but sometimes in distinction or even contradiction to each other. Any generalisation, therefore, runs the risk of serious inaccuracy. Nonetheless, it might be ventured that communists were often considered more extreme in their opposition to the status quo, and more likely to reject altogether a money system for exchange.

This is not to say that socialists, including communists, agreed on much amongst themselves, even in terms of their criticisms of commercial societies. Socialism embraces almost any policy from mild redistribution of income and wealth within a capitalist economy to highly egalitarian and revolutionary conspiracies to institute workers' control of the international economy. Perhaps by way of generalisation it might be said that socialists agree that 'society' exists apart from individual preferences and actions, and that it incorporates obligations and responsibilities to move resources towards those who cannot obtain a living through their own activities in the market place for goods and labour.

Specifically communist solutions to the social question were, in general, either directed to humanising the work environment, or to minimising the time spent there. In this way, communists engaged explicitly with issues of size and degree: large factories to gain the benefits of productivity, or small ones to reinforce affective ties and mutual help amongst workers; continually advancing technology in order to gain the benefits of innovation, or emphasis on aesthetic craftwork and human-scale tools; national and worldwide solidarity, or small-scale 'utopian' communities. Perhaps the most radical vision was Charles Fourier's, as he merged work, aesthetics, pleasure and leisure together in small-scale 'phalansteries'. Contributions to production were to be arranged according to natural inclination, and rewards were to be communally allocated according to what people needed and what they deserved. Sharing applied to emotional and sexual relationships as well as to material goods and contributions, as only through the mutually agreed satisfaction of 'the passions' could social harmony be ensured (Poster 1971).

In a rather different way, ideals of Christian charity and self-effacement surfaced in organised movements to save 'souls' from material as well as spiritual deprivation. Amongst the more extreme versions of this were the Shaker communities, in which sexual abstinence was an absolute rule, although mutuality in sharing tasks and in the consumption of goods was the norm. Some communities pursued technological innovation, in order to maximise time for collective worship, and some were commercially successful in marketing seeds and other goods, retaining surplus funds for communally determined use.

These examples could be multiplied many times in several directions: there were elaborated schemes to be managed by authoritarian 'scientists of society'; paternalistic schemes for model factories and workers' communities; democratic plans for national workshops to equalise disparities between effort and reward; nostalgic efforts to revive the guilds of the middle ages; emigrations to distant islands to begin the world anew. Communist and socialist ideas and experiments flourished from the mid seventeenth to the mid nineteenth centuries in what has been described as a 'wonderland' of practical experimentation on several continents. There was also a vast library of theoretically varied and innovative tracts, schemes and manifestos in innumerable languages (Claeys, 1987). But by the later nineteenth century the verdict was in on most of the experiments, and the intellectual debate had solidified around one overwhelmingly influential doctrine: Marxism.

Marx and Engels

Karl Marx and Friedrich Engels devoted their careers to the communist cause, though one (Engels) worked for years managing his father's factories in order to support the other (Marx) through the tribulations of his vocation as communist. Both were in sympathy from an early age with radical ideas concerning redistribution in response to the increasingly obvious difficulties of the agricultural, and particularly the industrial, labouring poor. Both were also enamoured of the power of modern energy sources and of the productivity of modern factory production. But in certain terms they then distinguished themselves quite self-consciously from some aspects of the communist tradition, and in that way they functioned as systematisers more than innovators. Above all they were determined to enter, indeed create, an age of mass politics on a national and international scale.

In the context of mid nineteenth century Europe, mass politics was in some places barely tolerated. In most areas, it was generally repressed. The French Revolution represented the most visible and highly publicised intrusion of mass participation and representative institutions into a politics of authoritarian kings, emperors and princelings. Marx and Engels aligned themselves in sympathy and doctrine with the normally clandestine, and only periodically visible, movement for constitutional rule, legislative assemblies, independent judges and responsible executives. Both expected this movement to grow and intensify through its own momentum; what they planned to contribute was an economic analysis critical of commercialism and the commercial classes or 'bourgeoisie'.

Marx and Engels took a systemic rather than a merely redistributive view. Marx in particular spent a lifetime analysing and documenting the proposition that monetary exchange is at the root of a self-replicating cycle of poverty amongst workers (or the 'proletariat') and of accumulating surpluses amongst owners of productive resources (or the 'bourgeoisie'). Neither Marx nor Engels was ever at all friendly towards 'utopians' for a number of reasons. First, Marx and Engels never favoured a politics of small-scale or 'experimental' schemes or communities, as opposed to large-scale nation-wide effusions of practical political activity. Second, they did not desire the rejection of modern technology and were not prepared to argue against further innovations. Third, they refused to look back to any ideal society or golden age. The one famous passage about hunting in the morning, fishing in the afternoon, rearing cattle in the evening and criticising after dinner is anomalous in their œuvre and ambiguous as a palimpsest (Carver, 1988). Fourth, they had no truck with religious ideas or ideals, moral feelings or even ethical norms such as 'justice' in any but the most covert ways. Fifth, neither was prepared to play the part of a real, or would-be, leader, patriarch, founder or authoritative source of wisdom. And sixth, they never showed any real dedication to organisations, parties or even discussion groups, newspapers being the sole regular exception (Marx and Engels, 1848). The wonder is that anyone 'followed' them at all, as it was so difficult to find them politically, in order to do so. To make matters worse, neither Marx nor Engels offered much in the way of recognition to their followers.

Perhaps there was some allure in the mystery and novelty of their approach. Both Marx and Engels pursued popular journalism, but editorial control and state censorship restricted their ability to propagandise openly for their brand of communism, and audiences, whilst widespread in Europe and North America, were comparatively small for any given series of articles. Marx in particular aimed to put his views persuasively to relatively small circles of intellectuals, some of them communists or socialists (on various self-understandings of these terms), some of them democrats moved by political inequalities, and some of them reforming radicals concerned with economic inequalities. Neither Marx nor Engels recognised that women were particularly oppressed in ways other than political and economic disadvantage conventionally understood – notwithstanding Engels' late attempts to respond to the 'woman question'. Although women appear in communist and socialist texts from time to time (Carver, 1985) their position in society was overlooked by all the widely published (male) theorists of the era. The communist and socialist perspective on women is thus necessarily partial and ill-informed. Women's and indeed feminist activity of that era is today still largely unrecovered, as it most probably took sparsely recorded forms of teaching and practice. Perhaps Mother Ann Lee of the Shakers could stand for the moment as the merest indication of other contributors who remain anonymous, though not necessarily without enduring influence. The same could be said of numerous pamphleteers, speech writers and organisers (of either sex), whose contributions were not then nor are today specially marked out as of historical significance.

From the time of Marx and Engels onwards, modern means of communication and increasing literacy allowed the practice of mass politics at a distance via the written word. The apparent aloofness of these two German intellectuals is perhaps an effect of this development. The communist tradition was not merely recorded in an intellectualised form; the activity of pursuing communism became itself an intellectualised endeavour. By the end of the nineteenth century the works of Engels, and numerous other systematic critics of existing society, became popular items of study for workers. Theory came to co-exist alongside and inside political organisations and movements as major activities. As a consequence Marx and Engels were amongst the first to move the masses beyond a politics of ideas to a politics of theory, and Engels in particular took on the burden of popularising the more forbidding tomes that Marx eventually produced.

Though denying that he was a 'Marxist', Marx was a fervent communist, and in the context sketched above the association between his name and the avant-garde of the movement became almost unbreakable. All Marxists were communists in some sense, and the chances of communism existing independently of Marxism became virtually nil. A further factor promoting this process was the internationalist perspective adopted by Marx and Engels from their earliest days. This provides in part an explanation for their lack of personal involvement in partisan activity at the national level; a further reason was their lifetime exile in England after 1848. Marx and Engels even advised communists that they should not form party organisations, independent of other democratic or specifically working-class parties – nearly all of which in 1848 were illegal or clandestine. Instead, they were to work as individuals, or in small groups, to promote the constitutional revolutions of mass (or at least large-scale) suffrage and to push economic reorganisation onto the national political agenda (Marx and Engels, 1848, section IV). Marx and Engels themselves almost always worked at the level of international information-exchange and co-operation. They were committed not only to setting agreed goals and definitions amongst allied groups and parties pledging to assist one another, but to ensuring that working-class co-operation took precedence over the conventional 'ruling class' politics of national interest.

As communism and Marxism became synonymous with one another, so the political agenda developed to promote the staged introduction of the new economic order, for which the founders provided notes rather than blueprints. Broadly speaking, the 'battle for democracy' occupied the first attentions of communists. This referred to the overthrow of authoritarian non-constitutional regimes that excluded working men from political power (women were not specifically acknowledged in this context). Change of this order was assumed to require a violent struggle, in order to resist the attacks or counter-attacks of authoritarian forces protecting the interests of large-scale holders of property or representing the interests of those aspiring thereto. A series of 'despotic inroads on the right to property' would ensure a redistribution under 'socialism' of income, wealth, power and ownership to the mass of the people organised within a democratic state. Pay would be proportional to the labour contributed. Central to the system was the distinction between on the one hand 'means of production' in land and in capital generally, which would be centrally controlled, and on the other 'private property' in items for personal use and consumption, which would be safeguarded, indeed increased qualitatively and quantitatively, for ordinary people (Marx and Engels, 1848, section II).

The line between this 'socialist' stage and communism itself was deliberately vague. As the point of socialism was to create communism through practical activity and participatory politics, individual interests were presumed to be converging upon the collective good. At that point, a labour contribution from individuals according to ability (rather than as a response to material reward) would be the norm. Technological productivity, planned production and consumption, reduced hours of work, and personal fulfilment through the productive and social aspects of the labour process would obviate the need for money as a mediator between working hours and consumption goods. The material means of life would then be distributed according to need (Marx, 1875). Neither the political details concerning the administration of such a scheme and the resolution of any residual conflicts of interest, nor the economic details concerning the planning process for nation-wide schedules of production and consumption (and international arrangements mirroring these principles between countries), were ever spelled out. Nor was the political perspective of contemporary pre-literate or non-European peoples ever explored in depth by Marx *vis-à-vis* the forced introduction of trading relations and the domination entailed in colonial rule on which he commented in his books and articles.

Even more seriously neither Marx nor Engels produced any usable theories concerning the organisation and mission of political parties at any stage, or of the principled criteria for intra-party or society-wide democracy (though there are sketches suggesting that Marx supported arrangements of workplace democracy and representative bodies taking decisions at successively higher levels). The way was open therefore for later theorists to fill these gaps in their own way, with their own personal predilections and political circumstances in mind. In this manner, the political function of communism in the very late nineteenth century and throughout the twentieth century has come to deviate very sharply from the theories and practice of Marx and Engels, and, even more noticeably, from virtually all aspects of the communist tradition up to that time.

Communism versus community

The more this deviation occurred, the more efforts were made on the 'communist' side to invoke the authority of 'founders', and a mirror-like process of confirmation developed on the 'Western' or 'non-communist' side. Both sides generated a politicised form of scholarship and a curiously similar demonisation of ideas. Attempts to trace the roots or origins of twentieth century 'communism' in the ideas (most usually) or practice (very occasionally) of pre-twentieth century communism became by the 1950s a sizeable academic and indeed political industry in the 'West'. The effort to produce a genealogy was predicated on the view that criticism of current 'communists' was not sufficient in itself. Similar malpractices were bound to crop up unless communist ideas themselves were shown to be 'linked' to twentieth century events and then 'refuted' once and for all. Thus many mid twentieth century accounts of the communist tradition suffer in varying degrees from a process of inscription – reading current political circumstances and judgements into what were presumed to be canonical texts, which were presumed to have 'forebears'. With the collapse of the former Soviet Union and the dissolution of 'superpower conflict' as an intellectual template, it is now possible to take a more dispassionate view.

Parallel to the association between Marxism and communism was a further association between both and 'revolution'. This was particularly influential throughout the 'developing' world, most notably in China, Cuba and Vietnam, where anti-imperialist struggles for national liberation took place. Very few successful revolutions were of the constitutional and democratic sort that Marx envisaged, although many participants may have associated themselves with revolutionary movements on the understanding that this would be the case. Nonetheless, through the late nineteenth and early twentieth centuries, and by a variety of means, an apparatus of representative government became widely established. Thus, the original link between the need for popular revolutionary force and communist politics should well have weakened, and there is some evidence in the correspondence of the later Marx to suggest that he had taken peaceful transitions to socialism on board.

Within the Marxist tradition, however, communism remained a doctrine of revolution; a guide for revolutionaries and the presumed authorisation for armed struggle. In part, this association remained valid on Marx's terms. Anti-authoritarian movements and anti-colonialist peoples struggled for local democratic rule, though such societies were often far from instantiating the benefits of modern material production that formed a necessary basis for the kind of socialist measures that Marx and Engels had wanted. The international co-operation between democratic movements that the two envisaged was rarely achieved either, as national and nationalist interests generally took precedence over collaboration. The most influential model for party organisation was derived from the writings of V. I. Lenin and from his experiences in fighting authoritarian rule in Russia; from his attempts to exercise political power in a war-torn society further troubled by civil war and foreign invasion; and from Stalin's consolidation of one-party rule and the establishment of a highly centralised system of economic management. Elements of representative democracy within party and state structures evolved but in a sham-like way.

The 'totalitarian' model, as applied by 'Western' commentators to 'communism', underestimated the need for, and the practice of, politics in an authoritarian system. But no model of democracy independent of self-description or elaborated excuses could save, then or now, the notion that the Communist Party of the Soviet Union, and the Soviet Union itself, were 'democratic'. None of the 'communists' of that regime, its satellites, or any other Marxist regime or movement appealed with any clarity or enthusiasm to any of the non-democratic models of rule available within the communist tradition itself. As noted above, these included 'philosopher kings' in Plato, patriarchal authority in More, or other versions of an administrative or religious elite. Thus, it is difficult to see how one of the great political movements of the twentieth century conformed at all to any aspect of communism as a pre-existing tradition, other than to institute elements of the sort of redistributive policies that have sometimes emerged within the socialist programmes of representative democracies.

What divides redistributive socialism from Marx's communism, and indeed almost any other communism in the tradition, is the presumed continuation of the money economy, rather than the managed obsolescence of monetary exchange itself. Nowhere in the 'communist' world was this ever seriously envisaged. The claims propounded by the Soviet Union that, for example, 1936 marked the 'victory of socialism'; that 1959 marked the beginning of 'the full scale construction of communist society'; and that in 1961 the transition from 'socialism to communism' would be complete 'in the main' within twenty years, inspired little confidence either inside or outside its boundaries.

Indeed, backtracking began in the 1970s, and by the beginning of the 1980s 'developed socialism' was said to be a lengthy historical stage, even a whole historical epoch in which progress would be merely gradual. Comments on the relative unimportance of rosy futures suggested that the communist ideal had been officially shelved. Furthermore it cannot be said that dissidence within the various 'communist' regimes flourished as much as it did because of any underground communist movement objecting, on specifically and traditionally communist grounds, either to the maintenance of monetary relations in society or to the undemocratic party and state structures that dominated the process of economic planning (Crouch, 1989).

Clearly the abolition of private ownership of the means of production in itself did not even begin the process of socialising production through democratic planning that Marx and Engels had envisaged. Futhermore, the imposition of authoritarian rule via self-selecting (and self-purging) parties, and the accumulation of political and economic privileges (by cadres and apparatchiks) did not match any previous model of communist society. It is difficult to see how these arrangements, which have been described by their originators and participants as 'communist', could possibly conform to any notion of shared control and use within a co-operative community. If that is what communism has come to mean, then Orwellian language has indeed triumphed.

The future of communism

Communism still has a future as a critical perspective on an economic system based on private property, or so-called private property – enormous resources are now owned and controlled by 'artificial persons' or 'private' companies. The relation of these entities to an economic and legal doctrine of 'individual' ownership and property rights remains politically obscure. The extent to which the current commercial system is founded on, and indeed continually recreates, wasteful and unjustified inequalities of income and wealth is always worth considering. The proposition that only 'effective demand', i.e. access to money or credit, is the sole necessary, efficient and desirable gateway to consumption goods has been in recent years loudly defended and, some would say, politically manipulated. Some of the regulation and control of the 'means of production' that democratic states have come to exercise has recently been weakened or abandoned. Some of the redistributive measures giving access to goods on the basis of need (rather than monetary resources, however derived) have been dismantled. Insofar as the counter-argument that society has a role in the productive process (beyond that of securing 'private property'), and that the 'individual' may claim resources on a basis other than commercial acumen (or charity), is still pertinent, then a communitarian critique of 'economic man' (*sic*) may rightly appeal to the communist tradition. After all, communists developed their systems for just this purpose.

The millennarian view amongst communists that competitive commercial individualism is fundamentally flawed, and that the wholesale substitution of communitarian relations is the sole logical and practical response, may have been a discursive strategy or trope within the communist genre. But critics, who argue that communists are necessarily extremists who want to sweep away entire existing societies, are not always reading the texts politically. Communists may well want to work within an existing democratic system to achieve their goals; occasionally they have claimed the right to do so. That said, there is always likely to be a continuing pattern of counter-cultural movements rejecting economic individualism and attempting to 'opt out'. In that mode, the communist tradition runs within and alongside a recurring vein of religious and secular experimentation.

The use and control of material resources is a necessary and increasingly divisive feature of human society. How these resources are 'owned' and 'shared' will be continually debated. Communists have argued influentially against a thoroughgoing individualist view. The extent to which an individualistic economics and politics are permeated by what is in reality an apparatus of regulation and control is perhaps testimony to the necessity for at least some communism in practice, even in a world where 'luxury' and 'surplus' are the name of the game.

References

Carver, T. (1985), 'Engels's Feminism', *History of Political Thought*, Vol. 6, No. 3, pp. 479–89

— (1988), 'Communism for Critical Critics? A New Look at The German Ideology', *History of Political Thought*, Vol. 9, No. 1, pp. 129–36

Claeys, G. (1987), *Machinery, Money and the Millenium: From Moral Economy to Socialism 1815–60*, Cambridge, Polity

Coole, D. (1992), *Women in Political Theory: From Ancient Misogyny to Contemporary Feminism*, 2nd edition, London, Harvester Wheatsheaf

Crouch, M. (1989), *Revolution and Evolution: Gorbachev and Soviet Politics*, Hemel Hempstead, Philip Allan

Marx, K. (1852), *The Eighteenth Brumaire of Louis Bonaparte* (various editions)

— (1857), Introduction to the *Grundrisse* (various editions)

— (1875), *Critique of the Gotha Programme* (various editions)

Marx, K. and Engels, F. (1848), *The Communist Manifesto* (various editions)

More, T. (1516), *Utopia* (various editions)

Plato, *The Republic* (various editions)

Poster, M. (ed.) (1971), *Harmonian Man: Selected Writings of Charles Fourier*, Garden City, New York, Doubleday

Seery, J. E. (1990), *Political Returns: Irony in Politics and Theory*, Boulder CO, Westview Press

Further Reading

Beilharz, P. (1992), *Labour's Utopias: Bolshevism, Fabianism and Social Democracy*, London and New York, Routledge

Nove, A. (1991), *The Economics of Feasible Socialism Revisited*, London, HarperCollins

Wright, A. (1987), *Socialisms: Theories and Practices*, Oxford University Press

Conservatism

There is no single corpus of conservative dogma, no particular text which conservatives can hold aloft as representing the basis of their beliefs. There has generally been an absence of what Gillian Peele (1976, p. 13) has called 'magisterial theorists' to whom conservatives can turn for inspiration. That has been the case particularly with conservatives in the English-speaking, as opposed to the continental tradition.

To be a conservative is to hold a particular view of human nature and of society, but it is a view that is largely antithetical to the generation of grand theories, of abstract vision of a society yet to exist. Exponents of conservatism are notable for eschewing such terms as ideology, some even avoiding reference to principles, preferring instead to refer to attitudes or, in the case of Michael Oakeshott (1962, p. 168), dispositions. The distinction is an important one. For to have a particular disposition is to have a feeling about the way things should be; the implication is that it is inherent and natural. Conservatives feel comfortable with such natural dispositions and as such feel little need to articulate them; they are personal and they are part of the way of the world.

A further discouragement to spending time articulating a coherent set of guiding principles has been, in the case especially of Britain, the long periods which conservatives have spent in government. 'Political parties seldom philosophise when in office' (Blake, 1976, p. 1). A combination of electoral success and an unwillingness to engage in expounding the essentials of a philosophy has led many observers to assume that there is little more to the British Conservative Party than a desire to be in government. 'Of all the features of the Conservative Party', wrote Richard Rose (1965, p. 143), 'the intense concern with winning elections and holding office is its most notable'. Attempts to locate and delineate the body of principles of conservatism have been rare. Conservatives see little need for such an exercise. Critics believe there is nothing to explore.

However, conservatives do not operate in some philosophical vacuum. Policies are not spun out of thin air. Even the Oakeshottian perception that the purpose of government is to keep 'the ship of state afloat' involves a certain view of the necessity to maintain the ship as well as an inferred need for a view as to how the ship may be maintained. Conservative pragmatism, as Lord Coleraine (1970, p. 20) noted, 'even when it seems to be second nature, is not simply instinctive. It is based on a certain reading of history, a certain interpretation of experience. Even the most hidebound of conservatives is more rational and less intuitive in his political attitudes than he, or anyone else, supposes.'

What, then, are the basic dispositions and tenets of conservative faith? At the heart of conservatism, especially that which predominates in the English-speaking world, are two basic dispositions. One is a scepticism as to the power of man's reason. Individual reason is seen as imperfect and limited. Man is a mix of emotion, instinct and habit as well as thought. The imperfections of man prevent the bringing about of utopia. Present society is the product of impersonal forces, of the accumulated wisdom of generations. No individual or group of individuals could ever achieve such a result, nor improve significantly upon it. There is thus a wariness towards, and distrust of, abstract ideas, untested by experience.

From this flows both an anti-intellectual streak – few conservative thinkers, as Tibor Szamuely (1968, p. 7) observed, would have dreamt of describing themselves as intellectuals – and a sceptical attitude toward what government may achieve. The capacity of government to change man's nature is limited and no one individual or collection of individuals is gifted with the ability to foresee fully the consequences of the actions of government. Efforts to remedy existing evils may result in even greater ones. Learning – and the practice of government – cannot be divorced from the appreciation of experience, that is, history. For those keen to identify from a priori reasoning what *should* be, the conservative tempers the debate by asking what *can* be.

The second disposition is, in large measure, a corollary of the first. This comprises a concern for, and in essence an adherence to, society as it presently exists. There is an appreciation of both the complexity and the conveniences of society as presently constituted, as well as of the forces that brought it about. For the conservative, the present is not necessarily the ideal, but it is the real. 'It is a measure of how things are, the conveniences, but also the inconveniences, of a style of living' (Norton and Aughey, 1981, p. 19). There is an attachment to those institutions which form and help shape society, institutions which exist, which are real, and which – in the absence of any clear evidence to the contrary – are deemed to fulfil some purpose. The effects of their removal are likely to be unknowable, but as with chopping off part of the human body, the presumption is that the surgery would be painful, with consequences for the rest of the societal body. If surgery is necessary, it should be as limited as possible, designed to strengthen – not weaken – the product of generations of accumulated wisdom. Even then, many conservatives prefer the natural solution of self-healing to the surgical knife of government.

For the conservative, then, the real and knowable are to be preferred over the abstract and the unknowable. Hence, whenever established norms and institutions – be it the crown or the police force – are under attack, the conservative disposition is to spring to their defence. In English history, this disposition is longstanding and its exposition can be traced back to Richard Hooker in the sixteenth century (Hearnshaw, 1933; Kirk, 1953). Conservatism then became, in the words of Hearnshaw, a 'continuing spirit', finding its later and most articulate expression in the eighteenth century writings of Edmund Burke.

Basic tenets

From these dispositions may be extracted some basic tenets. First, there is a belief in the *organic nature of society*. Society is seen as a historical product, a thing of slow, natural growth – a 'spiritual organism' in Hearnshaw's apt description. Right is a function of time rather than of present rationality.

The analogy with an organism has, as Lincoln Allison noted, both negative and positive connotations. Negatively, by stressing the complex interrelationships between the parts of the organism, it emphasises the difficulties attached to achieving change. On the positive side, it stresses that the individual is part of an entity with a character of its own beyond the complete control of conscious plans. 'His incorporation into this larger entity gives his life meaning, place and purpose. It makes him belong' (Allison, 1984, pp. 16–17).

Second, given that society is viewed as evolutionary and not static, a necessary consequence is an *acceptance of some change*. However, that same perception dictates a particular kind of change. Change that is wholescale and threatens the existing fabric of society is anathema to the conservative. So too is change for change's sake. The purpose of change must be to improve that which exists, to correct proven and palpable ills, doing so in order to strengthen – not destroy – the existing social fabric. 'Change should come in small gradations; by way of evolution not revolution; by adaptation and not destruction' (Gash, 1977, p. 27). It was Burke, responding to the excesses of the French Revolution, who provided the most cogent articulation of the belief in an evolutionary society and it was he who summed up the conservative approach to change in the aphorism: 'A state without the means of some change is without the means of its own conservation'.

Third, it is an axiom of conservative thought that there must be *order and discipline in society*, and that this should flow from a *deep respect for the institutions of state and society*. 'Order rests on the exercise of authority, on its embodiment in the institutions of society and on the acceptance of those institutions as legitimate' (Clarke, 1973, p. 11). The role of institutions is functional and symbolic: they represent continuity with the past and they embody the unity of society and the norms and conduct of that society. Those institutions, like the citizen, are subject to the rule of law, which regulates definitively the relations between citizens. The rule of law applies equally to governors and the governed. 'When injustice arises, the cause usually is not so much the content of the law as a failure to apply it impartially' (Patterson, 1973, p. 16). A stable social order is thus dependent on the maintenance of the rule of law.

Order, thus defined, is a condition of freedom. It provides a basic framework within which citizens can interact, pursue their diverse pleasures, achieve their own goals, without direction from above. In essence, a society characterised by Oakeshott as 'societas' – entailing a tolerance of diversity in social life and a natural harmony borne of the 'conversation of mankind' – as opposed to a utopian 'universitas', seeking some centrally imposed future goal for which all must strive.

Fourth, there is an attachment to the *ownership of property*. 'The possession of property by the individual', declared Quintin Hogg in 1947 (p. 99), echoing Burke, 'is the essential condition of liberty'. Property is seen as an extension of personality. It is a joy, something to be developed in one's own image. It ensures a sense of belonging and, concomitantly, imparts duties as well as rights. It is also a stimulus to future development. Property, declared Clinton Rossiter (quoted in Harbour, 1982, p. 150), 'provides the main incentive for productive work. Human nature being what it is and always will be, the desire to acquire and hold property is essential to progress'.

The ownership of property also contributes to stability. It imparts a sense of responsibility and a desire to protect one's possessions. It provides a bulwark against an overmighty state. It diffuses economic power and ensures the independence of the owner. Such independence, as Rossiter noted, can never be achieved by one who has to rely on others for shelter and material comforts.

Fifth, conservatives accord a role to government, but for limited purposes. They are, as we have seen, wary of government, especially that bent on the realisation of abstract designs. Unfettered government is a threat to liberty. Consequently, *limited government* should be realised through a series of checks and balances, both formal and informal, through an array of state institutions and of 'small battalions'. A plural society is a *sine qua non* of limited government.

Government nonetheless is necessary to fulfil those enduring tasks which government alone can fulfil: essentially defence of the realm abroad and the maintenance of peace at home. It is also necessary to intervene to check or prevent abuse, when there is a demonstrable need to do so. Conservatives have never rejected strong government, as long as the use of power has been justified by the special circumstances of the case. But even strong government must be accountable.

Sixth, conservatives have always accepted the importance of *creating wealth*. Burke had been influenced by liberal economic theory and wrote, in *Thoughts and Details on Scarcity* (1795), that 'the laws of commerce' were 'the terms of nature and consequently the laws of God'.

Central to wealth creation is a belief in the superiority of market forces over government intervention. Government intervention, it is argued, can lead only to inefficiency, monopoly and a decline in the ability of the nation to compete internationally. Allowing the free interplay of market forces is both a guarantee of individual freedom and an essential dynamic of national prosperity. The purpose of government is to maintain the social disciplines of capitalism, not to run the economy.

British conservatism has also witnessed the acquisition of two further tenets, the consequence of Disraeli's leadership of the Conservative Party. One is the concept of *one nation at home*, an acceptance of a role for government in some social provision for those unable to help themselves. 'Our policy', declared Neville Chamberlain in 1925 (quoted in Bellairs, 1977, p. 31), 'is to use the great resources of the state, not for the distribution of an indiscriminate largesse, but to help those who have the will and desire to raise themselves to higher and better things'. The other is *one nation abroad*, a belief in the need to defend and promote British interests abroad. Conservatives believe they have a unique perception of British interests abroad. 'The function of an enlightened foreign policy', declared Lord Hugh Cecil (1912, p. 211), 'is to uphold national greatness with due regard to the place of other nations in the world'. Disraeli played the imperial card. Empire was seen as the projection of British greatness on a global scale. More recently, some conservatives have seen the European Community as offering the means for the country to once again play a leading role on the international stage.

These various tenets suggest a richness of conservative thought. From them may also be inferred some inherent tensions.

Inherent tensions

The tenets we have identified are not necessarily compatible with one another. Indeed, three separate but interrelated tensions can be identified.

One is between continuity and change. There is a natural tendency to protect and preserve, to nurture the existing society. There is also a recognition that change may be needed to correct some abuse or to assist in wealth generation. The conundrum for conservatives is determining the point at which change becomes necessary. The need must be clear, but there are no hard rules, no prescriptive criteria, to determine when that point has been reached. Some conservatives will place greater emphasis on one tenet than another, resulting in some being more disposed than others to accept the need for change.

The second tension may be subsumed within that of continuity and change but has a distinct character of its own, and that is the tension between the free market emphasis of wealth creation and the willingness to contemplate government intervention. The emphasis on the need to maintain the social fabric and, in Britain, the 'one nation' tradition predispose some conservatives to sanction government intervention in economic affairs. The free market emphasis generates a principled opposition to such intervention. That tension was marked in the British Conservative Party in the early 1980s, though ironically prime minister Margaret Thatcher was forced to generate a strong state in order to force the conditions necessary for a free economy (Gamble, 1988).

The third tension is essentially a corollary of the second and that is the tension between the individual and society. Society is seen as greater than the collection of individuals that inhabit it. There is also a recognition that those individuals are different, naturally so. The problem arises in that there is, in a part of the free market philosophy acquired in the nineteenth century, a particular emphasis on the individual, to the extent that the role of society is diminished or denied altogether. The emphasis on the autonomous individual – what Allison (1984, p. 12) has termed the extreme form of 'marketism' – is rare within the British Conservative Party but it informs part of a particular strand of thought within the party. In as much as it does so, it generates a dialogue and occasional tension within conservative discourse.

Such tensions can produce splits within conservative ranks. Over time, they have resulted in different varieties of conservative thought. Continental conservatives have tended to be less empirical than conservatives in the English-speaking world (Schuettinger, 1969). Within British conservatism, several strands of thought are discernible (Norton and Aughey, 1981).

Yet they are also creative tensions. The basic scepticism of conservatism ensures that no one view of society is accepted unquestionably as the correct one. Conservatives must temper one emphasis against another. By such a process, the most appropriate response is likely to emerge. What Aubrey Jones (1946, pp. 160–1) perceived in the nature of society – 'there is more than an even chance that the generations of the past, swaying now to this now to that side of the see-saw, will in the end have struck the true balance of authority and power' – is seen also as a feature of the discourse of conservativism.

That discourse has both negative and positive connotations. Negatively, it reinforces the not unjustified perception that conservatives are more likely to know what they are against than what they are for. Positively, it means that conservatives are not constrained by some philosophic straitjacket. The result, in the English-speaking countries, has been a flexibility that may be the explanation for electoral success.

References

Allison, L. (1984), *Right Principles*, Oxford, Basil Blackwell

Bellairs, C. (1977), *Conservative Social and Industrial Reform*, London, Conservative Political Centre

Blake, R. (1976), 'A Changed Climate', in Lord Blake and J. Patten (eds.), *The Conservative Opportunity*, London, Macmillan

Cecil, Lord H. (1912), *Conservatism*, London, Williams and Norgate

Clarke, D. (1973), *The Conservative Party*, London, Conservative Central Office

Coleraine, Lord (1970), *For Conservatives Only*, London, Tom Stacey

Gamble, A. (1988), *The Free Economy and the Strong State*, London, Macmillan

Gash, N. (1977), 'From the Origins to Sir Robert Peel', in Lord Butler (ed.), *The Conservatives*, London, George Allen and Unwin

Harbour, W. R. (1982), *The Foundations of Conservative Thought*, University of Notre Dame Press

Hearnshaw, F. J. C. (1933), *Conservatism in England*, London, Macmillan
Hogg, Q. (1947), *The Case for Conservatism*, Harmondsworth, Penguin
Jones, A. (1946), *The Pendulum of Politics*, London, Faber
Norton, P. and Aughey, A. (1981), *Conservatives and Conservatism*, London, Temple Smith
Oakeshott, M. (1962), *Rationalism in Politics and Other Essays*, London, Methuen
Patterson, B. (1973), *The Character of Conservatism*, London, Conservative Political Centre
Peele, G. (1976), 'The Conservative Dilemma', in Lord Blake and J. Patten (eds.), *The Conservative Opportunity*, London, Macmillan
Rose, R. (1965), *Politics in England*, London, Faber
Schuettinger, R. L. (1969), 'Varieties of Conservatism', *Swinton Journal*, 15 (spring)
Szamuely, T. (1968), 'Intellectuals and Conservativism', *Swinton Journal*, 14 (spring)

Further Reading
O'Sullivan, N. (1976), *Conservatism*, London, Dent
Scruton, R. (1980), *The Meaning of Conservatism*, Harmondsworth, Penguin
Willetts, David (1992), *Modern Conservatism*, Harmondsworth, Penguin

The market

The market can be defined as the free exchange of goods and services at a price determined by the balance of supply and demand. Markets as social institutions have existed for many centuries. But thinking about the market as a sophisticated system dates back to the eighteenth century and the great philosophers of the Scottish enlightenment – notably Adam Smith and David Hume.

Adam Smith's *Wealth of Nations*, published in 1776, is the first and perhaps the finest attempt at a coherent overall account of market thinking. The foundations on which the structure of his argument rests are really very simple. He recognises that economic advance rests on the interaction of three forces. First, there is the instinct to 'truck, barter and exchange' (Smith, 1937, p. 13). This is a necessary condition for the second crucial factor in economic advance – specialisation of labour. The engine of ever-increasing prosperity starts turning as people specialise more and more in particular tasks which they carry out with greater efficiency. Exchange allows specialisation which drives the wealth of nations. Self-sufficiency is the sure route to poverty. Third, there is the recognition that we have unsatisfied wants. Our instinct to better our condition provides the essential impetus which drives forward the mechanisms of exchange and specialisation.

This way of thinking, the market way of thinking, has been the dominant intellectual current in political and economic thought for the past two centuries. It stands in contrast to a very different way of thinking which preceded it and still rivals it. Mercantilism was the dominant economic doctrine in Western Europe in the seventeenth and eighteenth centuries. Nations were seen as being in a state of economic war with each other – with their economies directed by their governments just as their armies were. During the nineteenth century free market thinking achieved almost total intellectual ascendancy. But during the twentieth century we have seen the revival of mercantilism in a new and more sophisticated form – corporatism. We can better understand the political economy of the free market if we identify the three crucial respects in which it can be differentiated from mercantilism and corporatism.

First, mercantilists believe that economic relationships must take the form of one person exploiting another. If one person gains, it can only be at the expense of another. They believe that if you are poor it is because he is rich. Trade, be it domestic or international, is not seen as something of mutual benefit – on the contrary it is a refined form of theft. If we all produced exactly the same things in the same way and had exactly the same tastes then the mercantilists would be correct. At best trade would be useless; at worst it would be exploitation. But fortunately we are all different, both in what we produce and in what we wish to consume – that is why we can exchange with each other to mutual benefit. Every schoolboy knows that if I exchange my old pop record for your football poster we can both be better off. It is this belief in the mutual benefits of exchange which lies behind the belief in free trade, both domestically and internationally.

The second crucial distinction is that mercantilists and corporatists look at economics from the perspective of producers, whereas free marketeers regard the consumer as sovereign. The market is an economic democracy in which we all vote with our pounds. Adam Smith robustly stated (1937, p. 625) that 'consumption is the sole end and purpose of all production'. But our interests as consumers are dissipated; our interests as producers are much more narrowly focused and vivid. It is tempting therefore to look at an economic system from the producer's perspective, not the consumer's. Many businessmen, for example, believe that we would be richer if only the Japanese were not so good at making cars and hi-fi equipment. But whilst the Japanese might make life difficult for our manufacturers, they enrich us all as consumers. We are better off if a Japanese manufacturer makes a more reliable and cheaper car than anyone has in the past.

The third crucial proposition is the recognition that we have unsatisfied demands and there is always scope for human ingenuity to increase our productive capacity too. Mercantilists see the world as a closed system, a zero sum gain. In this grim world it looks logical to cure unemployment, for example, by compulsorily taking some people out of the labour-force – normally picking on weaker groups such as the young, the old and women. This only makes sense if one assumes all demands are being satisfied and that therefore there is only a fixed amount of work to be done. The excitement of Smith's system is that it is open-ended: there is always scope for increasing consumption and production. Our unsatisfied wants and free trade create an ever-expanding range of opportunities and products. And because it is open, we can thrive without injuring others.

The market and economics: perfect competition

During the second half of the nineteenth century and early in the twentieth century market thinking was captured in increasingly rigorous economic theory. This gave it enormous intellectual authority, though it also took it a long way from its intellectual roots. It can now be proved mathematically that under a certain set of strict conditions free markets maximise the benefit to consumers from scarce resources. This model is called 'perfect competition'. The first term of most undergraduate economics courses is devoted to explaining it. The trouble is that the conditions required for it to generate the right conclusions are very stringent. There have to be so many competing firms they are all price takers rather than able to influence the price themselves. There should be no brand loyalty from consumers; no barriers against anyone entering the market; no transport costs.

The rest of the university economics course then consists of evidence that markets fail to live up to these rigorous conditions. If there is any competition at all, it is at best 'imperfect' (this should strictly be a technical term to describe some forms of markets, but the implied value judgement could not be stronger). The policy conclusion, sometimes explicit and sometimes implicit, is that as competition is imperfect, governments can intervene as much as they like.

J. K. Galbraith, probably the most overrated post-war economist in my opinion, mocked the obvious failings of the perfect competition theory. He saw the modern business corporation as a big bureaucracy, undisturbed by risk or competition because of the power it exerted over its customers, easily seduced by advertising. Adam Smith's entrepreneur had degenerated into Galbraith's middle-ranking corporate bureaucrat, more concerned with politicking his way up the corporation than with customers out there in the real world (Galbraith, 1974). But the fate of firms such as Dunlop or British Leyland, once-great companies brought low because they failed to keep up with their rivals and to satisfy their consumers, suggests that even enormous corporations are under sustained competitive pressure. Indeed, the competition faced by big corporations is in some ways more intense than that faced by small firms in a perfectly competitive market who can sell however much barley they produce at the going price.

There is more to markets than perfect competition. This is captured in what is called the Austrian school of economics (stretching back from Friedrich Hayek through Ludwig von Mises to Carl Menger). This goes beyond the mathematics of perfect competition back to the flesh and blood of Adam Smith's original conception. The perfectly competitive model is static. The free markets of economics textbooks are eviscerated, sterilised sorts of markets with no risk, no uncertainty, no new discoveries; just costs and prices and economic agents. In such a world there are indeed no entrepreneurs – because there are no information gaps for them to fill, or opportunities for them to seize. It is a view of the world captured in the story of two believers in perfect competition walking down the street. One spots a five-pound note lying on the pavement and the other comments, 'There can't be, if there were, somebody would have picked it up'. Such are the blinkers of the textbook orthodoxy. The Austrian school by contrast places the entrepreneur back at the centre of the economic process.

Austrian economists also understand that some of the knowledge which economic agents work on is intuitive; it is not explicit and cannot be written down. It is tacit knowledge – what they cannot teach you at Harvard Business School.

This sort of knowledge is an escapable part of the operation of any economy; it shows why full-scale economic planning is not simply impractical but theoretically impossible.

The market and politics: civil society

Adam Smith did not call his economic theory capitalism (that term was coined by its socialist critics in the early nineteenth century); nor did he call it free enterprise (the term coined later in the century by its American advocates). He called it 'a system of natural liberty'. That best conveys the political as much as the economic significance of the market. It is a system of political economy which begins with human beings acting freely and shows that, provided there is a clear legal framework, this does not lead to anarchy and confusion, but to a spontaneous, yet properly integrated, economic system. It no more needs an overarching explicit plan than a thriving forest needs someone to decide what the ants should do and which acorns should produce oaks. Order can be spontaneous; it need not be planned. Indeed it is beyond human capacity to plan it all or know it all.

There is a close connection between the free market and the modern liberal state. The theorists debate whether or not this is a logically necessary connection but there is certainly, at the very least, a striking correlation between free market economies and political liberty. Some of the reasons are obvious. The opening definition of the market made it clear that the private contract has a crucial role in the operation of a market system. That in turn has to be policed by an independent authority with greater power than any individual contract maker. Free markets require an independent judiciary which in turn is a necessary condition for our civil liberties.

The distinction between the market and the corporatist approach to economics can now be seen equally to apply to politics. Corporatists in economics see the nation-state as a purposeful organisation, like an army. For a free marketeer the nation-state is a place for people to pursue their own purposes without interfering with others. It is certainly not 'United Kingdom Ltd'.

The market and psychology: motive and intention

Perhaps the greatest confusion which arises in the interpretation of market thinking is the belief that it is somehow a psychological theory. This belief is understandable as many of the original advocates of the free market expressed in psychological terms ideas which would now be expressed in economic or philosophical terms. We have already seen that one of the foundations of Smith's system was what he called a desire to better oneself, but which modern economics would simply call unsatisfied wants.

Perhaps the most widespread criticism of the market is the belief that it has a debased view of human nature in which we are driven by greed and self-aggrandisement. But free market political economy does not claim to be a psychological theory. It is not an account of human motivation. In order to analyse its behavioural assumptions more thoroughly we need first to look at our behaviour as consumers, then as producers.

Markets give consumers power over producers, whereas in a planned economy, producers have power over consumers. Markets transmit consumer wants and ensure that they are satisfied. Some of these wants may be elevated and others ignoble; the market treats them alike. It will generate supplies of heroin or incense, depending on what it is that we demand. It is value-neutral. It will not impose on us higher tastes, nor will it debase our tastes lower than they already are. Adam Smith observed (1937, p. 343): 'It is not the multitude of ale-houses ... that occasions a general disposition to drunkenness among the common people; but that disposition arising from other causes necessarily gives employment to a multitude of ale-houses.' The market is a mirror which reflects back at us our wants and desires.

The left-wing critics of capitalist consumerism will not be satisifed with this reply. They fear that markets encourage materialism. The usual response of an economist charged with materialism is to plead guilty and say: so what? Free market economies have been very successful at generating more and more material goods. There is more to life than that, but material prosperity does not do any harm. Whilst we have unmet material demands, there is nothing wrong with us trying to satisfy more of them. And anyway, socialist planning is equally materialistic – just less successful at it.

The argument that capitalism reflects a debased view of human nature does not just depend on our role as consumers; we also need to consider our role as producers. Adam Smith famously observed (1937, p. 14) that: 'It is not from the benevolence of the butcher, the brewer, or the baker that we expect our dinner, but from their regard to their own interest.' Is this fair to bakers, brewers and butchers? The local butcher is doing his job for a whole mixture of motives. Maybe his father set up the shop and he is carrying on the business out of family duty. Maybe he likes chatting to his customers and would hate working on a noisy production line, even though he could earn twice as much. Surely, the critics say, capitalist theory simply fails to acknowledge this great variety in human motivation.

The answer is that apart from one or two basic assumptions (such as unmet material wants), modern free market economics makes no claim to be a psychological theory of behaviour. Individual economic agents have a host of different motives. The point is that they operate within an economic structure which means that they must at least use their resources efficiently enough to ensure their income exceeds their costs. Whatever the reasons for being a butcher, and however noble these may be, he can only survive as a butcher if he earns enough profit to sustain his minimum acceptable standard of living (or can be subsidised by something else that passes that test).

Believers in free markets are no more committed to saying that everyone is motivated by personal greed than to saying that every tennis-player at Wimbledon is simply motivated to win by the prize money. They are in fact driven by everything from pride to wishing to please their parents. But we can say that, by and large, the best tennis comes from matches in which the players compete to win.

Ultimately, advocates of free markets are making certain claims about the benefits of particular economic arrangements; they are not making claims about the details of human motivation. Personal motives are irrelevant to the beneficial consequences of certain sorts of economic organisations.

The market's critics: Marx and Schumpeter

Marxism claimed to have a scientific account of the course of human history in which the internal contradictions of capitalism, particularly the tendency of ever-increasing numbers of workers to become ever-poorer, eventually leads to revolutionary transformation into communism. In so far as any such theory can be open to refutation, it has been. The idea of capitalism collapsing because of failure to generate and then spread material wealth has been manifestly proved false by events. The free market enables the wheels of mass production to turn and, as Schumpeter observed (1954), mass production must inevitably be production for the masses. We need not allow the Marxist line of criticism to detain us any longer.

But there is another very different criticism of capitalism which requires much more serious attention. This argues that capitalism will destroy itself, not because of its failure but, paradoxically, because of its success. The pessimists fear that capitalism could destroy the very values that are necessary for its own survival. These pessimists (notably Joseph Schumpeter and, on some readings, Adam Smith himself), argue that successful capitalism requires what sociologists call 'deferred gratification' to yield the savings that make investment and economic growth possible. But the triumph of the consumer becomes also the triumph of what the classical philosophers called the appetites; epitomised by the advertisement for a credit card with the slogan 'Access takes the waiting out of wanting.'

At the same time, the pessimists fear capitalism unleashes a corrosive rationalism which undermines the values and institutions sustaining the markets. Schumpeter thought capitalism was incapable of defining any point at which the process of rational calculation stops. Everything is treated as an instrument, a means to something else, particularly one's own personal satisfaction (Schumpeter, 1954).

The most convicing reply to this critique is both theoretical and empirical. It argues that capitalism also generates ties of loyalty and affiliation – such as to the firm where one works or the neighbourhood where one has chosen to live. Indeed, successful modern capitalist societies are able to draw on sources of legitimacy and values outside capitalism itself: Germany's social market, the American Constitution, Britain's extraordinary historical continuity, Japan's unique national religion.

In so far as it creates an instrumentalist cast of mind in which people want even greater material prosperity, it also is alone able by and large to deliver the sustained economic growth necessary to satisfy that desire. Whatever the discontents of modern capitalist societies, they are more robust than any alternatives.

Limits of the market: internal and external

Many market theorists have written of the market as if it floats free of any cultural or institutional constraints. It is just a world of rational economic agents entering into contracts with each other. But perhaps the most interesting aspect of thinking about the market nowadays is the willingness of at least some economic liberals to recognise that the market is constrained both from above and from below. The market operates within a series of external constraints – cultural, moral and legal – which define its area of activity. Similarly, there comes a point at which micro institutions – firms, families etc. – cease to apply market principles to their own internal organisations. The real debate about the market nowadays is about the mutual dependence between this enormous middle area of the market and the cultural atmosphere within which it operates and the mode in which the particular institutions which it comprise manage their internal affairs. We look at the external and internal limits of the market in turn.

The free market revolution in the Soviet bloc and much of the third world represents the biggest single intellectual victory for economic liberalism since the British political elite was converted to that cause at the beginning of the nineteenth century. Yet the difficulties which these newly liberated countries have experienced in implementing free market reforms remind us of the moral, cultural and legal framework which is necessary in order to sustain a market. There has to be some acceptance of the legitimacy of the distribution of resources in society, yet if the main holders of cash are either old communist apparatchiks or Mafia criminals then the very idea of allocating control over assets in accordance with people's financial resources itself lacks legitimacy. Similarly if there is no tradition of defining the point at which market transactions cease and criminal activity begins it is very difficult to regard trade as other than theft. And if the judges are all left over from the old communist regime how can they be relied on independently to enforce contracts? These societies suddenly have to face explicitly questions which rarely seem problematic in the West. It is just accepted that you can buy and sell your labour and that your income is largely determined by market transactions whereas you cannot buy and sell votes or decisions of the courts. The recognition of the limits to market transactions is paradoxically one of the preconditions for the successful operation of a market economy.

There are equally constraints on the operation of the market at the micro level. The rational economic agents which are the key components of any market economy are rarely unencumbered individuals – they are firms or families. These organisations do not rigorously apply the principles of the market in their internal arrangements. Employees are not, by and large, hired each day for a day at prices set in open competition. In the family the parents do not hand out wages to their children and sell them their breakfast. Successful firms and stable families both operate with a subtle mixture of authority and co-operation rather than relying on market transactions.

One of the striking empirical developments of the past twenty years has been the spread of market style transactions at this micro level encouraged by the information technology making the pricing of individual transactions much easier. A firm might now buy in its security services or its catering services rather than manage them itself as a core function of the firm. Similarly financial obligations between members of the same family are now becoming more explicit and codified – as seen most recently in the Child Support Act setting out the responsibility of absent parents for the maintenance of their children. Similarly, the internal market is increasingly being applied across large areas of the public sector, such as the health service or local government. Analysing the ways in which market transactions within social institutions make them more efficient and flexible, and when they instead become futile or destructive and alternative forms of organisation take over, is one of the liveliest intellectual challenges facing market thinking today.

References
Galbraith, J. K. (1974), *The New Industrial State*, 2nd edition, Harmondsworth, Penguin
Schumpeter, J. S. (1954), *Capitalism, Socialism and Democracy*, 4th edition, London, Allen and Unwin
Smith, A. (1937), *The Wealth of Nations*, ed. E. Cannan, intro. M. Lerner, New York, Random House

Further Reading
Brittan, S. (1988), *A Restatement of Economic Liberalism*, Basingstoke, Macmillan
Gray, J. (1984), *Hayek on Liberty*, Oxford, Blackwell
Hayek, F. A. (1960), *The Constitution of Liberty*, London, Routledge and Kegan Paul
Willetts, D. (1992), *Modern Conservatism*, Harmondsworth, Penguin

Nationalism

'Nationalism' is an elusive concept. Throughout most of history humans have lived in small groups with only or mainly a local consciousness. Nations emerge when supra-local social exchanges make wider solidarities possible. Nations are only cultural if supra-local populations are identified by a common culture. We cannot say precisely when a culture-group becomes a nation, as there is no consensus on the usage of the term 'nation'. Nations should, however, be defined by both objective and subjective criteria: they are supra-local groups with common cultures that recognize themselves and/or are recognized by others as nations. Nationalism is the doctrine that attributes primary value to nations. Political nationalism mobilizes nations for political ends.

Origins and associations

The origin of nationalism is often located in the French Revolution of 1789, but nationalism can be found in the Old Testament. There we read of a people with a common culture, sharing a belief in a common history, associated with a particular territory and creating a common political rule. This religious nationalism was challenged by Christian universalism. The other-worldliness of Christianity has had to accommodate itself, however, to the demands of this-worldly politics. In the era of dynastic monarchies Christianity generally served to legitimate political regimes and thus found itself confined to various territorial states. With the decline of religion in the Enlightenment, nationalism came to perform the legitimating and mobilizing functions previously carried out by religion.

It has been suggested that nationalism is a functional requisite of industrial capitalism. On this view, capitalist markets destroyed localism and industrialism demanded a national-popular culture. But modern territorial states became nationalistic long before attempts were made to democratize national cultures, while nationalism spread in the nineteenth and twentieth centuries by imitation of and defensive reaction against the imperialistic nationalisms of Western

Europe. Thus nationalism played an important role in societies very different from those in which it first arose, both in the second ('socialist') and third worlds.

Modern nationalism is based on the concept of self-determination. Again, we should note that this is an ancient idea, for peoples throughout history have resisted domination by aliens. However, when Christian-monarchical authority came into question, the notion that the 'self' should determine its own destiny became an alternative basis for political legitimation. If the 'self' were conceived as individual, it gave rise to such ideas as individual natural rights and the social contract. But, in resistance to the claims of absolute monarchy, the 'self' with the right to self-determination came also to be thought of as 'the people' or 'the nation'. Thus 'self-determination' was interpreted as the sovereignty of the people or the nation.

At the birth of modern politics, therefore, the idea of democracy as popular sovereignty and the concept of national self-determination were closely related. However, the link between democracy and nationalism was smashed by French nationalistic imperialism of the Napoleonic period. This stimulated defensive nationalism in the lands conquered by the French, especially in Germany. Cultural nationalism had already had a long history there, and in the nineteenth century this was politicized in the drive for German self-assertion. The democratic element in this movement was weak and authoritarian German nationalism was to find its extreme expression in Nazism.

Nationalism became, therefore, 'progressive' in so far as it sought to mobilize nations for collective self-development, but also 'reactionary' because it sought to defend national cultures against modernizing forces. It could launch popular-revolutionary attacks on conservative regimes, but it could also legitimate authoritarian restorations in times of turbulent change. It could represent liberal claims to self-determination; it could also resist liberal subversions of national traditions. In the French Revolution authority was derived from the nation. In conditions unfavourable to democracy national authority was expressed through dictatorship: the nation became not simply authoritative but also authoritarian.

Active and reactive nationalism in the twentieth century

Nationalism values the unity of nations. It distinguishes nationals from aliens. Nations can have benevolent attitudes to foreigners, but nationalism tends to view aliens with suspicion, if not with hostility. Peoples and states have always been rivals and often enemies; nation-states became rivals and enemies on nationalist grounds.

With the collapse of the multinational Ottoman and Austro-Hungarian Empires at the end of the First World War, the League of Nations endorsed the principle of national self-determination but failed to find a stable political form for the multinational patchwork of Europe. The aggressive nationalism of Germany had been frustrated by defeat in the war and by the humiliating terms of the peace settlement. The national socialism of Hitler appealed to wounded German national pride, as well as to economic grievances, and began its expansion with claims based on kinship with the 'Germans' of Austria and Czechoslovakia. This new German expansionism, together with Japanese expansion in Asia, provoked the Second World War.

The destructiveness of the two world wars brought nationalism into some disrepute, yet it was partly on behalf of threatened nationalisms that the wars were fought. Thus, at the end of the Second World War the organization of the new world order chose to form itself as the United Nations. Even though the UN Charter followed the long-established practice of international law of conceiving its principal task to be the regulation of relations among states, it was now taken for granted that the peoples of the world were organized into nations represented by member-states at the UN. The UN Universal Declaration of Human Rights (1948) reflected not only the need to protect individuals against states but also, following the Great Depression of the 1930s, the obligations of states to care for the material needs of their citizens. The nation-state was becoming, at least in theory, the welfare state.

The claim that the member-states of the UN represented the nations of the world was soon shown to be hollow. The principal allies victorious in the Second World War had been the USA, Britain, France, the USSR and China. Britain and France were imperial powers facing nationalist oppositions. China was governed by a nationalist party but faced a challenge by communist rebels who disputed the nationalist credentials of the government. The USSR had fought the war on the platform of Soviet nationalism, was officially committed to the Leninist doctrine of anti-imperialism, but was in fact itself a multinational empire. The USA was a nationalist power with anti-imperialist roots.

The British and French had educated native elites to administer their empires, but these elites had learned with their bureaucratic skills European ideas of nationalism, liberalism and socialism. Pre-modern empires provoked resistance, but opposition to empire in the twentieth century was cast in the idiom of nationalism commonly combined with either social democracy or Marxism-Leninism. This opposition pre-dated the Second World War, but the war had both weakened the European imperial powers and, especially in East Asia, strengthened the hand of nationalist, anti-imperialist forces. After the war, therefore, the French faced nationalist resistance in Indochina, while the British faced challenges throughout their empire. The USA was at first sympathetic to anti-imperialistic nationalism, partly because of its own anti-imperialist origins and partly because it saw economic opportunities in the decline of European imperialism.

When the Cold War began between the USA and the USSR, with their respective allies, the third world became a surrogate battleground, with the USSR taking up the anti-imperialist cause, and the USA retreating into a conservative defence of the status quo. When the communists came to power in China in 1949 and later broke with the USSR they presented themselves as the champions of third world nationalism. As European imperialism retreated in the face of the nationalist challenge the USA took up the anti-nationalist reins in the name of anti-communism.

The successful nationalist movement against European colonialism had replaced the European empires with a large number of new nation-states, some of which were populated mainly by ancient peoples, but many of which had been artificially constructed by European imperialism, so that the task of 'nation-building' remained to be done by the new nationalist elites. This was a daunting challenge, since these societies were unfavourably placed in the post-war international economic system. Some aligned themselves with the West, others with the USSR or China; many sought non-alignment in order to play each side of the Cold War against the other. In most cases these new nation-states had little impact on the global political and economic systems, and were unable to generate either economic development or political stability at home. A few, mainly in East Asia, eventually achieved economic take-off, while many tottered on the brink of economic disaster and/or collapsed into prolonged civil war. Post-war nation-building in the third world has had varied success, and in some societies almost none at all. The 'nation-state' remains largely fictional throughout much of the world. Many member states of the UN represent peoples who do not constitute nations and who are not at all united.

The right of 'peoples' to self-determination was written into international law to legitimate third world anti-colonialism, but proved embarrassing when ethnic minorities in the third world nation-states claimed the same right. During the Cold War there was an inter-state consensus that the existing nation-state system should be stabilized, except for the removal of the vestiges of European colonialism. Third world states were therefore generally supported against rebellious minorities. The secession of Bangladesh from Pakistan was exceptional. Since the end of the Cold War and the disintegration of the USSR, the integrity of post-colonial nation-states has become more questionable.

Third world nationalism had consequences in the first world. The successful struggles of black Africans influenced the campaign for civil rights by black Americans. A number of minority nationalities in the rich Western states began to claim the right to self-determination (Kellas, 1991). Some of these movements turned to terrorism. Some states have more or less completely defused these protests by combinations of repression and concession, while others have found such violent nationalist campaigns to be intractable.

In Western Europe an attempt to go beyond nationalism has been made through the European Community. Whatever its economic achievements, it has done little to reduce nationalism. Although a supranational, European identity has been created among some elites, moves towards European integration have stimulated previously quiet nationalisms, have been accompanied by the rise of neo-fascist nationalist groups and have encouraged some frustrated 'regional' nationalisms to seek European solutions.

Post-Soviet nationalism

The USSR was recognized by the international community as a nation-state. From the point of view of non-Russian nationalists, however, it was an empire. The Stalinist system had both encouraged and repressed nationalist sentiment within the USSR, thereby causing nationalist resentment against the Soviet system. The USSR collapsed as a result of economic crisis and pressure from internal nationalisms. The collapse began with declarations of independence by the three Baltic states (Estonia, Latvia and Lithuania) that had been annexed by the USSR during the Second World War. The further disintegration of the USSR was led by Ukraine, which had never been an independent nation-state. Thus Ukrainian nationalism, like many nationalisms, was the product of alien rule rather than a pre-existing internal development.

The nation-states of Eastern Europe outside the USSR had strong pre-communist nationalisms that the communist regimes sought to control by various mixtures of repression and accommodation. Popular uprisings in Hungary in 1956 and Czechoslovakia in 1968 were put down by the USSR. Polish nationalism had always been restive under Soviet-backed communist rule. In 1989 the communist house collapsed. Resistance to political repression, economic nationalism frustrated by its deprivation relative to the West and cultural assertiveness against the sovietization of life all contributed to the anti-communist revolution. German nationalism played a special role. After the Second World War Germany had been divided into the capitalist West and the communist East. German nationalists had dreamed of reunification. Thus the disintegration of the communist Eastern bloc into its component nation-states was accompanied by the reintegration of Germany as the most powerful nation-state in Europe.

Soviet imperialism in Eastern Europe was supposed to be followed by the liberalization and democratization of the region's nation-states. Both the economic and the political tasks of the transition from communism have proved extremely difficult, however. Marketization threatens particular economic interests, creates general insecurity and divides societies. Nationalistic solidarity has tended to fill the political and cultural vacuum. Consequently liberal democracy has been threatened by anti-democratic forms of nationalism. Socialism, though professing internationalism, had always accommodated itself to nationalism. The post-communist picture in Central and Eastern Europe is complex. Poland, the Czech Republic and Hungary are democratically inclined, although democracy is tinged by right-wing nationalism in both Poland and Hungary. Slovakia seceded from Czechoslovakia on 1 January 1993 under a somewhat authoritarian nationalist leadership. Bulgaria is a still rather unstable democracy with right-wing, authoritarian elements. Romania is highly national-istic and not at all democratic. But the worst case has been Yugoslavia which, under pressure from the aggressive, authoritarian nationalist leadership of the Serbian president, Slobodan Miloševíc, broke up in a savage civil war. Slovenia,

Croatia and Bosnia have become independent nation-states. But while the ethnically homogeneous Slovenia has been able to keep clear of the fighting, Croatia
and Bosnia have been devastated by nationalist hatreds. This has led not only to
numerous atrocities but to a nationalist authoritarianism that has both constructed and sought to enforce national identities. Meanwhile Macedonia is
denied recognition as a nation-state because of Greek nationalist objections and
Macedonian nationalists have also to contend with the fact that none of their
neighbours regards them as a nation. Some post-communist states of Eastern
Europe have also manifested a kind of 'transnational nationalism'; the government of Hungary, for example, claims the right to be concerned with ethnic
Hungarians, wherever they reside and whatever their national citizenship. Such
claims are not unprecedented: Israel grants absolute right of immigration to all
Jews, the Republic of China (Taiwan) has granted political representation to
overseas Chinese, and Germany recognizes as fellow-nationals ethnic Germans
who are citizens of other states.

The national–transnational dysfunction

The end of the twentieth century is witnessing two apparently contradictory
tendencies relating to nationalism. On the one hand, the remit of scientific
rationalism is imperialistic in scale. Culture, economics and politics are
becoming increasingly transnational in the process known as globalization. On
the other hand, particularistic solidarities are becoming more intense. Some of
these are nationalistic, and the resurgence of nationalism has taken place in the
former first, second and third worlds. The economic world-system is dominated
by the USA, the European Community and Japan, the second (former Soviet)
world is struggling with the transition from socialism to capitalism accompanied
by relatively democratic or relatively authoritarian forms of nationalism, while
third world states pursue policies of economic nationalism with varying degrees
of success. The international demand that states meet the welfare needs of their
citizens, though promoted in the language of universal rights, has encouraged an
introverted nationalism such that nation-states tend to place the welfare of
their own citizens above their international obligations. The salience of economic
development in state policy-making has thus led to a kind of developmental
nationalism.

Yet many important solidarities are sub-national (e.g. tribal peoples) or transnational but not global (e.g. Islam). These movements are connected by the
tendency of the dominant global system to exclude and alienate many peoples,
who are seeking compensatory solidarity closer to home. In some cases the
nation-state seems too small (as an advanced economic unit, for example), in
other cases too big (to meet local needs), in still others about the right size (for
political representation in international fora). Liberal capitalism, though often
contained by the nation-state, has always had transnational tendencies. It has

consequently also tended to generate resistant solidarities among which nationalism has been prominent. This tension between liberal universalism and particularistic solidarity has been reflected in recent philosophical debates between 'liberals' and 'communitarians' (Mulhall and Swift, 1992). The latter have reaffirmed the moral and political value of the national community in what appears as a retreat from liberal cosmopolitanism and socialist internationalism. Notwithstanding globalizing pressures, the nation-state and nationalist sentiment remain strong bases of end-of-century economic and political policy-making. The savage war in the post-Yugoslavian states reminds us that nationalism remains attractive to some and destructive to others. The regulation of nationalism is at the top of the global political agenda at the end of the twentieth century as it was at its beginning.

Supra-local states are always more or less multicultural. Empires are multi-national. The normative ideal of the nation-state requires one nation, one state. The problem of the nation-state is that history has produced far more peoples than states, so that the normative ideal is unattainable and attempts to attain it are often grossly inhumane. Nationalism expresses pride but also resentment. It provides the security of solidarity while it may also coerce the deviant and expel or destroy the alien. Nationalism can inspire great art and genocide (Connor, 1972). It is because nationalism constructs a shared history that international conflicts are often prisoners of history. Nationalist history involves a shared remembering, a shared forgetting and shared participation in myth-making. Because it draws pride from the past, it often constructs a present of hostility and makes the construction of a more tolerant future more difficult.

The present configuration of nation-states is probably unstable and new nation-states may be formed in the near future. The late twentieth century tension between globalization and nation-building is generating massive population transfers, so that 'ethnic cleansing' and ethnic mixing are taking place simultaneously. Communications and transportation technology promote globalization and at the same time reactive nationalism. In contrast to persistent nationalist tendencies there exist not only the predominantly self-interested transnational powers but also a weak 'international community' seeking to maintain order and an international 'civil society', which includes transnational citizens' organizations concerned with peace, human rights, aid, environment etc.

The challenge of nationalism to political theory and political practice is to construct ways of organizing the polyethnic nation-state so that reasonable demands for self-determination can be met without violating the basic rights of individuals, of minorities and indeed of majorities. This presents us with a complex agenda. It has been rather neglected for most of the second half of the twentieth century. It is not likely to be in the twenty-first.

References

Connor, Walker (1972), 'Nation-Building or Nation-Destroying', *World Politics*, 24, pp. 320–55

Kellas, James G. (1991), *The Politics of Nationalism and Ethnicity*, Basingstoke, Macmillan
Mulhall, Stephen and Swift, Adam (1992), *Liberals and Communitarians*, Oxford,
   Blackwell

Further Reading
Anderson, Benedict (1983), *Imagined Communities: Reflections on the Origin and Spread of
   Nationalism*, London, Verso
Hobsbawm, E. J. (1992), *Nations and Nationalism Since 1870*, 2nd, rev. edition, Cambridge
   University Press
Mayall, James (1990), *Nationalism and International Society*, Cambridge University Press

Authoritarianism

Authoritarianism is the belief in the principle of authority as opposed to that of individual freedom. In its most developed form this becomes advocacy of orderly government under military or other dictatorship. Though as a philosophical position its antecedents are much older, reaching back at least to Joseph de Maistre (1773–1821) (Austern, 1974), the word 'authoritarian' dates only from 1879 and 'authoritarianism' from 1909 (*Oxford English Dictionary*). In both cases the words are used to designate a philosophical position antithetical to *liberalism* (*q.v.*), but otherwise not with clear ideological content. The term remained defined in essentially negative terms until well after 1945. In the *International Encyclopedia of the Social Sciences* (Sills, 1968), 'authoritarianism' was given no special treatment and was regarded simply as a concomitant of dictatorship (see also Neumann, 1957; Duverger, 1961).

However in the age of the Cold War (1946–90) a new term, *totalitarianism*, came into use in the West to describe a syndrome of features believed to be characteristic of both *fascism* in Hitler's Germany and *communism* in the Soviet Union, China and Eastern Europe. These states, it was thought, differed from all previous states in having both the will and the ability to exercise unlimited control over their populations (Friedrich and Brzezinski, 1975). By contrast the term 'authoritarian' gained a new popularity as a convenient term to designate more traditional dictatorships. The beliefs which underpinned such systems included: belief in the transcendental importance of the principle of authority; an emphasis on the exclusive use of political power, unfettered by juridical restraint or civil liberties; and a tendency to excuse the excesses either of arbitrary decision-making or of despotic methods of political and social control.

Such a use was consistent with the evolving use of the term 'authoritarian' in both psychology and sociology. In psychology it was employed by Theodor Adorno and his followers to designate a particular form of personality, the *authoritarian personality*, characterised by rigid and unbending beliefs. In this definitive work (Adorno *et al.*, 1964), both the political influence of the Frankfurt school and the social science methodologies of American functionalism combine to produce the 'T-scale', a measure of the propensity towards authoritarianism. Their further research concludes that authoritarianism is a tendency widely found throughout the populations not only of dictatorships but of the United States and other democratic countries. Authoritarian subjects do indeed (when they have the chance to do so) require obedience from others, but even more importantly they tend unquestioningly to accept the political leadership of others, and it is in this way that the 'cult of veneration among the masses' described by Robert Michels (1978, pp. 63–8) makes dictatorship possible. This thesis has since been widely accepted and a substantial amount of psychological research in this area continues to be conducted.

Authoritarianism in developing states

With the rapid decolonisation of the 1960s came first euphoria and then disillusion. Disillusion with the allegedly slow processes of democracy led to a wave of military coups in Africa and Asia. By 1970 military rule had spread to Turkey and Greece in Europe. In turn this prompted a fresh interest in authoritarianism as a concept which had a positive content, and was not merely defined by an absence of other features. In a key study Juan Linz (1970, p. 255) identified the new authoritarian states as 'political systems with limited, not responsible, political pluralism; without elaborate and guiding ideology (but with distinctive mentalities); without intensive nor extensive political mobilization (except at some point in their development); and in which a leader (or occasionally a small group) exercises power within formally ill-defined limits but actually quite predictable ones.' On the basis of Linz's definition it is possible to distinguish as he does between *new* and *old* authoritarian regimes. The longer established an authoritarian regime is, the less it needs to rely on the overt use of force and the more it tends to develop new forms of legitimacy. However, for Linz authoritarian government is always a transitional state, either towards democracy or towards totalitarianism.

In addition, Michael Sahlin (1977) suggests, it is also useful to distinguish between *protective authoritarianism* and *promotional authoritarianism*. Protective authoritarianism is the argument of those who intervene by force simply to protect the status quo and the position of those who benefit from it. Following a traditional military coup, which has only the limited aim of displacing the existing government, a period of emergency rule normally follows in which the armed forces emphasise the power available to them, their limited ambitions in making use of it, and their intention to return the country to civilian rule as soon as possible. Some regimes of this type, for example that of Franco's Spain, do survive for a long period and, Sahlin notes, become 'old' authoritarian regimes in Linz's terms, gaining a degree of legitimacy through force of habit, and, generally, needing to depend less on the overt use of force. However, their principal aims remain the same: the de-politicisation of issues and the demo-bilisation of the masses.

Promotional authoritarianism, by contrast, is characterised by a desire to promote change, by supplanting the existing government and establishing one which will stay in power for a period of years to pursue certain stated aims. Chief among these aims is economic development, the desire for which is in itself rooted in a nationalistic belief in the value of a strong state. But this requires a certain degree of mobilisation of the masses in the interests of productivity. For such *neo-authoritarian* regimes this can most safely be achieved by appealing to *nationalism (q.v.)*. However even this does not resolve, but only postpone, a fundamental conflict between the desire for economic mobilisation and the fear of political mobilisation. There are two possible ways in which this can be done; in each case, significantly, they involve maintaining and not jettisoning the forms of democracy.

Some authoritarian regimes are prepared to mobilise the popular sector for both political and economic purposes, and to live with the consequences. Regimes of this rare type can be classed as *authoritarian populist* regimes. The classic case of such a regime is to be found in Argentina under General Juan Domingo Perón (president 1946–55, 1973–4). Its success can be gauged by the fact that ever since the coup that displaced the regime in 1955, no government has long survived that did not come to terms with the Peronists. Despite his authoritarian ideology and emphasis on the role of the leader (known as 'verti-calism'), Perón was constitutionally elected and re-elected, and it took several attempts for the armed forces to overthrow him.

Other regimes have been able to achieve such a degree of economic success that their citizens are prepared to wait for democracy. It is probably not just coincidence that the so-called 'tiger' economies of East and South-East Asia – Singapore, Taiwan, South Korea, Malaysia and Thailand – are in states where for a variety of reasons and in varying degrees the governing style, and often the substance, is authoritarian.

Beginning with Brazil in 1964, several of a wave of new military governments in Latin America made the promotion of economic development a central plank of their policies (Malloy, 1977) and promised (or threatened) to stay in power for as long as it took to achieve these objectives. Hence 'a new set of hypotheses emerged which suggested that in late developing nations more advanced levels of industrialisation may coincide with the collapse of democracy and an increase in inequality' (Collier, 1979, p. 4). Within the then popular theory of dependency, this phenomenon was speedily linked by the political left to developments in the global economy. Specifically it was argued that such regimes were a reaction to the transnationalisation of Latin American economies and the economic crises generated by their insertion into the world capitalist economy.

Guillermo O'Donnell (1973) coined the new term *bureaucratic-authoritarian* to describe these governments, and this term has since achieved wide popularity. O'Donnell's theory envisages three stages of development of political systems. In the *oligarchic* stage the popular sector is not yet politicised, and so is neither mobilised nor incorporated in the state structure. In the *populist* stage, the popular sector is mobilised and incorporated. In the *bureaucratic-authoritarian* state it is then demobilised and excluded. For O'Donnell, the bureaucratic-authoritarian state 'guarantees and organizes the domination exercised through a class structure subordinated to the upper fractions of a highly oligopolized and transnationalized bourgeoisie' (1988, p. 31). Within the state structure two groups have decisive weight: specialists in coercion (the armed forces), whose job it is to exclude the 'popular sector' from power, and finance capitalists, whose role is to obtain the 'normalisation' of the economy, which performs the dual purpose of excluding the popular sector from economic power and promoting the interests of large oligopolistic interests. As part of the exclusion policy, social issues are depoliticised by being treated as a matter of narrow economic rationality, and direct access to government is limited to the armed forces, the state bureaucracy and leading industrialists and financiers.

Though applied in the first instance to Brazil, O'Donnell's model was derived from the experience of Argentina between 1966 and 1973, and, not surprisingly, fits it closely. Having failed in 1955 and 1962 permanently to exclude the Peronists from power by simple military coup, the promoters of what was grandiloquently (but not altogether inaccurately) termed the 'Argentine Revolution' in 1966 sought to stay in power for long enough to achieve that objective. However, the term bureaucractic-authoritarianism itself is misleading, in that it is military rule not bureaucracy that was its distinguishing characteristic, and the model does not fit the authoritarian regimes imposed in Brazil in 1964 (reinforced in 1968), in Uruguay and Chile in 1973 or in Argentina again in 1976 (Linz and Stepan, 1978). Not only were these states at very different levels of economic development, but in each case, as Collier (1979) noted, ideological polarisation was so marked, that an adequate explanation had to take account of political factors such as the nature of the party system and the strength of organised labour. Furthermore, these authoritarian regimes were not comparable to one another. Venezuela's mobilisation came at the end of its period of dictatorship and was accompanied by a deliberate and successful attempt to establish consensus as a basis for democratic government. The same was originally true for Mexico, which, though authoritarian, is closer to the liberal-democratic model than it is to the pattern envisaged by O'Donnell, and has been particularly successful in co-opting potential opposition. Both have relatively diversified and well-developed economies.

Authoritarianism in democratic states

In the United States, political authoritarianism received a new impetus from the Cold War and since the 1950s has come to combine anti-constitutional and anti-democratic elements (Kateb, in Connolly, 1984).

Anti-constitutional arguments used to justify emergency action in wartime were revived in the United States to defend the 'Imperial Presidency' both before and after the Watergate scandal. Richard M. Nixon and his supporters tried to assert a prerogative right of the presidency to freedom of action and immunity from scrutiny which ran counter to both the explicit and the implied intentions of the Constitution. Their arguments were to an extent underpinned by their belief that the danger presented to the United States by 'communist aggression' was such that the executive had to have the freedom to act in the national interest at very short notice. To this extent it was a new argument.

Anti-democratic sentiment, on the other hand, is as old as the American Republic itself. It centres on the belief that democracy works best when the masses leave politics to an educated minority – the theory of democratic elitism. In the 1960s the radical left, with or without the influence of Marxism, held that liberal democracy was simply a facade. The fall of Nixon, and the liberal 'human rights' policies of the Carter years, proved conclusively that this was at best an oversimplification and at worst entirely wrong. In the 1980s, however, with Ronald Reagan in the White House, the 'clear and present danger' argument was extended into 'plausible deniability' – the belief that agents of the president could and should act on his behalf, even without his knowledge. At the same time the administration returned to the original idea of the Nixon-Kissinger years that 'human rights' was only a problem in Eastern Europe.

Jeane Kirkpatrick, later Reagan's ambassador to the United Nations, in 'Dictatorships and Double Standards' (1979), argued indeed that the United States should actively support what she termed 'moderately repressive authoritarian governments' (MRAGs) to avert the more serious threat of totalitarianism. She supported this view with the contention that, with all their faults, authoritarian governments could in time become democratic, but from totalitarianism there was no return. In the event the Reagan administration found that the so-called MRAGs were not at all moderate, and that consequently the policy was at best dangerous and at worst unworkable. The attempt to use Argentine military personnel in El Salvador went badly wrong when Argentina invaded the Falkland Islands, and attempts to give positive support to the military authorities in Guatemala foundered when it became clear that though they were fighting against left-wing guerrillas, they were also engaged in a race war against their native American population.

After 1979 Britain undermined the liberal consensus that had prevailed in Europe since the end of the Second World War. 'Thatcherism' combined in a new synthesis two British political traditions: neo-liberalism in economic matters and authoritarian conservatism in social policy. In both its acceptance of the discipline of the market and its rejection of paternalism it owed much of its inspiration to the United States. However, lacking the protection of a written constitution, British citizens found that the Thatcher years were accompanied by a massive increase in the powers of central government. Time and again the law was used, in a manner reminiscent of Robespierre, to force people to be free. The government glorified the values of law and order and rejected the notions of society and of consensus (Hall and Jacques, 1983; Jessop *et al.*, 1988). Ministers systematically subverted the independence of local government and assumed extensive new powers to force schools, hospitals and other public bodies into a central framework, determined exclusively by narrowly defined considerations of economic 'rationality'. Welfare benefits failed to keep pace with the general rise in wages, leading to a widening gap between rich and poor. At the same time economic policy was conducted primarily in the interests of the financial services sector. Floating exchange rates, high fixed interest rates, sharp cuts in direct taxation, steep rises in indirect taxation and an overvalued currency reduced Britain's manufacturing base by about one-quarter between 1979 and 1982, leading to a fall of productivity that was not recouped until shortly before the onset of a further massive recession in 1989. Throughout it could be argued that the mass media played a key role in popularising and defending authoritarian solutions to problems that were often more imaginary than real. Though the nature of the coercion employed was of a very different order from that employed by the authoritarian populist regimes of Africa or Latin America, the significance of force was certainly not overlooked by the Thatcher government. Police and the armed services were the only sectors of the public service whose pay kept pace with the rapid inflation of the decade, and both public and private force was deployed during the miners' strike of 1984–5 to break the countervailing power of the trade unions.

More serious dangers lay in wait with the collapse of communist rule in Eastern Europe in 1989. The belief in the virtues of a 'hands-off' approach to the drastic changes taking place in East-Central Europe left the way open for a form of 'headless authoritarianism', in which the 'fear of freedom' described by Erich Fromm (1991) threatened to open the way for the rise of new authoritarian leaders. In Germany, disillusion with the high cost of reunification paved the way for a variety of neo-fascist movements. Yugoslavia first disintegrated and then dissolved into vicious inter-ethnic conflict because a generation of politicians schooled under authoritarian rule was unable or unwilling to recognise the strength of the forces they had let loose. Authoritarianism in liberal-democratic states, it is important to remember, is different from that of dictatorships only in degree, not in kind.

References

Adorno, Theodor W., Frenkel-Brunsik, Else, Levinson, Daniel J. and Sanford, R. Nevitt (1964), *The Authoritarian Personality* (first published 1950), New York, John Wiley

Austern, Donald M. (1974), 'The Political Theories of Edmund Burke and Joseph de Maistre as Representatives of the Schools of Conservative Libertarianism and Conservative Authoritarianism', Ph.D thesis, University of Massachusetts, University Microfilms

Collier, David (ed.) (1979), *The New Authoritarianism in Latin America*, Princeton University Press

Connolly, William (ed.) (1984), *Legitimacy and the State*, Oxford, Basil Blackwell

Duverger, Maurice (1961), *De la Dictature*, Paris, Juillard

Friedrich, Carl J. and Brzezinski, Zbigniew K. (1965), *Totalitarian Dictatorship and Autocracy* (2nd rev. edition 1965, first published 1956), Cambridge, MA, Harvard University Press

Fromm, E. (1991), *Fear of Freedom*, London, Routledge

Hall, S. and Jacques, M. (eds.) (1983), *The Politics of Thatcherism*, London, Lawrence and Wishart

Jessop, B., Bonnett, K., Bromley, S. and Long, T. (1988), *Thatcherism: A Tale of Two Nations*, Cambridge, Polity Press

Kateb, George (1984), 'On the "Legitimation Crisis" ', in William Connolly (ed.), *Legitimacy and the State*, Oxford, Basil Blackwell, pp. 180–200

Kirkpatrick, Jeane (1979), 'Dictatorships and Double Standards', *Commentary*, 68, November, pp. 34–45

Linz, Juan J. (1970), 'An Authoritarian Regime: Spain', in E. Allardt and S. Rokkan (eds.), *Mass Politics: Studies in Political Sociology*, New York, Free Press, p. 254

Linz, Juan J., and Stepan, Alfred (eds.) (1978), *The Breakdown of Democratic Regimes: Latin America*, Baltimore, MD, Johns Hopkins University Press

Malloy, James Michael (1977), *Authoritarianism and Corporatism in Latin America*, University of Pittsburgh Press

Michels, R. (1978), *Political Parties: A Sociological Study of the Oligarchical Tendencies of Modern Democracy*, New York, Dover

Neumann, Franz L. (1957), *The Democratic and the Authoritarian State: Essays in Political and Legal Theory*, Glencoe, IL, The Free Press

O'Donnell, Guillermo (1973), *Modernization and Bureaucratic-Authoritarianism: Studies in South American Politics*, Berkeley, University of California Press

— (1988), *Bureaucratic Authoritarianism: Argentina, 1966–1973, in Comparative Perspective*, Berkeley, University of California Press

Sahlin, Michael (1977), *Neo-Authoritarianism and the Problem of Legitimacy: A General Study and a Nigerian Example*, Stockholm, Rabén and Sjöyren for the Political Science Association

Sills, David A. (ed.) (1968), *International Encyclopedia of the Social Sciences*, New York, Macmillan Company and The Free Press

Further Reading

Bermeo, Nancy (1992), 'Democracy and the Lessons of Dictatorship', *Comparative Politics*, vol. 24, no. 3, April, pp. 273–91

Lacouture, Jean (1970), *The Demigods: Charismatic Leadership in the Third World*, New York, Alfred J. Knopf

Smith, William C. (1989), *Authoritarianism and the Crisis of the Argentine Political Economy*, Stanford University Press

Egalitarianism

The central questions and challenges societies face are universal: how is social order to be achieved and maintained? Is there to be leadership and by whom? How is envy to be controlled, inequality to be justified or condemned? Which dangers are to be confronted and which ignored? The questions are universal, the answers are different from culture to culture.

The answer of one culture, which I call 'hierarchical collectivism', is to impose order centrally through a division of labour. Inequality is deemed necessary to safeguard the collective, each element being taught to sacrifice for the whole. Envy is controlled by teaching people their places, by reserving ostentation for collective bodies (such as the state or church), and by examples of sacrificial behaviour by the elite.

The culture I call 'competitive individualism' imposes order by maintaining agreement on the basis of freedom of contract. Leaders are chosen like every other commodity, by bidding and bargaining. There is no permanent leadership, only different leaders for different purposes. Envy is mitigated by showing that everyone can have a chance, or by blaming failure on personal incapacity or bad luck. For individualists, risk is opportunity as long as winners can personally appropriate the rewards.

Taken together, the alliance of these two cultures – hierarchical and indivi-dualist cultures – constitutes the modern social establishment. From hierarchy comes order, including the rules for competition, and from individualism comes economic growth. To be sure, there are tensions between them: hierarchies care more about the strict division of labour, while individualists care more about results.

The proponents of what I call 'egalitarian sectarianism' are opposed to both establishment cultures. Where competitive individualists believe in equality of opportunity, egalitarian sectarians believe in equality of result. There is a world of difference beween those who wish to reduce authority so as to promote individual differences, and those who reject authority so as to reduce individual differences. While individualism encourages all transactions that maintain competition, sectarianism rejects all bargains that increase disparities among people.

At an individual level, radical egalitarianism has led to the diminution of distinctions that once separated moral from immoral behaviour, authority from disorder. Even a short list of eroded distinctions is impressive: those between male and female fashion; young and old; various types of sexual orientation and experience; the roles of parents and children, teachers and students. As old boundaries are breached, new ones begin to take their place. Smokers are separated from non-smokers, polluted areas from unspoiled nature, pure wilderness from impure money-making, affirmative discrimination from the negative kind.

Egalitarian sectarianism, I suggest, is at the root of this revolution in our times, and a new sectarian 'regime' is already emerging. Boundaries that supported past patterns of authority and morality are declining in favour of different distinctions. The rise of sectarianism is responsible, I contend, for many anomalies that puzzle us in our public life. When we ask why the public sector evokes such hostility from those who were and still are its strongest supporters; why the growth of the welfare state is severely criticised by those who demand it; why permissiveness in personal life goes hand-in-hand with regulation of public activity; and why there is condemnation of established authority without anything to take its place, the sectarian hypothesis offers a consistent and persuasive explanation.

Disintegrating institutions

The political consequences of sectarian culture are nowhere more apparent than in the changing fortunes of America's integrative and disintegrative institutions. In the United States today, every major integrative institution that must accommodate diverse interests – political parties, trade unions, mainline churches, the presidency – is under severe attack and is undergoing decline. By contrast, disintegrative movements – single-issue special interest groups, charismatic religions, candidate-centred political movements, a critical press – are flourishing.

Why have American political parties, for instance, declined in terms of membership, of allegiance among the citizenry, and of support by politicians? Why are they no longer able to keep divisive issues, like abortion, out of national life? Why have parties become less popular even while they reform their procedures to make themselves more democratic? The textbook definition of a political party is an organisation that nominates candidates for office. If this vital function is transferred to primaries, where voters cannot know the candidates, and where no deliberation about their qualifications can take place among knowledgeable politicians, parties can no longer integrate various political viewpoints. Coalitions that will help candidates govern cannot be formed before the election.

Nothing shows the strength of political sectarianism as much as the excess of issue-making over issue-containment. The desirability of issue-expression is a trademark of sectarianism. Political parties, sectarians argue, should be far apart; they should give voters a clear choice by differing sharply on as many issues as possible; they should stick to their principles without compromise; and, above all, they should not put the forming of coalitions to win elections ahead of maintaining the purity of their positions. Politics is dirty; only unyielding adherence to principle is clean. The more parties behave like sects, putting purity before politics, the less popular they are with voters. The same story is evident in Congress. The more Congress reforms itself by encouraging individual members to express themselves and show their moral sincerity, the worse its collective performance becomes. Thus egalitarians will agree that there ought to be confrontation over issues such as budget and taxation resolutions, but they cannot, of course, agree with others over what these levels should be; hence the stultification of Congress over the budget. Congressmen spend more time catering to their constituents today, and this affection is mutual. Voters love their members of Congress; it is only Congress they hate. As each member becomes more practised at self-expression – through less emphasis on seniority, better committee assignments, more staff, and other such equalising devices – Congress as a collectivity becomes less cohesive.

Studies of media elites reveal that they are disproportionately egalitarian. Aside from equalising income, which would hurt their pocketbooks, they are far more in favour of equalising differences among the general population than are most Americans. It is not so much party partisanship but opposition to authority as a form of inequality that characterises media elites.

Matching the failure in integrative institutions is the apparent success of disintegrative institutions. Single-issue special interest groups (the term now rolls off the tongue as if it were a single word) are known for what they do *not* do – taking positions on a wide range of issues and attempting to reconcile preferences and establish priorities among them. They are altruists for especially deserving interests, of course, while 'private-interest' groups are in it only for themselves. The purity of special interest groups lies in their motives, just as the impurity of the opposition (labour unions or corporations) lies in their devotion to material gain. These interest groups are no novelty in American life. But today integrative institutions, like political parties, Congress, and the presidency, are weak in resisting their claims. Demand making is on the rise in American politics, while demand shaping and demand resisting are on the decline.

Declining political institutions in the United States share three characteristics: they are organised on a hierarchical basis; they reconcile the preferences of their members or constituents on a wide variety of issues; and they attempt to integrate their views with those held by others of somewhat different persuasions. The ascendant organisations are just the opposite: they accept no authority unless it be the occasional charismatic leader (for instance, a Ralph Nader) who provides a substitute for that otherwise missing authority; they are single-, not multiple-, issue groups; and they reject rather than reconcile themselves with groups that differ from them. In a country characterised by the lack of hereditary hierarchy and the presence of strong individualism, socialism is not a real option. A culture of communes, moreover, each interacting on an equal basis under agreed rules, comes uncomfortably close to the individualism that egalitarians avoid. Far better for the egalitarians, who abhor compromise as insincerity, to remain faithful to the principle of pure criticism. Hence the search for a single issue – an unspoiled environment, for example, or complete safety – on which they can maintain a consistent stand.

Government contradictions

The dramatic turn the United States has taken from the welfare to the regulatory state is attributable to the egalitarian desire to punish departures from purity that are conceived of as implying inequality. Damage to nature, in the eyes of egalitarians, is a mirror of our damaged social relations. Endangered species are deprived people. Thus, egalitarians impose regulations on their enemies and affirm the connection between bad business ethics and poor health.

An egalitarian political culture demands both an increase in bureaucracy and a decrease in authority. This explains why, as scientists are increasingly involved in public policy debates, they are respected less and less. On the one hand, those who wish to show that the cultures they criticise cause contamination must invoke scientists and scientific knowledge on their side. On the other hand, their egalitarian social order has a congenital distrust of expertise because it is suggestive of inequality.

There is a catch. The denigration of scientific expertise can hurt people with whom egalitarians identify. Egalitarians identify with gays as an anti-establishment group in that they diminish differences among people. Hence they wish to dampen alarm about AIDS. But it may not prove so easy to urge people to follow mainstream scientific opinion on AIDS, while denigrating established scientific authority in regard to technological dangers, especially when it is alleged that scientific experts do not sufficiently warn the public (Wildavsky, 1987, p. 15).

To expand on the contradictions we are considering, why do the same people who support populist democracy (one person, one vote) also support judicial activism, which appears to negate this principle? Judicial activism is encouraged on behalf of causes that blame the system rather than the person, such as the abolition of the death penalty, due process for prisoners, the rights of the accused, and damage from defective products. 'Blaming the victim', as egalitarians see it, or 'personal responsibility', as the establishment calls it, justifies existing social relations. Blaming the system, requiring it to clean up its messes, and holding it responsible for untoward events are peculiarly useful to egalitarians who see themselves as judges of a corrupt society. The sea change in judicial interpretation from special protection of property to the preferred position currently accorded to civil rights and the corresponding secular movement of the law of personal injury (torts) from individual blame to system blame are but two indicators of egalitarian influence. Nor can one easily reconcile support for national defence with the belief that the system being defended is unworthy, that is, inegalitarian.

Foreign policy at home

A significant part of the opposition to the main lines of American defence policy is based on deep-seated objections to the United States's political and economic systems. This is not to say that existing defence policy is necessarily wise or that there may not be good or sufficient reasons for wishing to change it. Indeed, at any time and place the United States might well be overestimating threats to national security or using too much force. What is being suggested is that the across-the-board criticism of American policy as inherently aggressive and repressive, regardless of circumstance – a litany of criticism so constant that it does not alert us to the need for explanation – has its structural basis in the rise of a political culture opposed to existing authority.

To the extent that this criticism is structural – that is, inherent in domestic politics – the problem of fashioning foreign policies that can obtain widespread support is much more difficult than is commonly conceived. For if the objection is to American ways of life (and therefore to the government 'for which it stands'), only a transformation in the power relationships at home, together with a redistribution of economic resources, would satisfy these critics. Looking to changes in foreign policy to shore up domestic support radically confuses the causal connections and therefore the order of priorities. Unless or until people face an overwhelming external threat, how they wish to live with one another takes precedence over how they relate to foreigners. Foreign policy is fought at home.

While mass opinion is slightly more sceptical than it once was, elite opinion has turned against those authorities who formally determine foreign policy. Unfairness at home becomes transmuted into exploitation abroad. The third world serves as a surrogate proletariat, its poverty a result of United States-led domination by multinational capital. Inequalities within the United States thus spread their tentacles to the rest of the world. It follows that the United States owes redress to the poorer nations, just as it owes reparation to its own poor. Assuming, further, a fixed limit to the world's goods since egalitarians are also anti-capitalist, more for arms means less for welfare. In brief, the industrial North exploits the third world South; the United States rules the North; and capitalists rule the United States. Hence an end to inequality in the United States is necessary for social justice in the world.

The foreign policy of egalitarianism flows naturally from its commitment to redistribution. First is redistribution from rich to poor countries. Second is redistribution from defence to domestic welfare expenditure. Third is redistribution of authority from government officials to mass movements, from those now in power to those (to use their favourite phrase) left out of power. Aside from its effects on the government's ability to conduct consistent defence and foreign policies, this fundamental challenge to authority hits hardest the commander in chief and chief executive of the federal government, the president of the United States. Leadership is a prime instance of power asymmetry. Followership, to egalitarians, is subordination. Thus the series of failed presidencies in recent times – Johnson, Nixon, Carter, Reagan (almost), Bush – testifies not only to their incapacities but also to the animus against them (Wildavsky, 1991).

Programmed for failure

The anomalies in American politics that I have attributed to a rise in sectarianism may be summarised by saying that sectarians impose contradictory demands on government and society. They insist that equality increase, while demanding that government stay small. They insist on bureaucratic regulation, to show that government is ridding itself of moral impurities, while challenging governmental authority. The very government which sectarians call into action to enlighten the public is the same one that is always acting underhandedly to deceive the people.

The phenomenon of ungovernability, which has been said to afflict Western democracies in the era of the welfare state, undoubtedly has many causes. It may be, as both conservatives and Marxists contend, that buying votes leads to ever greater demands (the electoral spending cycle) until there is a 'fiscal crisis of capitalism'. Quite possibly, government has taken on tasks it cannot perform or that its people will not support. Were this the whole matter, the sense of crisis would not be in the air. Rather, one would hear of modest retrenchment, of a pause in the growth of the welfare state until the costs of oil or of pensions could better be accommodated. There is nothing surprising about outrunning one's resources, or spectacular about the difficulties of allocating a modest decline in standards of living. Why not just produce more and distribute more? No sweat. But when those who demand redistribution also oppose economic growth, and when those who expand government also condemn it for being too big we may be pardoned for thinking that government is being programmed for failure.

Collectivism and individualism are balanced cultures; the strong group boundaries and strong prescription of behavioural norms in hierarchies reinforce one another, as do the weak boundaries and lack of prescriptions in individualistic markets. The established cultures can govern alone; sectarian culture cannot. Sectarians make inconsistent demands because the rejection of authority and redistribution of resources cannot be reconciled.

In the past, the term sect was often preceded by the modifier 'powerless'. Sectarians either rejected the main society and moved to the wilderness, or so enraged the establishment that it destroyed them. Today, sectarians are part of the system that imposes regulations on their opponents. Their interaction with government means that they are powerless no longer. The use of computerised mailing lists permits sectarian entrepreneurs to tap contributions from large numbers of people who do not participate directly in their group activities. This opportunity for vicarious participation has not only produced ready cash but has also simplified the task of leadership. Instead of satisfying an active membership, which might make contradictory demands, only the top leadership need be considered. Sectarianism without sects is the clue to the comparative advantage of sectarianism in modern politics. Taken together as a statement of political economy, the costs of entry (a few dollars per mail-order member) and of activity (lobbying and legal work) in influencing government have been vastly reduced. The benefit of interaction with government has increased while the cost has declined. The egalitarian sectarians of the United States have succeeded in using government to coerce other interests without being responsible for the consequences. This makes sectarians very powerful. They must find the irony delicious: instead of being subject to other people's rules, they impose, through government, a large number of rules on their opponents. So sectarians get stronger as their opponents are made weaker.

Nevertheless, influence and access are not the same as government. It is not easy for egalitarians to govern; that is why the historical record offers so few examples. Nor is it likely that a unicultural party will gain office or keep it for long, precisely because of its adherents' objections to compromise and coalition, both of which to them signify selling out (Ellis and Wildavsky, 1989). Democrats do too much to satisfy individualists and too little to satisfy egalitarians, as it is not easy to diminish differences among people. Whatever egalitarianism they do possess leads them to the adoption of nation-wide hierarchical solutions, which causes discomfort to their individualists. Whether it is Walter Mondale's embrace of 'special interests' or Michael Dukakis's avoidance of them, Democrats do not satisfy either the individualists or the egalitarians. Republicans, aside from their uneasy alliance of individualism and hierarchy, lack sufficient egalitarianism to attract the largest and most rapidly growing minorities. They can take advantage of Democratic egalitarianism, which has alienated many white Christian males, but they cannot extend their reach into Congress so as to govern by themselves. Perhaps now we understand why everyone in office seems to do so poorly but no one can take advantage of the fact.

The problematic nature of egalitarian leadership

Who, if anyone, will today's egalitarians ally themselves with? The use of central government to redistribute resources suggests that modern-day egalitarians are willing to ally themselves with hierarchical forces. The centralising principle is there, we all see that, but not the centralisers. Egalitarians appear hostile to social no less than economic conservatives; hierarchists appear too weak to be worth allying with. Can egalitarians rule by themselves? It appears very unlikely, as there is virtually no precedent for a unicultural regime in American experience. The real question, therefore, is whether an egalitarian party like the Democrats can work closely enough with hierarchists to remain in power and further its aims. That there appears to be no American historical precedent for an egalitarian–hierarchical coalition (Wildavsky, 1988) makes President Clinton's Democratic administration especially worth watching.

The dilemma of those who attempt to lead an egalitarian party is that they will be judged too weak and too strong at the same time and by the same people. It cannot be easy to lead a party whose activists do not believe in leadership. It is even more difficult to lead party activists who call for leadership but who oppose compromise. President Clinton's problems will come far more from his supporters than from his opponents. Should Clinton (a) falter in pursuing egalitarian objectives, or (b) compromise in a perceived inegalitarian direction, or (c) encounter unanticipated and negative consequences for a policy previously believed to be desirable, circumstances likely to occur at some time or other, his supporters will turn on him with all the asperity of those who believe that virtue (that is, equality) has been betrayed.

Because egalitarians are basically concerned with a single value, equality of condition, they regard compromise as tantamount to corruption. Accusations that President Clinton is selling out the cause will, therefore, be common. Because egalitarians believe that human beings are born good but are corrupted by evil institutions, they will not accept excuses from their presumptive leaders. It is not bad luck or necessity or misjudgement, but wilful betrayal that they will convince themselves is responsible for the failure to enact the egalitarian agenda. Clinton can expect to be accused of being a political chameleon: an oreo (black on the outside, white on the inside), a radish (radical on the outside, conservative on the inside), or a banana (Asian on the outside, Caucasian on the inside). He was always a closet conservative, Clinton will be told, only now it is apparent. These accusations will be hard to bear not only for the president but for his family and friends. All this is difficult to believe now (after all, it did not happen in Arkansas where 'left' would be centre or right anywhere else). But it will.

As time goes on, especially as many egalitarian Democrats get re-elected on their own, the tide will turn against him. Foreign ventures will prove not so much dangerous as ambiguous. In domestic affairs, it will become more apparent that social justice (that is, equality of condition) is still a long way off. Errors or merely unfortunate events will cast their shadow over this new, Democratic happy warrior. Criticism will rise. Clinton's inevitably mixed record will bring forth opposing but negative reactions from his party's egalitarian activists. At one and the same time, President Clinton will be deemed too weak to make the structural changes in American political economy which egalitarians deem necessary to secure greater equality of condition, and too strong for the liberties of his people.

Why too strong? He will not be too strong by any objective standard, but rather his egalitarian followers will perceive him to be too powerful. The following circumstances can be envisaged: much higher taxes, with a far more progressive bent; more affirmative action in appointments; the maintenance of social welfare programmes, including universal access to health care; and much greater environmental regulation. Individualists will be beside themselves, fortified by those hurting in their pocketbooks. Hierarchists (social conservatives) will be unhappy for two different reasons. They will be dismayed at the deficit. This will remain large particularly because of the costs of maintaining existing welfare programmes. They also object to higher taxes. Both economic and social conservatives will be outraged by Clinton's social egalitarianism. Their concerns, while not decisive, will affect the climate of opinion.

When Clinton compromises to get more of what he wants, I expect to hear he has 'sold out'. If he does not get important legislation passed, I expect to hear he is another failed president. If, as is most likely, Clinton wins more than he loses, but implementation of his programmes creates no miracles, I expect to hear about a revival of the 'imperial presidency'. As Clinton appears to his followers to be becoming too important (i.e. to be more than a first among equals), I expect his followers to turn on him, both because he is judged too weak in achieving greater equality and because he is judged too strong in exercising his powers of office.

References

Ellis, R. and Wildavsky, A. (1989), *Dilemmas of Presidential Leadership from Washington through Lincoln*, New Brunswick, Transaction

Wildavsky, A. (1987), 'Choosing Preferences by Constructing Institutions; A Cultural Theory of Preference Formation', *American Political Science Review*, Vol. 81, No. 1, pp. 3–21

— (1988), 'Resolved, That Individualism and Egalitarianism Be Made Compatible in America: Political Cultural Roots of Exceptionalism', paper presented to the conference on American Exceptionalism at Nuffield College Oxford (14–16 April), pp. 1–43

— (1991), *The Beleaguered Presidency*, New Brunswick, Transaction

Feminism

Around 1972 the women's liberation movement discovered feminism. Before then, 'women's lib', as it was quickly dubbed by its detractors, had not seen itself as part of a tradition which boasted the admittance of women to Oxford University, or the right of married women to own property, as its finest achievements. The women's liberation movement saw its origins as entirely original; as belonging with the new world which a new political generation of the 1960s was creating. In its very essence, it was making a revolution, founding a new order, and, by its very existence, breaking all links with the past.

Its origin in the radical policies of the United States during 1966–8 demonstrated the new hegemony of American politics and culture for young Europeans. The modern women's liberation movement was an associate of an anti-war culture. This was a passionately democratic culture; a movement of young people that idealized direct action and spontaneity, that celebrated the expression of the self through sexuality, and which regarded all the institutions then existing, from orthodox political party to the family, as being part of the old order that had to be smashed. Founding members of women's liberation did not regard the bluestocking spinsters of inter-war feminism as their ancestors, nor the force-fed suffragettes as their founding mothers. In short, in origin women's liberation acknowledged no history.[1]

This changed from the early 1970s. By this time, thinking about the ideology and theory of women's liberation had developed, largely through pamphlets and papers produced for the network of groups and annual women's liberation conferences that made up a cohesive women-only movement. Both the ideas and the women-only practice created a cleavage within the general revolutionary movement. For a brief moment, this idea that women had created their own, original movement, and had brought themselves into being through a sort of self-generation, was the evidence of the movement's authenticity. Women were the authors of their own image and destiny.

Such moments cannot last. Women began to look backwards into women's history for their distinct and identifying past. By the early 1970s women's liberation had reclaimed the name 'feminism' from the dustbin of history, and began to excavate a continuous ideological thread, through time and across continents, which linked the exercise of political and economic power to the subjugation of women within the home.

The severance between feminists and their revolutionary socialist peers was never complete, and in fact, as feminism developed – fighting many battles along the way about the movement's right to be 'autonomous' – it generated its own divisions. From about 1976, all the divisions of a once unitary women's liberation claimed the name 'feminism', as in 'socialist feminism', 'radical feminism', 'revolutionary feminism'. The divisions were marked by separate conferences, divergent cultures and conflicting intellectual allegiances. By 1980, Marxism, post-structuralism, anthropology, psychoanalysis, mysticism, and social democracy were amongst the discourses which different feminists were adapting for their own use.

Despite these differences, the divisions have never been exclusive. The women's movement, with its characteristic rejection of para-party organization, has never reproduced the sectarianism of the socialist movement. As a lived political tradition, different approaches to feminism still affect and alter each other.

The age of feminism

Feminism is a little younger than nationalism, that is, approximately two hundred years old. As Eric Hobsbawm points out, nationalism, or the *idea* of a nation, pre-dates the reality of the nation-state, the latter only being recognized as a political actuality from the later nineteenth century (Hobsbawm, 1991). Women cannot demand entry into the political realm as citizens until the political nation has been conjured up. But rampant nationalism stifles feminist thought and action. When nationalism is all the rage, women must either be the helpmeets of men and mothers of the nation, or traitors to the cause.[2]

Feminism and nationalism are usually in opposition, but both ideologies are only made possible by some common conditions. One of these is a bourgeoisie that is not tied to the land, and for whose children education rivals money as a route to public life. The daughters can then see that lack of education, not inherent qualities of God's order, explains women's apparent inferiority. Another is the emergence of a 'political republic', meaning an assertive political society which is seen by its members as being both political and sovereign. This political realm, inside which all are equal individuals, displaces religion as the source of authority. Lastly the family has to lose its role as a unit in the political hierarchy. That is, kinship or clan have to be superseded by larger, non-dynastic communities in the transmission of power and authority. This process uproots women from their position within the order, but also sets women free to think of themselves as citizens. From these experiences, women can see themselves as having more in common with other women than with members of their family. The displacement of family is also a precursor of the foundation of political nations. It is only when these conditions exist that feminism is feasible.

Definition

Feminism cannot be defined as a theory of difference between men and women. That's what biology offers. Feminism is a *political* theory of why and how the male sex exercises power over the female sex, in actuality and symbolically. At different times, feminists may emphasize the potential for sameness or the actuality of sexual difference, depending on the political moment. As a theory, feminism operates on that border between imagining what could be and unmasking what is.

Feminism is also a political movement which challenges the power exercised by men, and it is a movement which creates a new political identity for those who engage in it. Feminism is, then, a practice for personal living and political action. It is a practice in which women can 'be themselves' and a theory which authenticates the need and right of women to assert a separate political being. Feminism has been most itself when at its most militant, and its apotheosis is a militancy of sexual rage (Holton, 1990).

Feminism is distinguished from doctrines of class or national liberation on two counts. As a theory of women's liberation, it cannot be universal; it does not offer men a theory or practice of self-realization. Second, feminists have not sought self-realization through the establishment of an endogenous, territorial, sovereign state. Arguments about statehood and nationhood have never been central to feminist theory, although arguments about citizenship have been.[3] Concepts of fraternity, virility, protection, gender itself and the public/private split have been as useful to feminist theory as conventional categories of liberty and the state.

As a consequence of these features, feminism has not provided an ideology of national government. Indeed, until recently, feminism has been a *contingent* ideology, responding to exogenous discourses (i.e. its characteristic mode was a critique of a mainstream discourse for ignoring gender). However, since the late 1970s, feminists have made headway in arguing feminism can be a hegemonic ideology. That is, feminist values of sexual equality, or of establishing a non-'macho' political practice, have become increasingly influential as values for political life in general, although they cannot be said to be dominant values. In Britain, the work which made the vital cross-over from the women's movement to a general political practice was *Beyond the Fragments* (Rowbotham *et al.*, 1979). But since the 1980s, the driving force for internal change in virtually all public organizations from right-wing parties to established churches has been an argument for the implementation of feminist values.

Like any group which 'forgets' its origin, its past and its defeats, feminism was unable to develop its own history or cultural tradition.[4] This is one reason why, until recently, there have been few standard 'great works' and no feminist canon. Without a canon, the evolution from a particular group or thinker into a sustained body of political theory does not take place. Some early feminist works, like Mary Astell's *A Serious Proposal to the Ladies* or, most famously, Mary Wollstonecraft's *A Vindication of the Rights of Women*, have taken their place as early classics of feminism because modern feminists have reclaimed them.

Feminism has therefore had a desultory intellectual tradition and, until recently, relatively few intellectuals it could call its own. Historians of feminism must track the ideas in obscure journals and pamphlets. Much of the early history of post-1968 feminism is still locked in the memories of its makers and in duplicated papers, most written by collectives rather than named individuals. Only the opening of higher education to women and the greater willingness of publishers to take feminism seriously (or at least, the market demand for feminist studies seriously) is laying down a body of feminist theoretical work. This suggests feminism, for the first time in two hundred years, has crossed the threshold from defeat into assimilation.

This pattern of creation, oblivion, re-creation and re-writing the past is a characteristic of feminism, as of all contingent ideologies. The history of feminism is contingent on other political and social changes. As a political ideology, feminism has been made by women through different campaigns and moral surges. Its goals and ethos change through time. What has remained constant has been the focus on social and domestic life as the origin of sexual inequality. The distinctive politics of feminism has consisted of identifying the power relations of domestic and social life as unequal, unjust and artificial and dubbing these 'political'. There was thus no absolute distinction between the realm over which the citizen, or government, exercised judgement and made laws and the private realm which the father governed with natural authority. Although traditional political theory had recognized the organic link between the authority exercised by the man as citizen in the 'polis' and the man as despot or partner in the household, theorists from Aristotle to Locke saw the household realm as lying beyond state jurisdiction and the authority of the father or parent as deriving from natural qualities. The jurisdiction of the state began at the border with nature's domain. It was these distinct qualities of the household realm which feminists have consistently challenged. Feminism has thus implicitly, or explicitly, always constituted a new definition of what is political.

The most distinctive slogan of the post-1968 women's movement was 'The personal is political' (used by Carol Hanisch in her essay 'The Personal is Political' in Agel, 1971). The axiom of self-liberation – common to all liberation movements – gave feminism one of its most distinctive forms, the consciousness-raising group. The slogan and the movement made possible a novel political practice, in which conflict over who cooked the dinner or the evasive orgasm were judged to be as valid as demonstrations or elections. The practice also contains the central paradox of modern feminism: an essentially collective practice stressing what all women have in common, yet aiming at the individual self-realization of each woman. The paradox is expressed by Catherine MacKinnon (1989) in the following terms: 'Feminism's search for a ground is a search for the truth of all women's collectivity in the face of the enforced lie that all women are the same'. It is not surprising that the modern movement has had such an affinity with psycho-therapy and self-help groups.

Although a women's movement has occasionally produced a women's political party, these parties have been the exceptions which prove the rule – the rule being that feminism does not constitute an ideology of national government. The authority of feminism derives from its particular challenge to the power relations between women and men. It cannot move far from this authentic basis without becoming totalitarian or separatist. It risks becoming totalitarian by obliterating any distinction between the political and the rest of the world. No part of life is therefore left outside the rule of a single ideology – feminism. Separatism comes when women abandon their attempts to change gender relations and, without bidding to form their own government, return to an ideology of defeat.

The divisions of feminism

By the 1980s it seemed impossible to talk simply of 'feminism', so varied and conflicting had the forms of feminism become. The distinctions stemmed from different analyses of the nature of the power which oppressed women and, therefore, what strategy of action could challenge that power.

Material/economic feminism
In the 1970s, socialist feminists saw power as originating in the ownership of property. Women's oppression was, at the least, reinforced and augmented by antagonistic class relations, if not caused by them. Most work within this trend followed Engels' approach, linking the development of the family with the ownership of property (Engels, 1940). Marriage was defined as an arrangement for the inheritance of property and the family was defined as the agency which reproduced labour power – a theory which made 'private' life an economic function of capitalism's needs. Arguments over the relation between class and gender were fierce and fruitful, especially in Britain, where feminists had a stronger relation to the labour movement than most. They produced influential studies on the domestic economy, and on the history of working-class and/or socialist women. Socialist feminists, heirs to the rationalist tradition, saw most sexual differences as a product of economic and social conditions, and women's particular oppression as contingent on the capitalist or imperialist order, rather than purposefully engineered by men for their immediate benefit. This approach generated fresh thinking on the nature of the state, particularly on its role in reinforcing women's dependence through welfare rules (Wilson, 1977; McIntosh, 1978). But it did not produce any wholesale rethinking about the formation of the state or the role of gender in the 'socialist' states.

The initial tendency towards economic functionalism, which retained the paramountcy of class relations in its analysis, was later amended or even jettisoned by socialist feminists who were influenced by the writings of French Marxists and post-Marxists, particularly Louis Althusser, Nicos Poulantzas, Michel Foucault and Jacques Lacan. They dethroned the idea of a single cause and aetiology of all oppressions. They also, in different ways, connected personal and family life to non-economic structures, especially the state.

Black and anti-racist feminism

Theoretically this has an affinity to socialist feminism in that it sees power as having a material base (e.g. the unequal ownership of wealth or property). But black feminists took a lead in pointing to the way apparently different oppressions in fact combined and reinforced one another, rather than coming in a simple hierarchy. In the United States they had had to direct arguments against those who asserted feminism was only an ideology of privileged white women, and against white feminists who were blind to the specific reality of black women's lives. The latter was contrary to the basic assertion that women's liberation was blind to all distinctions among women (Morgan, 1970). Racism was said to create a different form of sexual oppression for black women (Hooks, 1992). Black feminists have been instrumental in raising questions of national community and of where women 'belong', as well as, of course, in identifying the integral links between race and sex in the making of a national, or political community. Black feminists have thus been the bearers of the most integrationist view of feminism, while at the same time they have often been silenced by the conflict over where their political loyalties lie. They have also challenged white feminist conventions on the relation of 'the family' to wage labour and to the male state 'protectorate' (see below, and Hill Collins, 1990).

Sexual/personal feminism

Radical feminists identify men's exploitation of women as the originating conflict for power. Much radical feminist writing assumes a moment in historical time when men achieved some sort of victory over women. This is a variant of 'foundation' theory, in which the foundation of the community is imagined as a real event which then determines the subsequent nation, or political community. In this case, the foundation is of a male state which has conquered some form of matriarchal society. This has led to theories of the state which define it as a gendered system of jurisprudence (MacKinnon, 1989), rather than an institution or relationship which has to do with economic class.

The identification of sexuality itself as the quality to which men demand access and seek to control was initially made by radical feminist thinkers and developed through various campaigns on the vital link between sex and violence. From this, radical feminists named sexual terrorism as the means men use to maintain their power. Out of all the feminisms it has been the most likely to interpret men's actions as having the explicit purpose of oppressing women. It has thus tended to develop that familiar political trait of paranoia, meaning a belief that the actions of the other are directed at one's own destruction. Like other ideologies which focus on biological identity and on terrorism and violence, radical feminism tends to deny the political as a specific category.

Ecological feminism

There are many feminists who feel an easy affinity with ecological argument, but there is a particularly well-developed brand of 'gyn-ism' (see Mary Daly, 1979) which equates femaleness with wholeness and the earth, with natural cycles and the creation of life. It is contrasted with maleness which is seen as divisive and scientific, imposing abstract compartments on naturally whole processes. This strand was strongly boosted by the 1980s campaigns for ecological thinking, for 'alternative health' therapies, and against nuclear weapons in particular and high defence spending in general. As these concerns are not confined to women, it is here where feminism has been most obviously a dominant ideology.

Liberal/individual feminism

Liberal feminism has been the least concerned with historical explanation, tending to see sexual inequality as just one of the social inequalities that existed in prehistory. It has been most likely to see feminism as part of the general progress of modern society toward equal opportunity in which differences between individuals will not be vehicles for large economic differences. Liberal feminism, like other liberal ideologies, has focused on individual rights – constitutional and property-owning – as the measure of well-being. In consequence, those aspects of life which cannot be ordered into political, job or property rights – the domain of equal opportunities – are seen as beyond the feminist pale, and unreachable by political action. This form of feminism has been assimilated by many liberal and conservative parties. It would be wrong, however, to dismiss this liberal trend as conservative in nature. Liberal individualism has been a powerful theme of feminism, with its stress on the individual woman realizing her 'true self' by rejecting rigid sexual roles.

Psychoanalytic/symbolic/cultural feminism

Psychoanalytic feminism tends to explain differences between men and women by the actual and symbolic distinctions in the relations of male and female to parents, children and their own bodies and sexuality. It has the least obvious political implications, although this does not mean that its adherents advocate an apolitical approach. The first feminists to embrace Freud, in fact, tended to be socialist feminists, in part because of the importance of Juliet Mitchell's *Psychoanalysis and Feminism* (1974), in part because they had the least resistance to male theoretical writing. Since the 1970s, psychoanalysis has become a dominant influence on feminism, providing a rich theoretical and intellectual field for women's traditional concerns about the family, personal development and culture. It has also provided a rationalisation for the desire for self-realization (through therapy and analysis) which was a particularly powerful spring for the early women's liberation movement.

Postmodernist feminism

'Postmodern' feminism is a product both of the trends in socialist and psychoanalytic feminism, and also an attempt to adapt the approach of deconstruction and postmodernism to feminism. At its simplest, this means eschewing any absolute theoretical explanation based in any distinct material reality. It focuses on *how* gender is 'constructed' and 'represented' in all forms of communication or discourse. It thus tends to deny that there is some other reality lying outside the discourse which purports to represent it, and may deny the power inequality within that actuality (Flax, 1990). It thus becomes anti-political.

None of these trends is mutually exclusive in theory; and, in practice most actual feminists borrow from several feminist strands. They are all connected by the belief that the exploitation of female labour and sexuality is still widespread and profoundly shapes the lives of women and, thus, of society in general; an exploitation that still goes unrecognized.

Campaigns

Where does the politics of women's liberation lie? The great campaigning strands of feminism have been

(1) Sexual – White slaves; prostitution; pornography; sexual violence; abortion and contraception; sexual harassment.
(2) Educational – The idea that the inferiority of women is due to artifice and that access to reason will allow women to both develop the same intellectual qualities as men and to discover their own true interests; education is thus the route to equality, to authenticity and to self-possession. Institutional campaigns have been for admission on equal terms to educational institutes; the opening of all courses and forms of education to women as 'gender-free'.
(3) Employment – Pay, conditions, protective legislation, discrimination; the role of housework in the economy; the idea of women's 'double burden'.
(4) Motherhood – Childcare; safe maternity; the valuation of mothering and moral status of women; abortion and contraception; housework.
(5) Marriage – No longer a principal issue but, until the 1960s, at the forefront of women's campaigning on church and state, husbands and property law. Many forms of discrimination were not so much against women as such but against married women.
(6) Cultural – Ideas about women, men and gender. The representation of women, men and sexuality in art, literature, film, theatre etc. The gendered cultural heritage.

(7) Political – Women as citizens and members of the political community; the right to vote, to stand for office; to represent others, to be represented.

The course of feminism

What explains why women's separate voices emerge, and are heard, at some points in history, then subside, speak in unison or argue aloud? In Europe and the United States there have been three feminist 'moments'; the 1790s; a longer swell beginning in the mid nineteenth century, escalating in the 1880s and reaching an intense pitch in 1910–14; and the late 1960s, reaching a plateau around 1980. Between these moments feminist ideas were still discussed and campaigns waged, but they lacked the power of a movement.[5] Reasons for this erratic history have been variously attributed to technology and the forces of production, to political contingency, to national traditions.

Forces of production do change our ideas and actions, shifting our understanding of what is seen to be naturally right and what is humanly possible. But forces of production, including technology, are not political actors, and do not create ideas and desires. Women's lack of reproductive control has been due to political and moral prohibitions, not technology; the sheath, pessaries, the sponge and abortion were available in the nineteenth century. It was not technology but the state that closed the first American birth control clinic, opened by Margaret Sanger in 1916. Neither was it the forces of production which caused contraception to be advocated as a means of giving 'the more suitable races or strains of blood a better chance of prevailing over the less suitable' (in the words of Francis Galton, new president of the Eugenics Society, 1908; Hall, 1977).

A division of labour is clearly a fundamental shaper of social relations, but a division of labour is never an inanimate device for organizing labour and home life. All divisions of labour begin from hierarchies of power within an *existing* social order. Social orders which hold all people tight within family or political structures have inflexible economies. What causes these orders to weaken, loosening women and children as a new labour-force, or turning out both single men and whole communities as migrants, is a crucial question for historians and contemporary analysts of industrial development and migration.

Historically, the connection between the expression of feminist views and the size and nature of the female labour-force has been complex. It is not true that the larger the female labour-force, the louder the feminist voice. This is evident in the ex-socialist countries, one of whose defining characteristics is their use of a mass female labour-force without the engendering of a feminist political voice (Heitlinger, 1979). The nature of the work women do creates possibilities for feminism; but ideology about the role of women also determines how many women go out to work and what they do. This is one of the principal reasons for the historic association between modernism, feminism and the breakdown of traditional order.[6] Socially, the emergence of feminism is contingent on this loosening of the social and familiar order; politically it is contingent on the imagined creation of a man-made republic.[7]

Feminism as a political ideology depends on the idea that human beings make their own political destiny. This idea was born in the seventeenth century with the myth of the social contract, a myth of men founding their own political society. It was hotly contested at the end of the eighteenth by men like Edmund Burke, who saw political authority as derived from God, and Tom Paine (1987, p. 204), who insisted that: 'Every age and generation must be as free to act for itself, *in all cases*, as the ages and generations which preceded it.' Once the idea had taken root that men could make their own political destinies, there was no reasoned argument why women should not also make their own destinies. Other republican ideas, of universal reason, popular sovereignty, the corrupting effects of rank and inherited privilege, also made feminism possible. Women shared the aspirations of men to create a new public order but saw themselves as excluded and demeaned in the effort to make that order. Although the late eighteenth century witnessed the emergence of a recognizable feminist voice in the form of Mary Wollstonecraft, a republic was still regarded as contingent upon the demands voiced by men. In Britain, France and United States women concentrated on challenging the constrictions of the social realm, especially education, employment and the artifices of a new femininity (Rendall, 1985). Women identified social and domestic life and the rule of 'manners' as the sites of women's oppression, perhaps because the more clearly political demands of the new republicans were inextricably connected to the idea of manliness as *the* republican virtue.

At that time, citizenship was still linked to two key qualities, neither of which women possessed. The first was military potential. The 'virtue' (with its etymological root in 'vir' or man) of fighting for one's republic was not possessed by women, the lower orders or slaves, all of whom were debarred from the militias that prevailed through to the nineteenth century.[8]

The second quality was that of 'self-possession'; ideologically, the new political states from the seventeenth century were the creation of 'private' men who belonged to themselves, as marked by their possession of their own households and their domestic independence from the aristocracy. Women, servants and slaves did not possess themselves. Nor, as non-soldiers, did they belong to the nation. (The African–American leader Frederick Douglass urged blacks to enlist in the civil war with the argument 'He who fights the battles of America may claim America as his country and have that claim respected' (Berry, 1977, p. 93).) Rather they constituted a *protectorate*, whose destiny was under the command of the male colonizer. This definition applied only to white women whose fathers and husbands constituted the protectors by virtue of their position within the state. Ironically, the practice of slavery, which provided nineteenth century feminists with so much of their language of oppression, put black women in a fundamentally different relation to the dominant white male, i.e. they never constituted a protectorate (Hill Collins, 1990; Hooks, 1992).

Free women posed a threat to the social order, a threat that was reinforced by the destruction of the family order through industrial change, and the attachment of women in industrial areas to the Chartist cause along with its demands for citizenship (Taylor, 1983). Conservatives in the nineteenth century reverted to a pre-republican notion of fixed social orders. Faced with the erosion of male hegemony, potential war between women and men was resolved in the style perfected by their Cold War descendants; a line was drawn between women's territory and men's territory. The men's was called 'public' and women's 'private' or domestic or moral. The notion of 'separate spheres' defined by gender then took root. Feminists themselves adapted the new commanding ideology to their own purposes. By the end of the century, the argument for female suffrage was put precisely in terms of women's difference and the need to represent the separate sphere of femaledom, which also meant morality, in public life.

The hegemonic ideology of the nineteenth century was that of imperialism – meaning here the idea of an ordained destiny of the superior races to expand – e.g. Britain through the world, the United States across the American continent. Such races were destined to govern those who had *not* formed themselves into nations due, it was assumed, to racial (i.e. natural) inferiority or, in more benign language, 'immaturity'. White feminists were not immune to this trend. Some women did support the anti-slavery campaigns which strengthened the feminist language of human dignity and freedom and the link to political freedom (i.e. the right of self-possession and the command over one's own body). But often white feminists assimilated the imperialist and racist world view. The argument that middle class white women should be afforded the dignity of the vote, as a mark which distinguished them from the lower orders, from apolitical natives, from unfree slaves and from inferior black people, became a powerful part of the feminist demand for women's rights. Women want the vote, Florence Fenwick Miller of the Woman's Franchise League, told the World's Congress of Representative Women in 1894 because 'it is a slur and an insult that the most highly cultivated, the most competent, the most business-like, the best trained of women should be held incapable of giving any opinion on the affairs of their country, while the lowest, the most ignorant and the most illiterate of men is supposed to be equal to having such an opinion' (Sewall, 1894). This reality has often been expunged from the feminist record.

Significantly, it was American women who, around 1850, first launched a campaign for women's suffrage. It was described by Harriet Taylor Mill, in 1851, as 'new, and even unheard-of, as a subject for public meetings and practical political action' (Taylor Mill, 1983). The existence of the United States as a political republic and the anti-slavery agitation were two of the causes of the pioneering role of American women in the suffrage issue.

The emergence of social Darwinism, and thence eugenics, as part of the history of both imperialism and nationalism was a simple step, and many women took it with ease. If the new Darwinian social science successfully presented military and economic power as the evidence of innate racial superiority, then it became women's role to consolidate and enhance their superiority by reproducing the superior race. But there was another facet to this imperial outreach which had completely new implications for the role of women. The argument for separate spheres had been built on the idea that the men's world of running the empire and producing material goods was a thankless, exhausting and corrupting ordeal which demanded 'manly' qualities that had nothing to do with traditional goodness; when men stepped out of the house, they left behind their moral scruples. Ironically, the separation of human life into gender-based separate spheres removed one barrier to women's admittance to political life even while it was raising the ramparts to keep women out. Both the Aristotelian and the seventeenth century idea of the political realm assumed that political man entered the public realm from his secure domestic household, over which he exercised dominion. With the separation of his home from his public life, the master loses control over that which is his own – the household. Public life thus loses its distinct quality of being a realm in which men, in possession of their own selves, can exercise their independent, civic judgement over that which concerns the common good. In splitting life into two separate spheres, men had not only cut themselves loose from their private life (private also carrying that sense of that which belongs to oneself, and therefore which makes one unique), but also deprived themselves of their moral and life-creating selves. For domestic life is, *par excellence*, the arena in which life itself is created and sustained.

The new manliness developed in response to the demand for civic equality from women, Jews, blacks and 'natives', all of whom were said to have the feminine characteristics of weakness, disloyalty and lack of self-possession. The new manliness was also a denial of full humanity in men. The 'political' world of the modern nation was forged in this image. In exchange for the loss of their spiritual, domestic life men gained their communal identity as brothers. And this, more than anything, showed men belonged to the nation. As such the nation could demand – and it did – that they sacrifice their individual lives for its survival. Feminists at the turn of the century argued that if the political world was to represent moral qualities, it therefore had to admit women, now that they were the only bearers of domestic and spiritual experience.

Feminists also brought a particular twist to the 'separate sphere' ideology in their preoccupation with sexual disease and sexual purity. Syphilis was certainly a horrible and widespread disease which wrecked the health of many women and children. But the anger and intensity which many feminists brought to this campaign spoke also of the inexpressible anger felt about sexuality, abused and suppressed. This undoubtedly fuelled the campaign for the vote, not just with ideas about the 'unfitness' of men who did have the vote, but also with the readiness of women to martyr themselves in the holy war for women's righteousness. The 1910 campaign for a suffrage Bill was waged with 'an unparalleled intensity' (Strachey, 1976, p. 316). Thus this second, turn-of-the-century wave of feminism was a strange and potent mix of passions, for the dignity of the vote, for justice, and for escape from the artificial constraints on women's freedom, the arrogance of empire, the terrors of racial 'degradation', and the unspeakability of sexual rage.

The First World War destroyed men, national communities and the idea that men use politics to make their own destinies. If the mass destruction could not be attributed to a terrible nemesis, the military commanders and 'politicians' must take the blame. Even communists, who did uphold the potential of ordinary men and women to make their own lives, tended to see human destiny as the product of historical forces beyond political control.

Legislation giving women aged over thirty the vote was passed in Britain in 1918. In the United States all women were given the vote on the same basis as men in 1920. The vote was part of the settlement of war in which women had proved that they 'belonged' to the nation. Some campaigns, on maternity, contraception, employment and, later, family allowances, were pursued by women in the inter-war years. Pacifism and anti-militarism also remained a feminist cause. But feminism as a militant movement had been subdued. The items on the agenda of the National Union of Societies for Equal Citizenship were, according to its journal the *Woman's Leader*, 'not considered, even by the most ardent feminist, as being of such outstanding importance as the great problems in foreign politics, of international peace and reparations, and in home politics of unemployment, housing and public health' (Pugh, 1992, p. 62). Military thinking dominated the times, over which hovered the prospect of imminent apocalypse. Whether this would come through mass unemployment, the collapse of capitalism, the triumph of bolshevism or of fascism, or the millenarial rule of national socialism, the threats to national and international stability provided no fulcrum for feminist action.

Post-1968 feminism

By 1960 feminism survived as little more than a whisper of memory, of bloomers and blue-stockings and an indigestible paradox of violent action cloaked in the lady-like garb of the Edwardian era. Ten years later, the reputation of feminism had been transformed. There are many accounts of why women's liberation was born, but as in the nineteenth century, the initiative undoubtedly came from the United States where the experience of extra-party civil rights campaigning and political arguments for the equality of blacks profoundly affected white women.

The idea that the daughters of the white, professional middle class might deem themselves oppressed was risible and shocking. The violence of response from many men, once deemed comrades, to women abandoning 'proper' political meetings to go to women-only consciousness-raising groups, in turn shocked many of the women. It revealed a layer of sexual hostility from which most had been protected.

Socially, a new generation of women had entered what became known as 'civil society', where the persistence of low pay, poor conditions and lack of opportunity had no rationale in the public language of freedom and democracy. Post-war social democracy had engendered an ideology of equality and a belief that the public realm, specifically the state, should provide solutions for the deprivations suffered in social life, such as child care or low pay. Whether or not the state should intervene to change gender-based divisions of labour was a matter of contention between feminists and trade unionists in Britain. The contradictory trade union belief that the state should not intervene in free collective bargaining, but should nonetheless treat the female labour-force as a protectorate (through protective legislation), caused conflict. Intellectually, the conflict bore fruit in work on gender and the division of labour, and on why issues like abortion were a trade union responsibility. But by treating trade unions rather than political parties as the key agent for change, feminists contributed to trade union hubris, and also to the depletion of political debate both within the Labour Party and feminism.

Post-war social democracy had also shifted the boundaries of private and public in the other direction, to deem sexuality 'private' in the sense of permitting individuals to choose their own sexual practice, within as yet undefined limits. Rhetorically, personal destiny was a matter of individual choice. Only religious groups seriously contested the claim that whether or not to marry or have children was a matter of personal freedom. The intended beneficiaries of this shifting of the boundaries were men, specifically those whose homosexual practice was decriminalized by the 1967 Act in Britain, and those who did not have access to the sexual freedom or literature enjoyed by the elite.

Although these seismic shifts in the boundaries of private and public life were not intended to change gender relations, women's own frustration at the continued artificial constrictions on their lives, together with their appetite for a new freedom and a prevailing rhetoric of equality and freedom, meant that the boundaries were in fact reshaped by gender. This meant that instead of a new private domain being established, as MPs imagined (with the Acts of Parliament pushing back state restrictions on abortion and homosexuality) the distinction between private and public became ever more blurred. For it became clear that freedom for women meant *more* state intervention in the domestic domain. That is, for women's liberation to become an actuality, the state had to step inside the household and lay down the law against male violence, as well as making active provision for child care, contraception, and abortion.

How and why is post-1968 feminism different from what came before? Post-1968 feminism is caught on the same dilemma as early feminism: are women and men equal because they are the same, or are they equal but different? Undoubtedly, between the mid-1960s and 1980, feminism treated biological differences between men and women as lacking in social significance. If society could be reorganized, through personal change, industrial restructuring and massive state intervention, then sexual difference would have as little meaning as other biological differences (e.g. height or hair colouring). Feminist theoretical effort therefore went into proving that apparent differences were circumstantial or contingent.

The impact of changes which, by default, have been aggregated under the term postmodernism have been enormous. The focus of feminism as a 'discourse' has shifted from the phenomena of inequality – money, divisions of labour, child care etc. – to how masculinity and femininity, as disembodied qualities, are represented in words or visual images (Flax, 1990). In politics, postmodernism has assailed 'mono-morphism', meaning here that there can be no single cause of, or form for, either gender inequality or gender difference. By the same reasoning, there cannot be a hierarchy of oppressions either. Postmodernism thus takes the conflict, and the politics, out of feminism. Confined to the academy, preoccupied with defining differences rather than attacking unequal power relations, feminism becomes an intellectual discourse, not a political practice.

As in previous eras, feminism has been associated by conservatives with breaking down a traditional order, to the detriment of society. The social ills laid at the door of feminism are many and profound, particularly where feminism has been seen as recruiting the state to its service. The most aggressive charge has been that feminism has emasculated men and made fathers redundant. The redundancy of fathers, of masculinity itself, abetted by the state, is said to have led to the most damaging social ill of the late twentieth century – the single mother whose fatherless children are outside the social order altogether, rejecting education, engaging in riot and destruction, incapable of useful employment and, worst of all, perpetuating these asocial habits into the next generation. Feminism is also held culpable of having destroyed the culture, through its misappropriation of the very words and images which make up that culture. The bitterness of the charges against feminism is testament to the degree to which masculinity and male dominion over the household were seen as the foundations of the nation and its order.

It is also a testament to the degree to which feminist ideas have become integrated into a 'common sense' interpretation of life that the charges against feminism, though resonant, have not proved hegemonic. That is, feminist ideas have proved influential in interpreting social change, and have in particular stigmatised 'macho' behaviour (once revered as the stuff of national supremacy). Perhaps the greatest success of feminist ideas has been in the simple insistence that all social orders are shaped by, if not based on, gender, and any agency seeking interpretation or change must take this into account. The argument for the presence of women within political movements as a representation of wholeness, the feminine and the domestic has been assimilated into many political discourses, especially ecology, anti-war movements, and new-style social democracy.

The successive crises at the end of the twentieth century, of epidemic, famine and political collapse, of unemployment and social anomie, of pseudo-nationalist xenophobia and war, have all proved amenable to a feminist interpretation, if not feminist solution. And this is perhaps the limit of feminism.

Notes

1. In 'Women: the Longest Revolution', published in *New Left Review* in 1966, Juliet Mitchell connects her argument for action on women's oppression to the socialist tradition of the 'Woman question' (Mitchell, 1984). In *Woman's Estate*, published in 1971, she acknowledges that the contemporary women's movement 'is assimilated to the earlier feminist struggles', but that this 'obscures its novelty'.
2. This should be qualified by Richard Evans's view that the struggle for nationalism, especially in the Nordic countries, implied popular sovereignty and thus an extension of the suffrage (Evans, 1977). But this does not contradict the hypothesis that feminism is contingent on the demand of male peers for political sovereignty, but cannot flourish while that demand is at its most militant.
3. The question of why women should feel themselves obligated to civic allegiance was posed by Carol Pateman, in her highly subversive critique, *The Problem of Political Obligation* (1985), and the centrality of fraternity in *The Sexual Contract* (1988).
4. In 'What is a nation?', a lecture given in 1882, Ernest Renan (1990) argues that for a nation to exist, the acts of violence and the divergent groups which have made the nation have to be forgotten.
5. Although Martin Pugh (1992) titles his history of women's public actions in the period 1914–59 as a history of the women's movement, he does define the inter-war zeitgeist as 'the political containment of women' and 'the cult of domesticity'.
6. For a discussion of this see Mosse, 1985, or almost any play by Ibsen or G. B. Shaw.
7. The invaluable notion of nation as 'imagined community' comes from Benedict Anderson though sadly he does not discuss it in relation to imagined manliness or femininity (Anderson, 1983).
8. Military service as a prerequisite for citizenship was an explicit idea until the First World War. It was notoriously argued by Justice Roger Taney in the Dred Scot constitutional ruling (which ruled black Americans were not citizens): 'But why are the African race, born in the State, not permitted to share in any of the duties of the citizen? The answer is obvious; he is not, by the institutions and law of the State, numbered among its people. He forms no part of the sovereignty of the State, and is not, therefore, called upon to uphold and defend it' (Berry, 1977).

References

Agel, J. (ed.) (1971), *The Radical Therapist*, New York, Ballantine Books

Anderson, Benedict (1983), *Imagined Communities*, London, Verso

Astell, M. (1694), *A Serious Proposal to the Ladies* (pamphlet)

Berry, Mary Frances (1977), *Military Necessity and Civil Rights Policy: Citizenship and the Constitution*, New York, Kennikat Press

Bhabha, Homi K. (ed.) (1990), *Nation and Narration*, London, Routledge

Daly, Mary (1979), *Gyn/ecology: The Metaethics of Radical Feminism*, London, Women's Press

Engels, Friedrich (1940), *The Origin of the Family: Private Prosperity and the State*, London, Lawrence and Wishart

Evans, Richard J. (1977), *The Feminists*, London, Croom Helm

Flax, Jane (1990), 'Postmodernism and Gender Relations in Feminist Theory', in Linda J. Nicholson (ed.), *Feminism/Postmodernism*, London, Routledge

Hall, Ruth (1977), *Marie Stopes: A Biography*, London, Andre Deutsch

Heitlinger, Alena (1979), *Women and State Socialism*, London, Macmillan

Hill Collins, Patricia (1990), *Black Feminist Thought*, London, Unwin Hyman

Hobsbawm, Eric (1991), *Nations and Nationalism: Programme, Myth, Reality*, Cambridge University Press

Holton, Sandra Stanley (1990), 'In Sorrowful Wrath: Suffrage Militancy and the Romantic Feminism of Emmeline Pankurst', in Harold Smith (ed.), *British Feminism in the Twentieth Century*, Aldershot, Edward Elgar Publishing

Hooks, Bell (1992), *Ain't I a Woman* (first published 1982), London, Pluto Press

McIntosh, Mary (1978), 'The State and the Oppression of Women', in Annette Kuhn and AnnMarie Wolpe (eds.), *Feminism and Materialism: Women and Modes of Production*, London, Routledge and Kegan Paul

MacKinnon, Catherine (1989), *Toward a Feminist Theory of the State*, Cambridge, MA, Harvard University Press

Mitchell, Juliet (1971), *Woman's Estate*, Harmondsworth, Penguin

— (1974), *Psychoanalysis and Feminism*, London, Allen Lane

— (1984), *Women: The Longest Revolution*, London, Virago

Morgan, Robin (ed.) (1970), *Sisterhood is Powerful: An Anthology of Writings from the Women's Liberation Movement*, New York, Vintage Books, Random House

Mosse, George L. (1985), *Nationalism and Sexuality: Respectability and Abnormal Sexuality in Modern Europe*, New York, Howard Fertig

Paine, Thomas (1987), *Rights of Man* (first published 1791–2), in *Thomas Paine Reader*, Harmondsworth, Penguin

Pateman, Carole (1985), *The Problem of Political Obligation: A Critique of Liberal Theory* (first published 1979), Cambridge, Polity Press

— (1988), *The Sexual Contract*, Cambridge, Polity Press

Pugh, Martin (1992), *Women and the Women's Movement in Britain 1914–1959*, London, Macmillan Education

Renan, Ernest (1990), 'What is a Nation?', in Homi K. Bhabha (ed.), *Nation and Narration*, London, Routledge

Rendall, Jane (1985), *The Origins of Modern Feminism: Women in Britain, France and the United States 1780–1860*, London, Macmillan

Rowbotham, Sheila, Segal, Lynne, and Wainwright, Hilary (1979), *Beyond the Fragments: Feminism and the Making of Socialism*, London, Merlin Press

Sewall, May Wright (ed.) (1894), *The World's Congress of Representative Women* (proceedings), Chicago, Rand McNally and Co.

Strachey, Ray (1976), *The Cause: A Short History of Women's Movement in Great Britain* (first published 1928), London, Virago

Taylor, Barbara (1983), *Eve and the New Jerusalem*, London, Virago

Taylor Mill, Harriet (1983), *The Enfranchisement of Women* (first published 1851, reprinted with *The Subjection of Women*, by John Stuart Mill), London, Virago

Wilson, Elizabeth (1977), *Women and the Welfare State*, London, Tavistock Publications

Wollstonecraft, Mary (1992), *A Vindication of the Rights of Women* (first published 1792), ed. with intro. by Miriam Brady, Harmondsworth, Penguin

Further Reading

Kaplan, Marion A. (1979), *The Jewish Feminist Movement in Germany*, Connecticut, Greenwood Press

Reynolds, Sian (1986), *Women, State and Revolution: Essays on Power and Gender in Europe since 1979*, Brighton, Wheatsheaf. See especially the editor's own essay 'Marianne's Citizens? Women, the Republic and Universal Suffrage in France'

Weedon, Chris (1987), *Feminist Practice and Poststructuralist Theory*, Oxford, Blackwell

Religious fundamentalism

One notable feature of the last third of the twentieth century has been a particularly potent mixture of religion and politics. While the insertion of religion into the political process is scarcely new, 'fundamentalist' movements have so capably utilised the considerable resources at their command as to mount acute challenges almost everywhere to the political and social status quo. The very term has been invested with ideological meanings: for its adherents, fundamentalism is the standard of keeping faith in a morally bankrupt world; for its opponents – prevalent in policy, media, and even academic circles – it represents the antithesis of a tolerant, liberal order. This latter negative view owes much to Talcott Parsons' conceptualisation of the 'fundamentalist reaction', the desire to reconstruct an idealised past in order to mask the inadequacies of the present, which lay at the core of European fascism (Rose, 1990, p. 219).

The word 'fundamentalism' appears to have first made its appearance earlier in the century, in order to designate the crusade of an evangelical, largely Baptist, American Protestantism against 'modernism'. Curtis Lee Laws, the editor of the Baptist publication *Watchman–Examiner*, wrote in 1920: 'We here and now move that a new word be adopted to describe the men among us who insist that the landmarks shall not be removed . . . We suggest that those who still cling to the great fundamentals and who mean to do battle royal for the fundamentals shall be called "Fundamentalists" ' (cited in Shepard, 1987, p. 356). Over the intervening decades the word has attained a wider currency and is now applied, though not always uncritically, to those willing to engage in parallel 'battles royal' in the Catholic, Judaic, Islamic, Hindu, and Sikh traditions.

Features of religious fundamentalism

Observers, struck by the diversity of movements, have engaged in an energetic, though often sterile, debate over whether 'fundamentalism' is applicable to religious traditions dissimilar to those of a conservative American Protestantism.

It is often thought that, because either the essential characteristics of other faiths or the circumstances in which they operate are markedly different, the term is inappropriate and misleading. Constructs such as 'traditionalists' or 'neotraditionalists', 'evangelicals', 'militants', or 'intégristes' are thus often preferred to 'fundamentalists', but they possess no greater analytical clarity nor do they command any wider acceptance.

Attempts to delineate the contours of fundamentalism run the risk of engaging in an essentialism that would assume uniform and indisputable core principles exist. Does, for example, a belief in the inerrancy of scripture – a characteristic of Protestant fundamentalist groups and often predicated as common to all fundamentalists – mean anything in traditions such as Catholicism in which the *magisterium* of the church endows it with broad authority to interpret scriptural texts, or Islam in which all Muslims affirm God's revealed word to be literally true? It may appear to distort the differences among them to include in one generic analytical category Ayatollah Ruhollah Khomeini, the leader of the Iranian revolution, Jerry Falwell, an American Baptist preacher who headed the Moral Majority in the United States, and Rabbi Zvi Yehuda Kook, spiritual leader of Gush Emunim (Bloc of the Faithful) in Israel.

In the absence of a universally agreed definition of fundamentalism, however, an approach that delineates necessary, but not individually sufficient, characteristics of the phenomenon is advisable (e.g. Marty and Appleby, 1991, pp. 814–42). High on any such list of characteristics would be the belief that an indivisible body of revelation speaks directly to us and provides the timeless source of our identity. The New Christian Right in the United States asserts that America must be guided by the basic values elaborated in the Old and New Testaments and that it is as a Christian nation it must be known. Also characteristic of fundamentalists is the belief that boundaries must be drawn between the morally pure and impure, the incorruptible and corrupt. Moreover, fundamentalists self-confidently assert that they possess the authority – 'free of the complicating subordinate clauses of the religious liberals' (Sacks, 1990, p. 10) – to draw such boundaries. In this sense of ascribing to themselves the right to interpret revelation, they cannot be said to be simple literalists.

Netueri Karta, a zealous component of Eda Haredit (Pious Community) in Israel, seeks to maintain its quarter of Jerusalem for the pious (*haredim*), isolating it from the impious Jews nearby. In this defence of their morally superior realm, group members act not simply as interpreters of the written Torah (body of law and doctrine in Jewish scripture and traditions), but as 'authentic voices of the living [oral] Torah' (Lawrence, 1989, p. 139). For their part, many Sikh fundamentalists are secessionists, striving to create a state, Khalistan, which would separate them from the Hindus in India and be composed of baptised, purified ('Khalsa') Sikhs. In effect, the adherents of the Akali Dal (Band of Immortals) movement offer to draw such external and internal boundaries.

Also typical of fundamentalist movements is a strong sense of mission: to win converts to the Truth and to remake the world. Consistent with the appropriation of divine writ is their wish to attract followers. In the Catholic world, for example, Communione e Liberazione (Communion and Liberation) and Opus Dei (Work of God) are fundamentalist groups enjoying the patronage of Pope John Paul II. They undertake a responsibility to liberate Catholics from sin by demonstrating the relevance of the Gospels and church teachings to every realm of activity, and accordingly are vigorously engaged in missionary work. Latin America has become an important arena in which nondenominational Protestant evangelical groups, largely funded by North American churches, compete for adherents with old mainline Protestant groups such as Methodists and Baptists, new Pentecostal groups, and of course the Catholic Church. In India, Arya Samaj (Society of Aryas) is a Hindu fundamentalist movement founded in the nineteenth century which sees itself in the line of descent from the Aryas, the ancient Indo-Aryans who brought the Vedic scriptures. It has sent missionaries to the Pacific region, Caribbean, and sub-Saharan Africa where Arya communities were established and have prospered.

Allied with the obligation to proselytise, and often serving as a means to attract followers, is the compulsion to effect a social and political revolution. The world and its ways must be brought into line with the values of revelation. Some fundamentalist groups may believe that the construction of the pious society is best accomplished through the re-education of individuals and the gradual accumulation of godly deeds which have a 'spillover' effect on society – a revolution from 'below' – whereas others eschew gradualism in favour of direct confrontation with the impurities of society and government – revolution from 'above' (e.g. Kepel, 1990, pp. 42–73). As Ayatollah Khomeini famously exhorted, political activity is a form of worship.

Fundamentalist tactics of political engagement may thus vary from the operation of social welfare institutions such as schools and health clinics to the murder of political officials. Egyptian society has demonstrated the practice of both approaches. The Muslim Brotherhood and more radical groups have won followers through the effective provision of social assistance, such as in the wake of the earthquake that struck Cairo in October 1992. On this occasion and other more mundane ones, the contrast with the slow and inefficient state services could not have been more apparent. By way of contrast, the president (Anwar Sadat in 1981) as well as other high political functionaries have been assassinated in the expectation that such acts would facilitate the advent of the Islamic state.

Hindu fundamentalists are agitating for the recreation of India, away from the secular republic to a Rama Rajya ('God's Kingdom'), a Hindu state in which Muslims and others would not possess equal rights. Their dedication to overturning the status quo has been so emotionally charged that even Muslim monuments like the Taj Mahal have been threatened with destruction. In Ayodhya in December 1992, the Babri mosque, which was built in the sixteenth century, was demolished stone by stone. Fundamentalists had made it a symbol of Muslim intrusion on Hindu life because they believed that it had been built on the very birthplace of Ram, the incarnation of the god Vishnu.

The practice of fundamentalism

The conventional wisdom on fundamentalism obscures the realities of a complex political force and its often subtle workings, as the specific case of Islamic fundamentalism suggests. First, it is widely assumed that fundamentalism is anti-modern, harking back to the golden age of tradition. But this is not the case; the 'televangelism' of religious leaders like Pat Robertson, Jerry Falwell, and Jim and Tammy Bakker has become part of the landscape of American fundamentalism. Ayatollah Khomeini was often derided as a medieval turbaned cleric, censorious of, or oblivious to the complexities of, the modern age. However, the very same religious figure, steeped in the classical scholarship of *irfan* (gnostic knowledge) and *fiqh* (jurisprudence), cleverly launched a 'revolution-by-cassette' from his exile in Iraq and France, using technology to disseminate his moral sermons and political directives to networks of would-be revolutionaries inside Iran. Once in power, the Islamic revolutionaries – state fundamentalists – have repeatedly demonstrated their willingness to adapt to the needs of a modernising, oil producing economy and pursued a form of economic liberalisation. The Ayatollah's last will and testament does not hesitate to describe as 'idiotic' the accusation that Islam is anti-modern: Islam has never opposed the adoption of such 'manifestations of civilisation' as 'technical innovations, new products, new inventions, and advanced industrial techniques which aid in the progress of mankind' (Khomeini, n.d., p. 22).

In Algeria, the Front Islamique du Salut (FIS, Islamic Salvation Front) routinely deploys computers, tape recordings, videos, photocopier machines, and a range of other advanced equipment in its struggle against the secular state. An organisation known as the 'Fax Group', for example, has made an appearance. Some groups have even used the electronic news services of Internet to publicise their activities.

In addition to the willingness to use technology, fundamentalists have manipulated and reshaped the very traditions that they purportedly hope to defend. It is as true of Muslim fundamentalists as it is of Sikh fundamentalists that they are engaged in a 'selective appropriation of ... tradition in a manner which is simultaneously revivalist and futurist' (Madan, 1991, p. 619). The ideologies of Islamic fundamentalism are eclectic mixtures of ideas. FIS, for instance, combines calls for the supremacy of *shari'a* (Islamic law) with an endorsement of 'democracy'. The constitution of the Islamic republic of Iran affirms the ultimate sovereignty of Allah, yet the validity of the document rests on the approval of a national referendum; in addition, the constitution provides for elections and a national legislature. The Basic Law of Governance of Saudi Arabia refers to the Islamic duties of the monarchy, but outlines 'human rights' that are to be protected. Hamas (Harakat al-Muqawama al-Islamiyya, the Islamic Resistance Movement) in the West Bank and Gaza Strip refers to Palestine as an inalienable pious trust (*waqf*) of concern to all Muslims everywhere, while endorsing nationalism as 'a component of the faith'. Whether or not concepts such as democracy, human rights, and nationalism have firm Islamic roots, there is no doubt that ideological evolution has occurred and that fundamentalists have not stood aloof from this process.

Second, it is assumed by some that fundamentalist movements are mass-based, incorporating and organising the peasantry of the countryside as well as the urban poor. While they doubtless attract wide support, fundamentalists generally form elitist and cadre groups. In Israel, Gush Emunim found recruits among graduates of religious seminaries, new immigrants, and middle-class elements dissatisfied with prevailing political ideologies, and it established a large number of settlements in the West Bank. But it remained a 'small voluntary movement', its branches very often little more than a telephone-equipped small apartment (Sprinzak, 1993, p. 132). The Shi'i Islamic Call Party (Hizb al-Da'wa al-Islamiyya) in Iraq, like the Sunni al-Jama'at al-Islamiyya (Islamic Groups) in Egypt, functions along cell-based and hierarchical lines, thereby ensuring a tight organisation which renders penetration by the state's security apparatus all the more difficult.

The typical Muslim activist is male, young, urban, lower to middle class, and modern-educated. Large numbers are educated in the sciences or engineering, and many have attended Western universities at some point. This background helps to explain both why fundamentalist movements have been open to ideological evolution and why they have so effortlessly manipulated the means of modern mass communications to propagate their message. The implications of this form of organisation and social structure are not clear, however. While not including large numbers of people as its regular members, a fundamentalist movement may reach out to them and create circles of sympathy and support which sustain it. In this sense, the fundamentalist revolution can radiate outwards from a defining and mobilising centre. Yet the elitist nature of fundamentalism may also blunt its larger appeal and restrict the revolution to a small, unrepresentative core of militant activists. The former is a distinct possibility in Egypt, where almost daily acts of violence in the name of Islam have occurred since the late 1980s. But it may also be the case that the fear of fundamentalism has been overstated, the extent of its appeal exaggerated in proportion to its limited membership.

Third, and following from the second point, it is commonly feared that fundamentalist politics is dogmatic and uncompromising, a threat to liberal and participatory political orders. George Shultz, Secretary of State in the Reagan administration, warned of the inherent totalitarianism of a religious-based politics, in which the power of religious authority would not be balanced by other political forces but would instead become formally institutionalised (Shultz, 1985, p. 3). He clearly had in mind the Iranian revolutionary state, purportedly an extremist 'mullocracy', in which the mullahs subvert civil liberties by their exclusive and single-minded control of Islamic values and symbols. The same fear lay in part behind the Algerian military's opposition to FIS and other groups which achieved unanticipated successes in the elections of June 1990 and

December 1991. Notwithstanding the irony of overturning elections in order to ward off Islamic tyranny, the military and the *ancien régime* of the secular Front de Liberation Nationale feared a puritanical and intolerant fundamentalist revolution.

It would be foolish to deny that fundamentalists often make inflexible demands or are frequently uncompromising in conduct. The competition among fundamentalist movements may even encourage radicalisation: competing to certify themselves as the undisputed spokesman for authentic tradition, the truest of the true believers, they may – in a market metaphor – push the fundamentalist 'price' upward. In many countries of the Arab world, the Muslim Brotherhood (Ikwhan al-Muslimin) established in the late 1920s and once broadly seen as anti-establishment, has had to contend with not only the secular state, which it hopes to Islamise, but younger groups that have derided its willingness to co-operate with government. The new Islamic 'Young Turks' have thus condemned the Brotherhood as part of the establishment it had once hoped to undermine. The consequence has been a fierce debate within Islamist circles as to who among the believers have forfeited their claim to leadership and even their right to be called Muslim; the practice of *takfir*, pronouncing someone an infidel (*kafir*), and the use of violence against them have unavoidably followed, despite historic Islamic assumptions that only God could make judgements on one's faith.

Yet, as they are engaged in their high-stakes contest with governments and other fundamentalist groups, fundamentalists frequently change tactics, if not also strategy. Shrillness of rhetoric may mask compromise in practice, and the complicated political rivalries at work may yield tacit rules by which bargaining and a form of structured interaction can occur. American Protestant fundamentalists have distinguished themselves by the skill with which they use the political system – the media, political parties, local and national elections – to advance their viewpoints on abortion, homosexuality, and other 'family values'. One fundamentalist leader, Pat Robertson, even stood for the Republican presidential nomination in 1988. As they use the system for their own ends, fundamentalists are, however, transformed by the process, conceding – despite the language of holy war and demonisation of enemies – that pluralism and constitutional guarantees are unimpeachable.

In the case of Islam as well, *de facto* rules of the game emerge; to return to the market metaphor, 'prices' may be controlled. The Islamic Call Party in Iraq and the Muslim Brotherhood in Syria recognise that their weakness in the face of the power of the Ba'athist regimes in both countries requires them to reach accommodation with groups like the communists and secular nationalists. In Lebanon, the Shi'i Hizbollah (party of God), committed to the creation of an Islamic republic, has had to co-operate with, as well as oppose, Amal (Afwaj al-Muqawama al-Lubnaniyya, the Brigades of Islamic Resistance), a Shi'i group hoping to reform the Lebanese state from within. Hamas partly defines itself by way of opposition to the secularism of the Palestine Liberation Organisation, but it has had to work out a *modus vivendi* with it as the *intifada* (uprising) has proceeded since 1987.

The only sure conclusions that can be reached are that religious fundamentalism is not a monolithic phenomenon and that its course is not predetermined. Although all fundamentalists, whether anti-regime, under official patronage, or incorporated in the regime, display broad characteristics in common, they must be placed in the context of their societies and histories in order to comprehend them. Critics, but also creations, of the modern age, fundamentalists may be described in terms of both ambivalence and zealotry. While the spectre of radicalism and conflict is ever present in fundamentalist politics, it is also possible that the give-and-take of political contest will transform moral crusades and demystify the partisans of God.

References

Kepel, Gilles (1990), *La revanche de Dieu*, Paris, Editions de Seuil

Khomeini, Imam Ruhollah (n.d.) *Imam Khomeini's Last Will and Testament*, Washington, DC, Iranian Interests Section of the Embassy of Algeria

Lawrence, Bruce (1989), *Defenders of God: The Fundamentalist Revolt Against the Modern Age*, New York, Harper and Row

Madan, T. N. (1991), 'The Double-Edged Sword: Fundamentalism and the Sikh Religious Tradition', in Martin E. Marty and R. Scott Appleby (eds.), *Fundamentalisms Observed*, University of Chicago Press, pp. 594–627

Marty, Martin E. and Appleby, R. Scott (1991), 'Conclusion: An Interim Report on a Hypothetical Family', in Marty and Appleby (eds.), *Fundamentalisms Observed*, University of Chicago Press, pp. 814–42

Rose, Gregory F. (1990), 'Shi'i Islam: Bonyardgiri or Fundamentalism', in Emile Sahliyeh (ed.), *Religious Resurgence and Politics in the Contemporary World*, Albany, State University of New York Press, pp. 219–28

Sacks, Jonathan (1990), 'Fundamentalism' (Reith Lecture No. 5), *The Listener*, 13 December 1990, pp. 9–11

Shepard, William (1987), ' "Fundamentalism", Christian and Islamic', *Religion*, 17 (October), pp. 355–78

Shultz, George (1985), 'Welcoming Remarks to the Conference on Religious Liberty', *Department of State Press Release*, No. 72 (15 April)

Sprinzak, Ehud (1993), 'The Politics, Institutions, and Culture of Gush Emunim', in Laurence J. Silberstein (ed.), *Jewish Fundamentalism in Comparative Perspective; Religion, Ideology, and the Crisis of Modernity*, New York University Press, pp. 117–47

Further Reading

Marty, Martin E. and Appleby, R. Scott (eds.) (1994), *Accounting for Fundamentalisms*, University of Chicago Press

Environmentalism

The Earth Summit held in Rio de Janeiro in 1992 marked the coming of age of the environment as an object of public policy. Dozens of governments around the world attended the summit in the realisation that national and international action seemed necessary to head off a growing number of environmental dangers that threaten both human well-being and the integrity of the global ecosystem itself. The environmental movement that alerted the international community to these dangers has provided us with a new vocabulary of concern: words and phrases such as global warming, ozone depletion, deforestation, desertification and acid rain are all late twentieth century tokens of the damage we are capable of inflicting on ourselves and other species. While the scale of this damage is specifically modern, and while the environmental movement that confronts it is a very contemporary one, concern for the environment goes back further than most people think. The road to Rio has been a long one.

Old anxieties

There is evidence, for example, that entire ancient societies in Mesopotamia, the Indus Valley and South America collapsed through over-exploitation of local resources. More parochially and less spectacularly, concern in Britain over the scarcity of resources goes back at least as far as Tudor and Elizabethan times when attempts at building a navy to dominate the European seas threatened to destroy the country's forests. Resource conservation, as it has come to be known, is an important feature of modern environmentalism and its scientific roots go back nearly a hundred years. In the United States of America, for example, forests became the object of long-term strategic decision-making in the early twentieth century with the establishment of the Forest Service, headed by Gifford Pinchot, charged with the scientific and sustainable exploitation of woodlands.

During the same period in the United States, conservationists were confronted by preservationists who argued that tracts of wild land should be preserved whether they were useful to human beings or not. In contrast to Pinchot's economic concept of conservation, champion preservationist John Muir argued that 'mountain parks and reservations are useful not only as fountains of timber and irrigating rivers, but as fountains of life' (Strong, 1971, p. 98). The battle between Pinchot and Muir for the future of the United States's forests has been handed down to the modern environmental movement in the guise of those, on the one hand, who defend the natural world because of its usefulness to human beings, and those, on the other, who feel that parts of it should be preserved whether it is useful to us or not. The romantic poets of nineteenth century Britain and Germany played an important part in these debates too, and so once again modern arguments can be shown to have old resonances.

While resource questions will be central to any environmental politics, issues of pollution and waste play an essential role too. Acid rain and nuclear waste might excite the public's imagination today, but pollution is by no means a specifically modern phenomenon. In sixteenth and seventeenth century London coal-burning produced such pollution problems that at least one diarist, John Evelyn, complained of ubiquitous hacking coughs and rain that fell black and contaminated. As for waste, another seventeenth century London diarist, Samuel Pepys, had to contend with his neighbour's turds appearing in his cellar, and the river Seine in the eighteenth century had the reputation of an open air sewer. A clean environment has long been regarded as a precondition for good health, and despite Margaret Thatcher's apparently modern exhortation to 'bag it and bin it', the removal of rubbish and waste from the streets has in fact been an objective of public policy in Britain for over six hundred years.

Greens have become famous – even notorious – for their claim that the planet has a limited carrying capacity as far as population is concerned. If, as they argue, resources are limited, then the more people there are the more quickly they will be used up. Once again as the world's population pushes towards six billion this seems like a very modern problem, but Thomas Malthus first pointed it out nearly two hundred years ago. He argued that unchecked population growth increased in geometric ratio while food supplies increased only in arithmetic ratio. As he said, 'A slight acquaintance with numbers will shew the immensity of the first power in comparison with the second' (Malthus, 1969, p. 7), and this is exactly the same conclusion as that reached by the 1972 *Limits to Growth* (Meadows *et al.*) report on which so much modern environmentalism is based.

Finally, contemporary ecological economists take their more traditional colleagues to task for failing to realise that economic growth depends fundamentally on ready supplies of energy. Most of the energy we use today comes from non-renewable sources (coal, gas, oil), and the first law of thermodynamics tells us that once this energy is used it cannot be used again. The increasing growth to which we have become accustomed, and to which most major political parties continue to commit themselves, is therefore made possible only by the steady erosion of a fixed natural capital. When that capital runs out (as it must, claim ecological economists) growth will stop. The contemporary green conclusion reached is that a sustainable economics must be based on decreased throughput of resources, driven by renewable energy sources (sun, wind, geothermal). Once again, these arguments might seem new, but Anna Bramwell (1989) has pointed out that they were in fact anticipated by a number of British and German economists (such as Wilhelm Ostwald and Frederick Soddy) in the first quarter of this century.

Modern environmentalism

So if so much of what contemporary greens have to say appears to have been said already, why do we think of environmentalism as a specifically modern doctrine? In the first place the movement that articulates the doctrine is new. Campaigning organisations such as Friends of the Earth and Greenpeace were both founded in 1969, the first recognisably green political party was formed in New Zealand in 1972, and perhaps the most famous Green Party of them all – the German Greens – first gained parliamentary representation only in 1983.

Some theorists, most notably Ronald Inglehart (1977), have suggested that the rise of this movement is sociologically related to the growth of a generation of 'post-materialists', raised in the wealthy welfare states of post-war Europe. Inglehart's argument is that this generation had its immediate material needs satisfied to such an extent that it could devote itself to 'post-material' projects such as the defence of the natural world. It would be wrong to say that this class caused the environmental movement, but it is appropriate that a post-material ideology should encounter a post-material generation to articulate it.

Second, the scope of concerns in the modern age is new. All the resource, waste and pollution problems referred to above are characterised by their being fundamentally local. The modern movement is motivated by the belief that environmental degradation has taken on a global dimension – most obviously in cases such as global warming and ozone depletion, but also in view of the potentially global climatic implications of rainforest deforestation. Humans have always interacted with their environment, and not always wisely. But greens believe that in the modern age the scale of human activity relative to the biosphere's capacity to absorb and sustain it has increased to the point where long-term human survival and the biosphere's integrity are put in doubt. This view – right or wrong – has lent a sense of universality and urgency to the environmental movement which it lacked in its more *ad hoc* past.

Third, the new party political wing of the movement has grown up around the belief that pressure group and single-issue approaches to environmental problems do not address their seriousness at a sufficiently fundamental level. Green parties campaign against acid rain, deforestation and ozone depletion, of course, but they do so by arguing that these problems stem from basic political, social and economic relations that encourage unsustainable practices. Only when these relations are put on a different footing, they say, will sustainability be possible. So despite the fact that environmental problems have been with us for most of human history, it is their contemporary scale that has spawned both radical and wide-ranging prescriptions for change, and the vehicles – green political parties – for bringing it about.

Finally, the role of science has been crucial in lending legitimacy to the claims of environmentalists, and thereby helping to underpin the modern movement. It is unlikely that environmentalists would have made such inroads into public opinion or have persuaded governments to make environmental commitments in their manifestos, if scientific evidence – while not conclusive – had not lent respectability to their claims regarding (for instance) ozone depletion and global warming. In previous ages environmentalists have had a reputation as cranks, but now with significant parts of the scientific establishment behind them their claims are not so easily dismissed. Science has therefore lent a legitimacy and coherence to the modern movement that never existed before.

It is clear, then, that modern environmentalism is very different in scope and character to any of its previous incarnations. Less obvious, though, is what it takes to be an environmentalist. Some people will say that a concern for the environment, however expressed and of whatever sort, is enough to qualify for the title. But this would make just about anyone an environmentalist. Others have said that a commitment to sustainable ways of living is the mark of an environmentalist. But this is also too indistinct: who, after all, would support *un*sustainable ways of living if sustainable ones were on offer? In this respect environmentalism is similar to democracy: everyone is in favour of it and the real arguments revolve around what sort rather than its intrinsic desirability.

What we need, then, is a way of distinguishing between different sorts of environmentalism, and four themes can be used to illustrate the differences: first, attitudes to growth; second, the question of the proper relationship between human beings and the non-human natural world (the subject of 'environmental ethics'); third, economics (and particularly the role of the market); and fourth, the nature of political relationships in the sustainable society.

Growth

Green politics is popularly (but not wholly accurately) known as 'no-growth' politics. Growth is usually understood to mean an increase in the production and consumption of goods and services. Ever since (at least) the *Limits to Growth* report in 1972 greens have claimed that infinite growth in a finite system (such as the planet earth) is impossible both because resources are finite and because the ability of the biosphere's capacity to absorb the waste produced by human activity is limited. Greens have therefore proposed a 'steady-state' economy in which the total stock of people and goods would remain constant, instead of constantly increasing as at present. While this clearly involves limiting growth in general, it can be consistent with growth in certain sectors of the economy (such as alternative energy technology).

There are arguments within the green movement as to how best to bring about a steady-state economy, with some opting for selective taxation to encourage frugal resource use and discourage waste, while others advocate the political imposition of resource-use quotas. Indeed this latter suggestion has led to claims that the green programme harbours surreptitious temptations of authoritarianism. These are evidently disputes about means rather than ends, but there are still others who claim environmental credentials and yet reject the end itself. These people suggest that growth is essential to environmental stewardship because it creates the wealth to pay for the 'clean' technologies required. Mainstream greens usually reject such an approach on the grounds that the cure (growth) merely makes the illness (caused by growth) worse.

Environmental ethics

In respect of the second dimension, a split has occurred between those who think that the non-human natural world should be cared for because of its usefulness to human beings, and those who feel that it has value in itself irrespective of its human use-value. This is sometimes (but not completely accurately) cast as a debate between 'shallow' and 'deep' ecologists, or between 'anthropocentrics' and 'bio-' or 'ecocentrics'. The anthropocentric point of view has it that the rainforest (for example) should be preserved because it is a source of medicines or because it regulates the climate, while ecocentrics will say that it should be preserved because it has value in itself. Ecocentrics argue that in principle all species – including, of course, human beings – have equal value and that there is no a priori reason why human interests should always trump the interests of other species.

The ecocentric position has been attacked on the grounds that it can legitimise the loss of human life when the defence of the environment (or certain bits of it) is at stake. Indeed some political ecologists in the United States associated with the radical group Earth First! have been accused of welcoming mass starvation in Africa precisely because it reduces human populations. These are the roots of what has come to be known as 'ecofascism'. On the other hand ecocentrics criticise their anthropocentric counterparts on the grounds that anthropocentrism is part of the problem rather than part of the solution. Ecocentrics say that environmental degradation has been caused, in part, by regarding the environment as nothing more than a resource for human use. Even a more responsible version of this view, they argue, will leave vast tracts of the non-human natural world undefended because it is held to be of no use to us. Moreover, when an environment's value is calculated according to its use-value, it probably *will* be used – with the despoliation that goes along with it.

The market

The third dimension is an economic one, usually revolving around views concerning the proper role of the market. Some economists who claim environmental credentials (e.g. Pearce *et al.*, 1989) have argued strongly that the market can be adapted to deal with environmental problems. They recognise that up until now the market has treated environmental goods as free goods, and that this has underpinned their profligate and unsustainable use. The market will only recognise and react to goods that give off a price signal, and because there has been no market in environmental goods they have not acquired a price. Market-orientated environmental economists therefore advocate bringing the environment into the market place by pricing it. In this way, they argue, environmental goods will respond to the rules of supply and demand and more responsible treatment of them will follow – for good, hard-headed economic reasons.

Opponents of the market solution remind us that the economic system operates within the boundaries set by the larger biospherical system. As we saw above, the limits to growth are reached when the former butts up against the latter. This amounts to saying that the scale of the economic system must be kept within the resource and waste limits set by the biospherical system. The problem with the market from this point of view is that it has no eyes to see the scale of its operations. The market is very good at co-ordinating information internal to its operation, and it may also be an efficient (if unjust) allocator of goods and services, but it has no antennae to tell it when its scale of operations is in danger of undermining its very existence. The market's ecological opponents will therefore urge a planning role on governments that sits uneasily with free market intuitions.

Political organisation

The final dimension of disagreement concerns the political arrangements in a sustainable society. Some greens have famously urged us to 'act local, think global'. These greens argue that environmental charity begins at home in the sense that localised production and consumption involves less resource use of all kinds than that presupposed by a global economy that encourages the sale of New Zealand apples in Britain when perfectly good ones can be grown here. Such greens therefore show a marked preference for decentralised forms of politics. Others in the movement, though, recognise that decentralised politics can be disorganised politics. They argue that strategic decisions over resource use and distribution will still have to be made in a sustainable society, and that therefore there is room for the traditional political forms associated with the state. Still others stress that many of the environmental problems faced today are international problems, and that the most important organisations in a sustainable society will therefore be international ones.

Ecologism and the decline of environmentalism

So much for the different positions to be found within environmentalism. In practice, of course, groups and individuals will not be consistent across the dimensions, and they will choose postures without necessarily demanding internal coherence. I do think, though, that there is a radical combination of positions within these dimensions which amounts to an ideology which I prefer to call 'ecologism', in contrast to a less radical 'environmentalism'. In brief, political ecologists believe that the aspiration of infinite growth in a finite system is unsustainable and that present practices are characterised by precisely this aspiration; that the non-human natural world has value in itself and should not have to rely on its use-value to human beings for its defence; that the market cannot bring about sustainability on its own and that strategic planning is essential; and that decentralised political forms are preferable to centralised ones. The ramifications of these positions in social, political and economic terms amount to ecologism – the most recent addition to the list of modern political ideologies (see Dobson, 1990).

In the early and mid-1980s the environment seemed likely to spawn wholly new political practices. Public opinion was sensitised to the issue, green political parties piled success upon success, environmental pressure groups' coffers overflowed with donations, and major political parties were panicked into learning and deploying the new environmental vocabulary. In the 1990s nearly all this optimism has dissolved. The public still seems energised by the environment but refuses to prove it at the ballot box, green parties have imploded under the stress of internal and extenal tensions, pressure groups are making their workers redundant, and the major political parties have turned out to be an environmental king with no clothes. Is environmentalism, then, a blip on the screen of political history?

Some of the reasons for the decline of environmentalism are contingent. The recession that afflicts economies around the world makes the environment – in the eyes of some – a luxury that cannot be afforded in a time of general belt-tightening. More secure economic times would almost certainly herald a return for the environment to somewhere near centre-stage. It is also clear that those who peddle environmental disaster as their *raison d'être* need environmental disasters – or at least environmental bad news. It is no accident that the apogee of environmental concern peaked around the time of the Chernobyl nuclear disaster in 1986. Some will say that there is nothing wrong with the environmental movement that an environmental calamity would not put right.

But perhaps the environment's greatest misfortune was to have risen to prominence at a time when governments around the world, but particularly in Britain and the United States, were convincing themselves that the time had come to revert to the rigours and disciplines of the free market. It is not so much (necessarily) that the market is constitutionally unkind to the environment, but that in the 1980s every object of public policy was relegated to the status of a proving ground for the market. The environment, then, was converted into a challenge for the market rather than a object of public policy of primordial strategic importance in its own right. There are signs that the tide is turning as far as market dogmas are concerned, and once issues are treated once again on their own merits rather than as test-cases for the market then there is every possibility that the environment will recover the high profile it enjoyed so recently.

More generally, though, if the green analysis concerning limits to growth is correct then governments that claim to have 'dealt with' the environment by painting a green stripe on their red or blue flags will eventually be called to book. As with all political ideologies ecologism will stand and fall by the accuracy of its descriptions of, and the desirability of its prescriptions for, social and political life. As an uncertain future beckons it would be premature to bet against ecologism figuring prominently among the political options available to us in the twenty-first century.

References

Bramwell, A. (1989), *Ecology in the 20th Century: A History*, New Haven and London, Yale University Press

Dobson, A. (1990), *Green Political Thought*, London, Routledge

Inglehart, R. (1977), *The Silent Revolution: Changing Values and Political Styles Among Western Publics*, Princeton University Press

Malthus, R. T. (1969), 'An Essay on the Principle of Population' (first published in 1798), in G. Hardin (ed.), *Population, Evolution and Birth Control*, San Francisco, Freeman

Meadows, D. H. *et al.* (1972), *Limits to Growth*, New York, Universe Books

Pearce, D., Markandaya, A. and Barbier, E. (1989), *Blueprint for a Green Economy*, London, Earthscan

Strong, D. H. (1971), *Dreamers and Defenders: American Conservationists*, University of Nebraska Press

Further Reading

Eckersley, R. (1992), *Environmentalism and Political Theory: An Ecocentric Approach*, London, UCL Press

Goodin, R. (1992), *Green Political Theory*, Cambridge, Polity Press

McCormick, J. (1992), *The Global Environmental Movement*, London, Belhaven Press

European integration

'European integration' is an off-cited term of political discourse in contemporary Europe and one of the factors that has moulded political action in Western Europe since the war. States, governments, political leaders, parties and private agents have had to determine their attitude towards European integration and the development of the European Community as an economic space and a political arena. The term European Integration finds institutional expression in the myriad of regional organisations that mushroomed after the war. It is especially concerned with the European Community which, by the end of the 1980s, emerged as the core regional organisation for Western Europe if not the continent as a whole. From the outset, European integration was an ideal conjured up in phrases like 'Building Europe', a 'United States of Europe', the 'European idea' and 'European Unity'. Integration manifests itself in the economic sphere, in the evolution of transnational political processes and in a profusion of societal contacts. The essence of economic integration is the abolition of barriers to economic exchange between different national economies and the integration of these economies into a large market area. Political integration connotes a process of institution building, on the one hand, and an end state, a transnational polity, on the other. For the purposes of this essay, European integration is taken to mean the deliberate creation of institutionalised co-operation among states. It is acknowledged that this neglects extensive integration through informal processes of industrialisation and technological diffusion.

European integration, as an ideal, predates the Second World War. During Europe's transformation from political fragmentation and the transnational loyalties to empire and church to a Europe of nation-states, many thinkers and political activists advocated schemes to foster peace on the warring continent. There were suggestions for a European Senate at Utrecht with a European army (see Abbé de Saint Pierre), a European Estates General (see William Penn), a European Parliament (see Saint Simon) and a European Federation (see Rousseau). Such proposals appeared utopian and found little resonance in a continent absorbed with territorial consolidation, state-building and nationalism.

The international order established by the Congress of Vienna (1815) could not adjust to the weakening of multinational empires, to the onset of German unification, or to the rise of imperial rivalries. The European state system was highly competitive. Failure to contain this competition led to the First World War. After the First World War, Count Coudenhove-Kalergi founded the 'Pan Europe' movement and published the 'Pan Europe' Manifesto in 1924. His ideas were taken up by Astrid Briand, the French Foreign Minister, in 1930, and were debated in the League of Nations.

To understand how the 'European idea' was translated from ideal into the realm of political action, we must look to the Second World War and its immediate aftermath. European integration is the product of a particular set of geo-political circumstances – the Cold War, US Marshall Aid, and the division of Europe. The shadow of two world wars and the social upheavals of the depression underlined the need for a system of order above the level of the state. During the war, members of the resistance movements began to consider the post-war reconstruction of the continent. It is worth recalling the tenets of their thinking because it informed subsequent efforts towards the establishment of new political structures in Europe. Lipgens lists five main themes in resistance thinking about European unification. Its members felt:

- a strong antipathy towards the nation-state
- that European unity would prevent a recurrence of war
- that unity would solve the German problem
- that a united Europe would compete internationally
- that European unity would protect Europe in a bipolar world dominated by the superpowers

(1982, pp. 53–5)

This type of search for order and stability motivated the post-war reconstruction of Western Europe. Three powerful ideals informed the early post-war debate on integration, namely, peace, prosperity and supranationalism. The latter was based on a perceived need to go beyond the nation-state, to temper the excesses of nationalism in inter-state relations (Weiler, 1993). The first attempt at institution building, the Council of Europe, failed to live up to the grandiose expectations of the Hague Congress that had called for the creation of 'an economic and political union' and had declared that the 'European nations must transfer and merge some portion of their sovereign rights' (quoted in Vaughan, 1976, p. 37). The contentious debate about the Council's role and institutions brought sharply into focus a deep-rooted conflict between the United Kingdom and the Scandinavian states, on the one hand, and the continental states, on the other. The former favoured intergovernmental co-operation among sovereign states, whereas the continental states were willing to go beyond a narrow definition of sovereignty. They were willing to embrace a 'sharing of sovereignty'. Echoes of this conflict may still be heard in the contemporary debate about the future of integration.

Each state in Western Europe was faced with the challenge of economic and political reconstruction after the war. Political leaders had to find new paths to political and social stability. The search was particularly acute for those six continental states that had experienced the ravages of fascism and prolonged occupation. The French elite struggled for new ways of coming to terms with Germany. The Monnet Plan, announced by Robert Schuman, French Foreign Minister, in May 1950 proposed the establishment of the European Coal and Steel Community. By placing French and German coal and steel under joint management, the ECSC provided a framework for Franco-German reconciliation and established a powerful Paris–Bonn axis at the heart of the integration project. Schuman (1982, p. 48) presented the ECSC as a 'first concrete foundation for a European Federation'. With the failure of plans for a Defence Community and a federal Political Community in 1954, the advocates of the European project opted for co-operation in economic matters as the motor force for European integration. The strategy was to overcome the barriers of sovereignty indirectly by co-operation in low key non-controversial matters. The Rome Treaty (1958) heralded the establishment of the common market. This reflected and reinforced growing economic interdependence among these states.

A unique community

The European Community defies classification as a political entity. It is neither a traditional organisation nor a state. It represents an arena of political activity, a would-be polity, above the level of the state. Since 1958, the Community has expanded its policy remit, enlarged its membership and enhanced its role in international affairs. There has been a gradual Europeanisation of many issues that would once have been decided at national level. Because the Community's governance structures are not rooted in a state, law plays a critical role in the community. EC Treaties and the judicial review of the European Court of Justice create a constitutional framework for integration. EC institutions pass some 3,000 pieces of law each year that are binding on public and private authorities. The institutions are a curious mixture of intergovernmental and supranational traits. The Council of Ministers represents the interests of the member states; the Commission, Parliament, and the Court attempt to merge these interests into a European common good. Policies and laws emerge for a complex, multi-levelled system involving a myriad of actors at EC and national levels. Decision-making involves tortuous bargaining, negotiations, sidepayments and package deals. Most of the decisions are taken in rooms without windows. Notwithstanding the ideals of the founding fathers of the Community and the myth of its formation, pragmatic interest politics tend to predominate in day-to-day politics.

Following a period of stagnation in the 1970s, when the Western European states grappled with the end of the golden period of economic growth, the Community experienced a resurgence of integration with the signing of the

Single European Act in 1986. The 1992 programme held the promise of a Europe free of economic barriers with a vast unfettered market of 360 million people. The allure of a 'Europe without Frontiers' captured the imagination of many in Europe. A pervasive sense of Europe's economic decline and its inability to match Japan in many industrial sectors motivated those who negotiated the SEA. The deregulatory ethos of the internal market programme has been part of a general strengthening of market forces *vis-à-vis* public power in Europe and reflects the emergence of neo-liberal economic strategies during the 1980s.

The success of the SEA ushered in a period of confidence in Western Europe and in the relevance of the European Community. The Commission in Brussels, under the presidency of Jacques Delors, assumed a central role in the relaunching of European integration. Spurred on by the dynamism of the internal market, the member states and Commission set their sights on European Monetary Union, a single currency to match the single market. The collapse of communism and German unification came just at the time when the 'Twelve' were in the process of consolidating Western European integration. The consequences of the transition in Eastern Central Europe for European integration should not be underestimated. Europe is now facing a considerable period of uncertainty as states and regional organisations search for new ways of providing order for the continent as a whole. The EC states responded to German unification by negotiating the Maastricht Treaty on EMU and Political Union. The Treaty consisted of different pillars dealing with money, judicial co-operation, foreign policy and the traditional areas of EC policy. Nevertheless, it lacked a clear statement of objectives and goals. Furthermore, the Maastricht Treaty did not pass easily into law. A 'no' vote in the Danish referendum of 2 June 1992 triggered a profound crisis in European integration. Turmoil in the money markets led to the virtual abandonment of the ERM (Exchange Rate Mechanism), the framework for Monetary Union. The Maastricht crisis brought serious questions about the integration project to the fore.

State or market?

The European Community is both a union of states and a market. There is, however, a tension between those who place the main emphasis on a liberal, deregulated free trade area or market, under intergovernmental control, and those who see the need to regulate economic exchange at the EC level by means of a federal state. The polar extremes of this debate during the 1980s and early 1990s have been represented by the former British prime minister, Margaret Thatcher, on the one hand, and Jacques Delors, the Commission president, on the other. Jacques Delors' vision of Europe favours the strengthening of market forces in Europe, but he remains conscious of the social impact of economic integration. Delors pioneered the Social Charter as a counterweight to the 1992 programme. He sees the need to recreate at a European level a framework of

European rules to control unfettered market forces. Margaret Thatcher's view, on the other hand, sees Europe as a liberal economic trading area and is, therefore, deeply opposed to central EC institutions and an EC social policy. Thatcher declared that 'We haven't worked all these years to free Britain from the paralysis of socialism only to see it creep through the back door of central control and bureaucracy in Brussels' (quoted in *The Independent*, 15 October, 1988). During the negotiations of the Maastricht Treaty, the British government persisted with its objections to a Social Europe and insisted on an opt-out from the Maastricht social provisions. This ambiguity about the future direction of integration and the very different images of what constitutes the Community are likely to continue. It highlights a tension between an unfettered market and a regulated common economy, and between a diffuse set of policy regimes unattached to a state and a community with strong state-like properties. The complex, diffuse and obscure nature of the Community's political system raises difficult questions about political accountability and legitimacy in the system.

Democracy and integration

The integration project was designed and sustained by Europe's governmental and bureaucratic elites. Public opinion in most member states has tended to be favourable towards the 'idea of Europe', although popular sentiment has remained largely uninterested in the day-to-day workings of the EC. The EC's policy-making system strengthens executive power in relation to the powers of national parliaments and bureaucratic power over political power. Some 80 per cent of all EC laws are agreed by civil servants working in committees under the auspices of the Council of Ministers. Pragmatic interest politics predominate rather than debate about core issues of politics. Put simply, EC bargaining obscures politics behind a veil of technocracy. For example, fundamental questions about economic governance, that should have accompanied the debate on a single currency, were obscured in discussions on the statutes for a European Central Bank and the role of such a bank. Issues of accountability and norms of economic governance were hidden by the arcane language of central bankers.

The Maastricht ratification process that stretched over twenty-two months raised serious questions about the direction of European integration and the tension between integration and democracy. In many member states the debate on Maastricht suggested that popular sentiment was uneasy about European integration and the working methods of the Community. Questions were raised about the weakness of political accountability. This is an issue which has been further exacerbated by the increased use of qualified majority voting in the SEA whereby 'Member States are now in the situation of facing binding norms, adopted wholly or partially against their will, with direct effect in their national legal orders' (Weiler, 1991, p. 2443). The democratic deficit is now frequently analysed in terms of the powers of the European Parliament. Redressing the democratic deficit is often seen as being achieved by enhancing the powers of the Parliament. The problem is, however, much deeper than this. National politics still defines the public space. Habermas (1991) argues:

> That nation states constitute a problem along the thorny path to a European Union is however less due to their insurmountable claims to sovereignty than to another fact: Democratic processes have hitherto only functioned within national borders. So far, the political public sphere is fragmented into national units.

Solidarity and a commitment to the common good are still largely, although not exclusively, defined within national political systems. There is little evidence that the national idea is dying in Western Europe although most nationalisms have accommodated the integration project. Some nationalisms and nation-states are even reinforced by European integration. However, the integration project itself may be partly responsible for a revival of xenophobia in Europe as conservative forces react to the growing cosmopolitanism of European society.

Although the national idea is alive in Western Europe, this does not preclude the development of a European identity as one in a range of identities. From the outset, the Rome Treaty pronounced the goal 'of ever closer union among the peoples of Europe'. The EC now boasts a flag, an anthem, a common passport and a standard driving licence. Student exchange, regional networks of one kind or another, cross-national interest groups, links between new social movements point to the possibility of a European civil society in the future. The Maastricht Treaty has a section on citizenship that has transformed the status of non-nationals in any member state from that of 'privileged alien' into EC citizen. But citizenship implies inclusion and exclusion which raises a critical issue about Europe's boundaries and the meaning of a 'European identity' following the events of 1989.

Which Europe?

The year 1989 will go down in the history of Europe as an epoch-making year: the year when the post-war order came crashing down, bringing with it an end to the division of Europe and of Germany, but also great uncertainty about the European order and the place of European integration in this order. The division of Europe and the Cold War were a powerful cohesive force in Western Europe. The pervasive tendency to regard the European Community as synonymous with Western Europe, and even with Europe as a whole, no longer holds. The desire of the Eastern and Central European countries to 'rejoin' or 'return' to Europe raises the delicate issue of an eastward enlargement and an extension to the boundaries of the Community system in the next century. Difficult issues concerning agricultural reform, market access and redistribution to the East will have to be confronted. Immigration is likely to prove contentious as Western Europe confronts the prospect of large movements of people. Events in the former Yugoslavia highlight the Community's weak capacity for international action and the fragility of the state-system in the eastern half of the continent.

A period of profound transformation

Post-1989 Europe is in a period of profound transformation. European integration was a product of the need to reconstruct individual states and an inter-state system in Western Europe after the war. It allowed for economic reconstruction, Franco-German reconciliation and a sense of shared destiny among the continental states. It was motivated by the desire for peace, prosperity and the need to recast inter-state relations. European integration was an instrumental value in the search for order and stability in Europe. As Europe regained its economic well-being and political stability, the founding ideals had less resonance. When the scope of European integration widened and its membership grew, utilitarian pragmatic-interest politics came to dominate relationships. Economic integration provided Europe's governments and bureaucracies with an arena for the management of economic interdependence within a growing and privileged market. The formula of 'pooling sovereignty' allowed states to transform their relations, while maintaining the trappings of sovereignty. Nonetheless, the Community is much more than a creature of the member states. The impact of European integration on the Western European state is contested. Some writers see integration as undermining the state and state sovereignty. Others argue that integration has reinforced the state in an era of interdependence. Undoubtedly, the driving forces of integration can be found in the need of the contemporary state to marry state intervention with the international political economy.

There is little doubt that European integration has created a new forum for political action and a new style of politics among its member states. Each member state, and the social forces it represents, takes into account the existence of the Community and the other member states in the calculation of their interests and preferences. These states have autonomous political systems, but their politics, especially at a governmental level, are no longer autonomous. Democratic politics still remains national which makes the redress of the democratic deficit within the Community highly problematic. The tensions between democracy and integration, and between state and market, to a large extent mirror debates within the member states about governance in Western Europe.

Western Europe is still grappling with the need to recast its economies and economic management in the context of a liberalisation of economic exchange and a deregulation of financial markets. The emergence of neo-liberal economic strategies in the 1980s brought the public/private line sharply into focus in Western Europe. The debate on unemployment raises questions about the power of labour and corporatist structures in labour-market regulation. Social provision, a central element in Europe's post-war social order, is being buffeted by the demands for competitiveness and the costs of social transfers.

The future development of the EC is a subject of considerable contention and ambiguity revolving around Thatcher's neo-liberal dream and Delors' social Europe. The balance between deregulation and reregulation is still being worked out. The choice between an EC of highly diffuse policy regimes and one with strong central institutions buttressed by political accountabiity has not yet been made. The balance between autonomy for the member states and the need for collective action has not reached an equilibrium. And the place of European integration in the new Europe is unclear. The Community and its member states are still trying to work out their response to the events of 1989. They are torn between the desire to protect the gains of the Europe envisaged by the Monnet Plan, and the evident need to respond to the rest of Europe.

References

Habermas, J. (1991), 'Citizenship and National Identity: Some Reflections on the Future of Europe', paper given to a symposium on Identity and Diversity in a Democratic Europe: Theoretical Approaches and Institutional Practices, Brussels

Lipgens, W. (1982), *A History of European Integration: The Formation of the European Unity Movement 1945–47*, Oxford University Press

Resolution of the Political Committee of the Congress of Europe (1976), quoted in R. Vaughan, *Post-War Integration in Europe*, London, Edward Arnold

Schumann Declaration, 9 May 1950, quoted in European Parliament (1982), *Selection of Texts Concerning Institutional Matters of the Community from 1950–1982*, Luxemburg, European Parliament

Weiler, J. H. H. (1991), 'The Transformation of Europe', *The Yale Law Journal*, Vol. 100, No. 8, pp. 2403–85

— (1993), 'Fin-de-Siècle Europe', plenary address to the Third Biennial International Conference of the European Community Studies Assciation, May, Washington

Further Reading

Garcia, Soledad (ed.) (1993), *European Identity and the Search for Legitimacy*, London, Frances Pinter

Laffan, Brigid (1992), *Integration and Co-operation in Europe*, London, Routledge

Keohane, R. O. and Hoffmann, S. (1991), *The New European Community*, Boulder, CO, Westview Press

International organisation

There can be no question that, at the international level, one of the most far-reaching developments of the twentieth century has stemmed from the idea and practice of international organisation. But it is also true that the ultimate significance of this development is as yet uncertain. A hundred years hence it may be possible to say that the world's political structure has been fundamentally reshaped by the concept under discussion. Even, however, if a much more limited judgement is then required, it will still be of great moment. For already it is clear that in the present century – and more particularly its latter half – the society of sovereign states has, through international organisation, undergone something of a transformation in the way in which it conducts both its routine and its more important business.

The term 'international organisation' here refers to an organisational structure which has been set up by any number of sovereign states to deal with any kind of subject matter. Typically such an arrangement will include an assembly, in which all the member states are represented, and which meets annually; a smaller executive body, probably with a rotating membership; a variety of sub-committees, both permanent and *ad hoc*; and a secretariat to administer the organisation – a kind of international civil service, the head of which might be called the secretary-general or director-general. Usually, the decisions of the organisation on other than internal matters will require unanimity if they are to be legally binding on the member states. But recommendations may be passed by a majority vote.

Utility

The uncertainty about the long-term destination of international organisation reflects a duality in the source from which the contemporary concept has sprung. In the first place, the emphasis of the idea is basically utilitarian – international organisation being seen as a more efficient, or sometimes a necessary, means of dealing with certain sorts of matters. Putting the point more generally, it is one manifestation of the desire or need of states to co-operate with each other. This point is worth emphasising, for a not uncommon picture of the international scene is that of one dominated by the threat or actuality of armed conflict. But in fact co-operation – in the widest sense, so as to include bargaining – is, and always has been, a fundamental characteristic of international life. This, after all, is a large part of the reason why states have been represented abroad by diplomats ever since the beginnings of the contemporary international society in the late fifteenth century (Anderson, 1993).

At that time, however, and for a long while after, the tempo and substance of international relations was such that there was no requirement for any organisational superstructure. Bilateral diplomacy, occasionally supplemented by an international conference (especially at the end of a war), was entirely sufficient. But during the nineteenth century this situation began to change. Spurred on the one hand by technological developments arising from the industrial revolution, and on the other by the need to protect their interests in the altering environment, states found that certain matters called for frequent or even regular attention. This pointed towards some form of organisation. Thus, political conferences of the great powers were envisaged and duly held on a slightly more systematic basis – this practice was called the Concert of Europe. Permanent bodies were set up to handle communication across boundaries by postal and telegraphic means. In such ways states sought to cope more satisfactorily with the increasing number and complexity of their international contacts.

The political catastrophe and mass slaughter of the 1914–18 war, together with the rapid advances in technology during the early part of the twentieth century, prompted an increased interest in the potential benefits of international organisation. It was widely believed that if states had been associated in some organisation which had had the authority to call them together in conference, they might not have stumbled into carnage. The fact that there is considerable doubt about the historical credibility of such an analysis is irrelevant. It was in many quarters *believed* to be true. The co-operative activity which ensued produced the world's first international organisation of a political and potentially universal kind – the League of Nations (Zimmern, 1936). Pre-eminently, it was meant to provide a means whereby states could more effectively maintain international peace. As it happened, it was only twenty years before another world war broke out. But one of the most remarkable accompaniments of that war was the assumption that the idea of a general international organisation should not be cast to one side but reborn in a more effective format. 'The League is dead; long live the United Nations' was the cry of the victors of 1945. And in fact the treaty setting up the new body was signed before the war had fully ended (Russell, 1958).

The signatories, however, were very clear that what they were doing was firmly within the utilitarian mode. It is true that provision was made for the UN to act with much more power than its predecessor. But at bottom the organisation was nothing more than its member states. Accordingly, the UN could only act outside its debating chambers if a sufficient number of sufficiently powerful members were prepared to don the mantle of the organisation and use their power on its behalf. There was never any question of a body being established with a source of strength which was independent of the world's sovereign states. It was not a case of the UN versus the member states, but of those states acting in the UN's name as and when they were both legally entitled and politically willing to do so. And there was no doubt that in making such calculations the overriding criterion for each of the member states would, as always in international relations, be its individual national interest, nationally conceived (Brierly, 1947).

In other words, the UN was never meant, by its founding states, to be a world government, or anything like it. Nor were any other intergovernmental organisations – the roster of which before long amounted to about three hundred – meant to exercise independent governmental power. Rather, they were means for facilitating co-operative action. The organising principle of the political world was still the territorially demarcated sovereign state. International organisation was just a new way of doing intergovernmental business.

Reform

Throughout the twentieth century, however, the concept of international organisation has also been envisaged and advanced as a medium of reform, as a means of improving the quality of the business which goes on internationally, and even of altering the basis on which that business is done. This is the second aspect of the idea of international organisation. Its exponents see organisation at the international level as offering an escape route from what has often been pejoratively termed 'power politics'. They view it as a way of providing a criterion for international activity which has a much higher moral status than the traditional one of 'national interest', and also as a means of establishing the foundation for an alternative political arrangement of the world, in which states are relegated to a secondary position – if that.

It almost goes without saying that the advocates of such conceptions are predominantly found in unofficial circles, in the sense that they are not, at least at the time of their advocacy, the holders of governmental office. To them, the idea of international organisation is one which might clip the wings of their sovereign masters, channel them into better modes of behaviour, and perhaps bring them to the point of political salvation. Not surprisingly, the sovereign states have greeted such missionary zeal – in so far as it might affect their day to day positions – with something less than a convert's enthusiasm. A bureaucracy is never much enamoured of the suggestion that it should mend its ways, and even less of the idea that it should surrender some of its competence to a superior agency. Furthermore, such proposals are not the sort which, if rejected, might result in the loss of an election or the mounting of a successful coup. The campaigners have therefore made little direct progress.

And yet, it is also incontrovertibly the case that the conduct of international relations since 1945 has been much affected – many would say improved – by the idea and practice of international organisation. There are three intertwined reasons for this. The first is that among states the idea has become orthodox. This is seen most obviously in the case of the UN. For, on the one hand, the suggestion is never seriously made that the UN should be wound up. And, on the other, all sovereign states, except the most tiny, seek to join the organisation. This was vividly exemplified by the application and immediate admission of two of Europe's historical mini-states, Liechtenstein (1990) and San Marino (1992), the population of each of which is in the region of 25,000. Correspondingly, no state wishes to leave the UN, however dark its view of the organisation, or the UN's view of it. Thus membership of the UN has risen steadily upwards from the initial 51 of 1945 to no less than 179 in the autumn of 1992. (By contrast, many states left the League of Nations, and with little compunction.) It must also be noted that in most regions of the world there are political organisations to which virtually all eligible states belong. Evidently, international organisation is an idea whose time has come.

A second reason for the part which international organisation now plays is the sheer usefulness, indeed, necessity of the device. So much international business – both of a technical and a general political kind – has since 1945 demanded not just regular consultation but also continuing administrative follow-up. In any one year a large state, in its capacity as a member of international organisations, attends many hundreds of meetings. (During the nineteenth century the average was one per year.) In consequence, it is common for diplomats to spend a not insignificant part of their careers representing their states at international organisations, or dealing at home with organisational matters. 'Parliamentary' or 'multilateral' diplomacy (as the meetings of international organisations are called) has become an important feature of international life. Moreover, the position of permanent representative, or ambassador, to the UN has become one of the top jobs in all states' diplomatic services.

Beyond this utilitarian explanation, however, there is a third reason for the impact of international organisation on international relations, which again has little directly to do with the reform movement. It stems from the nature – between states as elsewhere – of the political process.

Politics

Many functioning organisations tend to acquire a momentum of their own. They become going concerns. In this process they may develop in ways which were unanticipated by their founders. For it is almost in the nature of things for an organisation to reflect changes in both its external and its internal environment, and these rarely stay still. More particularly, developments within the organisation will express its changing composition and concerns, as all the members try to use the organisation for their own individual purposes. The result will be an evolving organisational ethos, which will exert something in the nature of an independent influence on the membership.

The UN provides an excellent example of this process. It was set up after the Second World War to prevent the outbreak of a third global confrontation by the threat and, if necessary, the use of military force. Nevertheless, an overwhelming obstacle to the implementation of this prospectus was soon discovered: the loud break-up of the victorious alliance, leaving its former members as bitter Cold War enemies rather than comrades in arms. As a consequence, the UN became just a Western-dominated talking shop. But before long it took a stand against the punitive use of violence by Western states. The early fragmentation of European empires resulted in a flood of 'new' third world members to the UN. They used their numerical weight to castigate racism, to condemn any form of colonialism, and to call for what was grandly called a New International Economic Order. The UN also, in a more general way and in the cause of human rights, began to chip away at the hitherto well-established principle that outsiders should not poke their noses into a state's internal affairs. In these ways, the UN was to a large extent changed from a body committed to the support of the status quo, to one calling, often quite stridently, for what was seen as a radical conception of international justice (Claude, 1966). Was the UN turning out to be a Frankenstein's monster, mused the British prime minister as early as 1957?

One ground for his anxiety may well have been the UN's virtually unanimous condemnation of the armed Anglo-French attempt to take over the Suez Canal in 1956, plus the fact that the face-saving device which was used to speed the invaders' departure was a UN force – of the type which was soon to become known as 'peacekeeping'. These peacekeeping forces (and the observer groups which were included in the same category), although predominantly made up of military personnel, are characterised by their non-use of force (except in self-defence) and by their impartiality. Thus they rely on the co-operation of the parties, being meant to help them live in peace rather than to impose peace on them. The UN established about a dozen such bodies during the first forty years of its life and, with the end of the Cold War, as many again between 1988 and 1992. The UN has no monopoly of this kind of activity, but has become closely identified with it. In fact, peacekeeping has become the UN's chief operational contribution to the maintenance of international peace – and a most valuable one, too (James, 1990).

In connection with all the matters discussed in the previous two paragraphs, however, it is very important to remember that the UN does not have a power base which is independent of its member states. The UN as such, therefore, cannot raise money, conscript men, adjudicate on disputes, and deploy force. What has happened is that, using such diplomatic and physical resources as its members are prepared to put at its disposal, the UN has become a significant international forum and peace-helping tool. In the first of these capacities the members use it to try to bolster their own positions and undermine those of their adversaries. In the second they use it to take agreed action, of a limited kind, in support of peace. And it is very striking that the UN's imprimatur is now almost routinely regarded as, if not essential, at least highly desirable for major armed undertakings conducted on a national basis. Thus, during the Falklands crisis of 1982, Britain was exceedingly anxious to obtain, and retain, the support of the UN Security Council for the view that the Argentinian invasion represented an illegal use of force (Parsons, 1983). During the crisis of 1990–1 over the Iraqi invasion of Kuwait, the United States-led coalition also went to great trouble to ensure that it had the Security Council's authorisation for every step along the way to the forceful expulsion of Iraq (Taylor and Groom, 1992).

Too much should not be made of this last development. If a state deems a matter to be of the utmost importance, it will proceed along its own path, irrespective of what the UN thinks. And yet, the international world is now a very different place from what it was in 1945. In no small measure this is due to the play of politics having elevated the UN to a position of some eminence – and also to the imperatives of international co-operation having spawned a profusion of smaller institutions.

The future

Will the idea of international organisation become more influential than that of the individual sovereign state? If any number of the latter wish it, they could set up an organisation with 'real' power – so that it would, in effect, be a super-cum-federal authority within the area of its competence, with its member states being subordinate parts of a larger whole. It is also possible that an organisation which has been given complex and important tasks could, over time, become so indispensable that it would carry more weight than its supposed masters. To some extent the European Community exemplifies the first of these possibilities, and may be on the way to exemplifying the second. And as the Community's subject matter is so significant, such a development may herald its eventual transformation into a single state – which would be a triumph, of a kind, for the idea of international organisation against that of the sovereign state. But at the moment the individual member states of the Community are in the driving seat, and are unlikely easily to countenance their international demotion from sovereign entities to federal provinces (Puchala, 1993).

Furthermore, there are no other international developments which are even remotely comparable to the EC. Indeed, with the break-up of the Soviet empire and of Yugoslavia, and a number of vibrant secessionist movements elsewhere, the trend would appear to be very much in favour of the state. This is a reflection of the basic sociological and political fact that people everywhere want to be governed by those whom they can identify as of their own national kind (James, 1986). Thus international organisations remain firmly under the thumbs of their sovereign creators, and seem most unlikely to consume them. Although very unexpected things can happen in politics, this interim report on the idea of international organisation must conclude that, while it has had a marked impact on the conduct of international relations in the second half of the twentieth century and has become an essential vehicle for the conduct of much inter-state business, it remains subordinate to the idea of sovereignty. It is a servant of states rather than an instrument of basic international restructuring.

References

Anderson, M. S. (1993), *The Rise of Modern Diplomacy 1450–1919*, London, Longman

Brierly, James (1947), *The Covenant and the Charter*, Cambridge University Press; also to be found in James Leslie Brierly (1958), *The Basis of Obligation in International Law and Other Papers* (selected and ed. by Sir Hersch Lauterpacht and C. H. M. Waldock), Oxford, Clarendon Press, pp. 314–26

Claude, Inis L., Jr (1966), 'Collective Legitimization as a Political Function of the United Nations', *International Organization*, Vol. 20, No. 3 (summer), pp. 367–79

James, Alan (1986), *Sovereign Statehood: The Basis of International Society*, London, Allen and Unwin

— (1990), *Peacekeeping in International Politics*, Basingstoke and London, Macmillan, in association with the International Institute for Strategic Studies

Parsons, Sir Anthony (1983), 'The Falklands Crisis in the United Nations, 31 March–14 June 1982', *International Affairs*, Vol. 59, No. 2 (spring), pp. 169–78

Puchala, Donald J. (1993), 'Western Europe', in Robert H. Jackson and Alan James (eds.), *States in a Changing World: A Contemporary Analysis*, Oxford, Clarendon Press, pp. 69–92

Russell, Ruth B., assisted by Jeanette E. Muther (1958), *A History of the United Nations Charter: The Role of the United States 1940–1945*, Washington, DC, Brookings Institution

Taylor, Paul and A. J. R. Groom (1992), *The United Nations and the Gulf War, 1990–91: Back to the Future?*, London, Royal Institute of International Affairs

Zimmern, Alfred (1936), *The League of Nations and the Rule of Law 1918–1935*, London, Macmillan

Further Reading

Finkelstein, Lawrence S. (ed.) (1988), *Politics in the United Nations System*, Durham and London, Duke University Press

Jensen, Erik and Thomas Fisher (eds.) (1990), *The United Kingdom: The United Nations*, Houndmills and London, Macmillan

Riggs, Robert E. and Jack C. Plano (1988), *The United Nations: International Organization and World Politics*, Chicago, Dorsey

Collective security

The concept of collective security is a relatively simple one. It implies the organisation of many to deter or militarily punish the actions of an aggressor. By statement or, more significantly, by treaty obligation states in any particular system will provide collective guarantees for the security of others in the system. It is generally agreed that the major threat to international order is the use of violence by one state or by a group of states upon another state or states. Collective security is designed to alter the cost-benefit analysis of such aggressors in such a way as to convince them that such actions are bound to fail. Such security supposedly ensures that conflict is much less likely to occur; that the strong act in the interests of the weak; that the justice of independence and self-determination as rights are supported; that if violence is used by the world community it is seen as legitimate and defensive; and finally that it diminishes the possibility of a preponderant power emerging and threatening domination (e.g. Napoleonic France or Nazi Germany). Yet despite its relative simplicity, the concept of collective security is one that has been at the centre of much controversy in international relations.

Realists and utopians

One group of analysts, commonly referred to as *realists*, tends to deny the practical and indeed the theoretical utility of collective security. These analysts argue that states only act when it is in their national interests to do so: and nowhere is that more the case than in the use of force. Thus, a general collective security guarantee is of no utility, since individual states will decide whether to punish an aggressor militarily on specific, not general, grounds. Further, collective security implies the necessity of all in the system to take action against an aggressor, but realists argue that in fact it is only the important states, the 'great powers', whose actions matter. A focus on collective security implies an equality of states which, for realists, is a misunderstanding of the reality of power in international relations. Examining power leads many realists to suggest that the identification of an aggressor in a particular situation may not be a simple matter. Because great powers have allies and political interests, it means that military actions will be interpreted in different ways by different actors. For example, different states reacted in different ways to the Soviet intervention in Afghanistan and the American incursion into Grenada. Thus, truly collective action is impossible, unless the supreme national interests of all the major powers are involved. Even worse for realists is that a concentration on collective security would mean that more sensible routes to security (e.g. deterrence strategies based on collaborative military force in an alliance, as opposed to general collective strategies) might be forsaken. Hence, for realists, collective security does not work, and a reliance upon it in fact makes it more likely that aggressors will succeed in their actions (Waltz, 1993).

In sharp contrast, the *utopians* or *rationalists* argue that a truly secure world can only be based upon a system of collective security. If all the states in the world were to guarantee the security of all others, then it would be clear to any would-be aggressor that military action would be doomed to failure, since the range of forces arranged against it would be insuperable. Thus, an effective system of collective security would end the reliance purely on a balance of power for achieving security. The balance of power, some would argue, has had a very negative influence on the development of peaceful and legal processes in international relations. The operation of the balance of power has emphasised might over right, force over justice. It has given a stronger position to the powerful states, and often reduced the weaker states and peoples to a position of inferiority, being mere objects in the 'games' of the great powers. Thus, in the interests of peace, democracy and justice, it would be better to move from a balance of power system to one characterised by collective security. Such a move would lessen the legitimacy of the use of force, since military might would only be justifiable collectively and in defence of others, not in the interests of national aggrandisement. In addition, the operation of the balance of power system by the great powers is always subject to risk. As one state or group of states seeks to strengthen its position against its rival(s), there is always the danger of miscalculation and war. A system of collective security would eliminate such risks of accidental war on a global scale.

These arguments and ideas are not simply related to debates in the academic world. They have had an immediate and direct impact upon the history and shape of international relations in the twentieth century. It was the debate between those who supported and those who opposed the concept and implementation of collective security that shaped the origins and operation of the League of Nations, the creation of the United Nations, and the 'rebirth' of the United Nations in the post-Cold War era.

The limits of collaborative security

Arguments over the validity of collective security were central to the rise and, in many ways, the fall of the League of Nations. The central idea – of deterring potential aggressors by indicating that a united front of all other states would be formed in opposition to them – was critical to the deliberations over creating a new world order at the end of the First World War. At this time, many of the arguments of the utopians were politically significant, particularly the belief that, had Germany understood the scale of the opposition to its actions, then the First World War would never have begun. Under the strong encouragement of the American president, Woodrow Wilson, the peacemakers in the aftermath of the war attempted to create a League of Nations, and with it an arrangement for collective security. In the event the arrangement was compromised by the reality of international politics in the 1920s and 1930s. Article 10 of the League Covenant – on action against aggressors – was often seen by states to be significant only in a regional rather than a global context. Similarly, Article 16 of the Covenant, relating to sanctions, was widely regarded by governments to be a matter of selective obligation. Furthermore, given the absence of some of the major countries from the League – the United States and, for various periods, the Soviet Union, Germany and Japan amongst others – collective security never rested on an absolute preponderance of world power, but in practice depended on the leadership and efforts of the two remaining great powers in the League, Britain and France – i.e. the nations that became the bastions of appeasement in the 1930s.

Dispute still rages over whether the 'failure' of the League in the 1930s was due to the incorrect application of the principles of collective security, as the utopians would argue; or whether an international system based on collective security would inevitably have failed in the face of concerted aggression, as the realists would hold (Carr, 1939). Nevertheless, the 'failure' of the League in particular circumstances (e.g. over the outbreak of the Japanese–Chinese War in Manchuria in 1931–3, or over the Italian invasion of Ethiopia in 1935) illustrates many of the weaknesses of the collective security approach that realists believed needed to be corrected when, in the aftermath of the Second World War, debate again turned to the creation of a new world order.

In the formation of the United Nations, collective security was to be a compromised asset. Collective security was deemed to have failed in the inter-war and pre-war period, and therefore many of the arguments of the realists came to the fore in the construction of a new security arrangement. Collective security remained an ideal, but various measures of a more practical nature were insti-tuted in the new organisation. Responsibility for international security was to rest in the Security Council (Article 24 of the United Nations Charter), and as a consequence great influence was given to its Five Permanent Members (United States, USSR, Britain, France and the Republic of China). In this way, the interests of the great powers could be taken into account. It also made clear where responsibility for world peace was to be lodged (see Article 25 of the Charter in which all members agree to accept the decisions of the Security Council). However, this arrangement meant that collective security would, in effect, not apply when the interests of the Permanent Five were directly involved, as Hungarians, Czechoslovaks, Vietnamese and Cambodians amongst others were to find. The development of the Cold War made any attempt to institute global collective security doomed to failure. Finally, the weakening of the reliance upon collective security, by which an aggressor would be punished by the world community, was reaffirmed in the move away from the use of war by the international community to that of peacekeeping – a move necessitated by the deployment, or the threat of the deployment, of the great powers' veto during the Cold War. Although peacekeeping has achieved a number of valuable goals, for many it is still a second best to imposing a just status quo ante upon belligerents in the way that collective security would achieve, at least according to the conception held by many of the utopians. Ask the inhabitants of the Middle East in the 1970s and 1980s, for example, or the population of the former Yugoslavia in 1990s, about the utility of peacekeeping compared to military intervention by the international community to make peace.

For much of the Cold War period collective security was a legitimate term, but in effect an illegitimate practice for both East and West. Both sought to argue that it was they who stood for world unity, at least in the minimal sense of a world not threatened by the horrors of war. But the geopolitical and ideological division of the world into two meant that the practice of collective security was inconceivable, as the inactivity of the United Nations Military Staff Committee amply illustrated. Even the United Nations action in the Korean War (1950–3), supposedly in support of collective security, only took place in the context of the Soviet Union's absence from the Security Council, in the face of armed Chinese action (at that time not a member of the United Nations), and on the understanding that the United Nations forces would be based overwhelmingly on the military power of the United States. The term collective security became an element in the Cold War's language of division and argument. Nowhere was this more evident than in the terms and structure of the North Atlantic Treaty Organisation (NATO) and, to a lesser extent, the Warsaw Treaty Organisation (WTO). NATO and the WTO were set up ostensibly to further collective security through support of Article 51 of the United Nations Charter. This was spelt out in Article 5 of the North Atlantic Treaty, and Article 4 of the Warsaw Treaty. But in reality the limited collective security guarantee provided by the United Nations was supplanted, rather than supplemented, by specific security guarantees provided within the alliances.

Neither NATO nor the WTO were in reality organised around the concept of collective security. Both were collective *defence* organisations, and the differences between collective defence and collective security are quite profound. Collective defence implies that all in an alliance, or party to an agreement, will support any member that might be attacked. This is similar to the concept of collective security, but whereas the latter is designed to be inclusive, collective defence is designed to be exclusive. Collective security is supposed to protect all its members against any other member; collective defence is designed to protect its members against those outside the alliance. Thus, NATO was designed to protect its members against the Soviet 'threat'. Were NATO to have been a collective security arrangement, then it would have had to include the USSR as one of its members. Collective defence is a tool of the balance of power system. For some utopians, collective security is a central part of an international system that has moved beyond a reliance on the balance of power. Hence, while realists are quite comfortable with collective defence, utopians wish to move further towards collective security.

Collective security in the post-Cold War world

The end of the Cold War has done much to re-establish the concept of collective security as one worthy of consideration. The new post-Cold War environment has been much influenced by the action of many states to evict Iraq from its occupation of Kuwait in the spring of 1991. Was this an action of collective security? In some senses, it was. The United Nations, under Resolution 678, authorised collective military action for the first time since the specific circumstances of the Korean War some forty-one years earlier. The Iraqi invasion of 2 August 1990 provided the United Nations with a relatively clear-cut case of aggression, illustrated by the subsequent annexation of Kuwait by Iraq. Following a series of resolutions designed to apply increased pressure on Iraq, involving the imposition of mandatory economic sanctions and condemnations of its activities, the Security Council adopted Resolution 678 on 29 November 1990. This set a deadline of 15 January 1991 for the withdrawal of Iraq from Kuwait. Within a matter of weeks, Iraq had been driven from Kuwait by a combination of military forces including those from the United States, Saudi Arabia, Britain, Syria, France, Kuwait and Italy. But was this really a success for collective security?

For some, the successful implementation of United Nations Resolution 660 (calling for an Iraqi withdrawal) by force illustrated the success of collective security in the post-Cold War era (Hurrell, 1992). For utopians, it was a basis on which to build a more legitimate international order, one based more on collaboration and co-operation, with a general security guarantee for all as the ultimate goal. Yet there were others for whom Operation Desert Storm, as the military action was named, had less to do with collective security, and more to do with a collection of national interests. For some states, the war was about oil; for other countries, the action concerned regional and global prestige; elsewhere the war could be explained by national and personal antagonism to Iraq and President Saddam Hussein. Realists would suggest that it was not an action of collective security to liberate Kuwait, the victim of an aggressor, but a war that met a variety of individual needs. After all, if the Kuwaiti experience were to recur elsewhere with the invasion and annexation of another small state in Africa, Asia, or Latin America – would Desert Storm really be repeated, as the requirements of collective security would require?

United Nations Resolution 678 and the subsequent military action did not fully implement the principles of collective security in the way that those who drafted the Charter of the United Nations might have envisaged. Resolution 678, after all, was not passed unanimously. China abstained, and Yemen and Cuba voted against. Furthermore, Resolution 678 legitimised the actions of those conducting Desert Storm, but it did not take responsibility for those actions, nor take command of them as a United Nations operation. This may say more about the operation of collective security in the United Nations as an organisation, rather than about the principle of collective security itself. Nevertheless, it says much about the post–1945 period (at least up to 1993) that Deset Storm represents the nearest example to a full implementation of collective security in international relations.

What of the future for collective security? There has been some discussion about the implementation of the concept on a regional basis, as well as on a global basis, in the aftermath of the 1991 Gulf War. It is generally assumed that the most likely region for the implementation of collective security is post-Cold War Europe, particularly under the auspices of the Conference on Security and Cooperation in Europe (CSCE). During 1990 and 1991, as communism collapsed in Europe and new leaderships came to power in the states of Eastern Europe, many called for the replacement of collective defence, through NATO and the WTO, with collective security in Europe through the development of the CSCE. Such ideas were propounded by leaders such as President Havel of Czechoslovakia, President Gorbachev of the Soviet Union and President Mitterrand of France, and were supported by governments in Poland, Hungary, the Baltic states, Scandinavia and elsewhere. They were opposed, however, by a number of NATO governments, particularly those of Britain and the United States. For the latter, it was folly to abandon the tried and trusted method of collective defence for the untried collective security in the context of instability and uncertainty throughout much of Europe. While collective security was regarded as an asset by the British and American governments in the action against Iraq, they currently deem it to be a danger in creating a new post-Cold War environment in Europe.

It is, therefore, unclear what the future of the idea of collective security will be. As for much of the twentieth century, there are those both in the academic world and also in government who support the introduction of collective security; but there are many more opposed to the introduction of the concept on a global basis. Much will depend upon the future pattern of international relations.

References

Carr, E. H. (1939), *The Twenty Years Crisis*, London, Macmillan (reprinted many times subsequently)

Hurrell, A. (1992), 'Collective Security and International Order Revisited', *International Relations*, Vol. 11, No. 1 (April)

Waltz, K. (1993), 'The Emerging Structure of International Politics', *International Security*, Vol. 18, No. 2 (autumn)

Further Reading

Claude, I. (1962), *Power and International Relations*, New York, Random House

Rivlin, B. (1992), 'Regional Arrangements and the UN System for Collective Security', *International Relations*, Vol. 11, No. 2 (August)

Roberts, A. (1993), 'The UN and International Security', *Survival*, Vol. 35, No. 1 (spring)

Wolfers, A. (1962), *Discord and Collaboration*, Baltimore, Johns Hopkins University Press

Non-alignment

Non-alignment, in the post-war era, has been largely associated with the Non-Aligned Movement (NAM), but not entirely so. The Chinese, mindful of the superpower struggle, and seeking assured international space of their own, twice sought to establish a non-superpower bloc. First, by canvassing a third world alternative to the superpower-dominated United Nations in the 1960s. And second, by advancing a theory of international relations in the 1970s, in which China and the third world stood in unified opposition to the joint social and capitalist imperialisms of the Soviet Union and the United States (Chan, 1985).

The notion that the superpowers and their rivalry threatened the rest of the world, particularly the third world – just emerging into independence or beset by the problems of development – has lain at the heart of post-war non-alignment. Never susceptible to precise definition, it became a very loose condition articulated by a very loose international organisation, the NAM. It needed to be open-textured both ideologically and organisationally, to accommodate what became a large and diverse membership. It gave newly independent states, many not yet assured of their own nationalistic bases, a rudimentary form of supranational identity. Membership of the United Nations (UN) denoted statehood. Membership of regional organisations, like the Organisation of African Unity (OAU), denoted geographical and geopolitical space. With space and statehood having been established, membership of the NAM signified an intention not to be at the beck and call of the superpowers.

Non-alignment differs from neutrality, which is commonly a legal or constitutional position of the state concerned. Neutrality may be recognised or even guaranteed by other states. Non-alignment, by contrast, represents an interest in political space and in an identity independent, if not secure, from the stress of the superpower competition. 'The origins of non-alignment lie in identification, stress and interest' (Willets, 1978, p. 29).

Although a clearly defined number of third world leaders established the NAM, it was really only after the NAM's foundation that these leaders were able to interpret the past on the basis of having been 'traditionally' non-aligned.

While these cultural justifications were seldom seriously advanced, the organisation in a very real sense permitted the possibility of such a philosophy. Non-alignment came to mean first and foremost membership of the NAM. The rest of this chapter, therefore, is concerned with the history and the conduct of the NAM.

History of the NAM

The forerunner of the NAM is usually viewed as the 1955 Afro-Asian Conference at Bandung, Indonesia, but this assembly should more rightly be viewed as the precursor of a general third world agenda. It was the first large joint meeting of Asian and African states. Its main concern was with fair and reliable trading prices on the one hand, and with the third world having a guaranteed portion of global industrial output on the other. These concerns provided the basic negotiating themes in the UN Conference on Trade and Development (UNCTAD) and, before the debt crisis of the 1980s, constituted the skeleton agenda of the third world caucus within the UN itself, the Group of 77 (G77). The five political principles of Bandung, borrowed from the 1954 'Panshilah' agreements between China and India – respect for each other's territory, non-interference in internal affairs, equality and mutual benefit, peaceful co-existence, and non-aggression – became generalised standards of behaviour; not always observed by third world states themselves, but capable of being invoked whenever there was any hint of superpower incursion.

Bandung also foreshadowed an essential tension within the NAM itself. Though nominally non-aligned, many NAM members enjoyed close relations with one or other of the superpowers, more often than not the Soviet Union. At Bandung, great concern was expressed over communist subversion, particularly in South-East Asia, and this contributed to the conference's fragile sense of unity. Some were sympathetic to the communist cause, others greatly fearful. Chou En Lai's skilful speech defused some of the anti-communist feelings, but it did not dispel the idea that future third world conferences would only ever acquire a marginal form of co-operation. It seemed, from the outset, that non-alignment was to mean merely a stand against domination by one or other of the superpowers, not necessarily a lack of affiliation to them.

General Tito's idea of an alternative form of communism, for example, was closely associated with the rise of the NAM. Tito was instrumental in setting up Bandung. From mid-December 1954 to January 1955, Tito stayed three weeks in India and five days in Burma. He met with Abdel Nasser in Egypt on his way home to Yugoslavia. After Bandung, in July 1956, Tito organised a meeting with himself, Nasser, and India's Jawaharlal Nehru, on the Yugoslav island of Brioni. This was followed up at the fifteenth session of the UN General Assembly in September 1960 when Tito, Nasser, Nehru, Indonesia's Sukarno and Ghana's Nkrumah met in New York to urge a dialogue between the superpowers. In fact, these leaders were preparing for the first official NAM meeting.

Tito's interest in the NAM had a strong Yugoslavian element to it. Tito viewed non-alignment, and organised the NAM, as a means of keeping the Soviet Union at arm's length while he set about creating a non-Stalinist form of communism. He pursued this task on various fronts, one of which was the creation of the NAM; another was Yugoslavia's successful application to become an associate member of the Organization for Economic Co-operation and Development (OECD – the 'club' of the Western capitalist nations).

Once identified with the NAM, Tito remained a prominent figure within it. He and the other four leaders who had met in New York became acknowledged as the founding fathers not only of the NAM but of non-alignment itself – even though Nehru had entertained early doubts on the matter. On 5–12 June 1961, twenty-one countries met in Cairo to attend a preparatory meeting for the first NAM conference.

The first NAM summit was duly convened in Belgrade later in 1961. Tito's address set the theme: 'We shall render a great service to the world if we indicate clearly and resolutely the road towards the freedom, equality and peaceful co-operation of all nations'. International tension was the summit's major concern. This was understandable given the crises in Berlin, the Congo, and Algeria at that time; but the call to solve issues other than by force reflected also the military vulnerability that member states felt towards more powerful nations. Belgrade papered over the cracks between radical nations seeking to blame the West and colonialism for all third world ills, and others (e.g. India) who advanced less politicised ideas of world peace. Non-alignment, and the NAM, began in Belgrade as a generalised middle point not only between two superpowers, but between concepts of blame in the international system.

Surprisingly, of the next seven summits – Cairo in 1964, Lusaka in 1970, Algiers in 1973, Colombo in 1976, Havana in 1979, New Delhi in 1983, and Harare in 1986 – as many as five had basically economic themes. The problems of development, endemic in a basically third world organisation, were experienced early in the NAM's history. It has often been said that the third world has had two major organisations representing its interests – the G77 for economic matters and the NAM for political matters. Nevertheless, the NAM has always had its own economic agenda, foreshadowed at Bandung, and making itself felt from its 1964 Cairo summit onwards (Avramovic, 1983). As described below, it was the Algiers summit of 1973 that inaugurated the decade-long campaign for a New International Economic Order (NIEO).

Conduct of the NAM

Although the NAM has been characterised as having no secretariat and revolving around the irregular summit meetings (Mphaisha, 1983), the 1973 Algiers summit did establish a small Co-ordinating Bureau of Non-Aligned Countries.

This provides a device for maintaining contact between summits in the shape of ministerial meetings, seminars and collaborative groups specialising in particular areas. The most notable examples of the latter have included specialist groupings on technical co-operation (co-ordinated by India), on scientific and technological development (Algeria), on international co-operation for development (Egypt), on trade, transport and industry (Guyana), on monetary and financial co-operation (Yugoslavia), and on disarmament and international security (co-ordinated by the Bureau itself).

Despite the existence of the Bureau and its various groupings, the overriding importance of the NAM resides in its summit meetings. Apart from constituting the largest series of summits in international history, the spectacle of so many world leaders in one place suggests the possibility of co-operation. Precisely because they are leaders at a summit, however, the NAM is an elite organisation. The summits are some distance above the constituencies they claim to represent and, in every summit, a substantial proportion of the government leaders present have not been elected in the competitive sense of having defeated other leadership aspirants in open multi-party elections, or have not been elected in any sense at all. Of all the seven summit locations (eight including Bandung), only Colombo, New Delhi and Harare had any sustained history of multi-party democracy (and that in Harare was young and unstable in 1986).

In this respect the 1973 summit in Algiers stood out from the others in at least seeming to take action for the benefit of the poorest citizens within the NAM states. The summit pressed for a NIEO, but the impetus of 'muscle' behind the NIEO campaign really came from the Organisation of Petroleum Exporting Countries (OPEC) and its policy of quadrupling oil prices in that year. For the first time, the third world felt that it had some leverage in the international political economy, even if this meant that many, if not most, NAM members had to pay higher oil prices alongside the Western members of the 'old' international economic order. The NAM summit, together with the OPEC price rises, led directly to the Sixth Special Session of the UN General Assembly in 1974 where the NIEO theme was pursued in earnest.

In retrospect, the entire NIEO episode seems naive. But the feeling of triumph drawn from the West's discomfort over the oil price rise was palpable. The NAM, while an instigator of the NIEO campaign, soon gave way to a third world lobby that found expression in other organisations – so, naive, triumphalist or otherwise, the episode belongs to a much wider history than the NAM's alone. What is significant is that although the *West* was attacked for its monopoly of the international economic order, what was proposed as a *new* order in its place was not anything structurally new. What was proposed was not a mixture of Western and Eastern economic order, but simply a fairer 'old' economic order. There was, therefore, something equivocal about the Algiers summit – simultaneously against dependency but seeking a more humanised dependency. The Algiers conference also rejected a proposal for a NAM Charter and, after a debate instigated by Libya as to what non-alignment actually meant, settled on a bottom-line criterion of not being in formal military alliance with either of the superpowers. Despite the efforts at Algiers to clarify the NAM, the definition of the movement remained as imprecise as ever. The movement was also beginning to show a fundamental flaw in the notion of non-alignment itself, and this at the NAM's most active and perhaps most successful hour: that even though non-alignment might be some place between East and West, it was, economically at least, more dependent on the West than the East, and that this relationship with the West determined the agenda of non-alignment.

The same problems of definition and disposition afflicted the 1976 Colombo summit. By 1979, it would have been time in any case for a review of what non-alignment was and where the NAM stood in the international system. The fact that the 1979 conference was held in Havana guaranteed to raise the NAM's consciousness with respect to its relationship with the West. Castro's transparency in advocating closer ties to the communist bloc was, in the end, largely refuted by the Indians and Tanzanians who reasserted the 'non-bloc factor' of non-alignment. Even so, Cuba's anti-imperialist views were reflected in the final declaration or communiqué of the summit. (A few years later, Khan and Mostafa's (1983) study of African states in the NAM revealed that the 'non-bloc factor' had in fact been compromised in the foreign and defence politics of several states.)

By the time of the Havana conference, there had been a substantial turnover of heads of state and government despite the undemocratic nature of many NAM countries. Each new president adopted the non-aligned stance of his predecessor, whether or not he had violently overthrown the previous government. The anti-imperialist rhetoric sounded a note of protest against an international system dominated by others, but the generality of non-alignment meant that there was never a high price to pay for commitment to the NAM. High oil prices were, as noted above, an OPEC instrument and no one saw the NAM as being to blame for their impact on third world economies. All the same, the Havana summit sought to use the NAM's linkage with OPEC to guarantee oil supplies to the poorest third world countries.

Despite the debates in Havana on the meaning of non-alignment, nothing of importance was settled. The dispute, in clearing the air, seemed to have served its purpose. The next conference took place in New Delhi in 1983. Given the accumulated effects of the oil price rises and the recession in the capitalist West, the NAM returned to economic issues, but this time couched in more sober language. The Soviet invasion of Afghanistan was dealt with through low key support of the UN's position. The question of which was the legitimate government of Cambodia was postponed. Libya sought to have Egypt expelled from the NAM and Egypt responded in kind by seeking the suspension of Libya. And attempts to mediate between the two sides in the Iran-Iraq Gulf conflict came to nothing. No political issue was pursued to a point of crisis within an obviously divided movement. The stress fractures within the NAM were not resolved so much as concealed in the face of deteriorating international economic conditions.

If a sense of NAM decline was cloaked in New Delhi, it was disguised still further in Harare in 1986. With South Africa as a real antagonist immediately south of the Zimbabwean border, the attention of all delegates was drawn to the question of the regional depredation occasioned by Pretoria's military adventurism. An air of unreality overcame the summit as both the Indians and Zimbabweans extemporised on the possibility of sending NAM troops to safeguard the front-line southern African states. But the financial costs and the logistics were not thought through. Neither was South Africa's response to such an operation dealt with at length. A fund was proposed and accepted, but it was never well supported.

The plan revealed the essential drawback of policy-making by heads of state and government in their own conclaves, isolated from technical and staff inputs. At the Harare summit, both Libya and Iran questioned the worth of the NAM, but by now Colonel Gaddafi appeared to be treating the occasion as a fashion parade for his gold-braided white uniforms. His otherwise serious criticism of the movement was lost amidst the fanciful flights of policy towards South Africa. Despite Gaddafi, the Iranians had a serious point – namely that the NAM had not stopped the war with Iraq. Some commentators have speculated that the death of Mozambique's Samora Machel shortly after the Harare summit was Pretoria's way of stating bluntly that the NAM could not stop South African policy (Chan, 1990, pp. 53–4).

By 1989 the NAM summit was back in Yugoslavia where it all began, and the Soviet bloc was collapsing around the ears of the non-aligned. The demise of Eastern Europe as part of the eastern bloc, and the subsequent demise of the Soviet Union itself, marked the end of bloc politics and presumably the end of an organisation that made a virtue of not being aligned to either bloc. Yugoslavia did not address the issue of the NAM's redundancy, but the demise of Yugoslavia itself in 1992 might well suggest that the movement General Tito had spawned, had also come full circle.

It is hard to say how seriously either bloc ever took the NAM. In the early days of African independence, Khrushchev spent large amounts of aid to woo the new states to the Eastern bloc flag. In his mind, a country not aligned to the West was an automatic gain for the East, and the idea of an intermediate category did not occur to him (Ogunbadejo, 1980). Certainly, by the time of the Havana summit, the Soviet Union would have been happy to have had a NAM more biased towards Moscow, but it hardly viewed Castro's failure to accomplish this as a foreign policy disaster. The United States never treated the NAM as a serious player in global politics. The Western academic profession of international relations, either in its traditional geo-strategic guise, or in its paradigmatic debates, never sought to theorise about non-alignment. As late as 1987, the Indian academic, A. P. Rana, stated that it was time to start an effort towards theorisation. This in itself implied that in the thirty-two years since Bandung and the twenty-six years since Belgrade, Indian academics, citizens of a founder member of the NAM, had not seen much value in making such an intellectual effort. The history of thought on non-alignment, where it exists at all, is nothing but generality.

References
Avramovic, D. (1983), *South-South Financial Co-operation*, London, Frances Pinter
Chan, S. (1985), 'China's Foreign Policy and Africa: The Rise and Fall of China's Three World Theory', *Round Table*, 296, pp. 376–84
— (1990), *Exporting Apartheid: Foreign Policies in Southern Africa 1978–1988*, London, Macmillan
Khan, A. D. and Mostafa, M. G. (1983), 'A Self-Scrutiny of the Non-aligned Movement: The African Members' Perspective', *Bangladesh Institute of International and Strategic Studies Journal*
Mphaisha, C. J. J. (1983), 'Diplomacy by Conference: Principles, Goals and Problems of NAM', *India Quarterly*, 39
Ogunbadejo, O. (1980), 'Soviet Politics in Africa', *African Affairs*, 79
Rana, A. P. (1987), 'The Legitimacy Crisis of Contemporary Non-alignment: A Paradigmatic Enquiry and Research Proposal': *Paradigms*, I, pp. 89–103
Willets, P. (1978), *The Non-aligned Movement*, London, Frances Pinter

Further Reading
Jackson, R. L. (1987), *The Nonaligned, the United Nations and the Superpowers*, New York, Praeger
Singham, A. W. and Hune, S. (1986), *Non-Alignment in an Age of Alignments*, London, Zed
Williams, G. (1987), *Third World Political Organizations*, London, Macmillan
Williams, M. (1991), *Third World Cooperation: The Group of 77 in UNCTAD*, London, Frances Pinter

Nuclear strategy

If we get our approach to nuclear strategy wrong, then the societies in which people think about and act upon the political ideas discussed in this book could be destroyed. The question of how to respond to the potential for rapid, certain and enormous nuclear destruction has generated a vast academic literature and has been the main driving force behind the development of strategic studies (Brodie, 1946; Jervis, 1984, 1989; Kaplan 1984; Herken, 1987; Kull, 1988; Trachtenberg, 1988; Freedman, 1989; Baylis and Garnett, 1991). The debate about the implications of nuclear weapons has also penetrated popular consciousness worldwide to produce waves of activism by citizens, mainly in liberal democratic states and especially in the 1960s and early 1980s.

Mutually Assured Destruction versus warfighting

The main debate within nuclear strategy has been about the requirements for deterrence. The participants in the debate have divided into the advocates of nuclear warfighting and those who prefer Mutually Assured Destruction (MAD) (Keeny and Panofsky, 1981–2; Glaser, 1990). That debate has revolved around a number of key questions which are now discussed in turn.

Is denial or punishment more important?

An important distinction in nuclear strategy is deterrence by threat of punishment (retaliatory deterrence) and deterrence by threat of denial (warfighting in order to prevent the opponent from achieving its objectives). Denial strategies can be adopted even with relatively small forces (for example, this has been the approach of China), but US and Soviet leaders have preferred much larger forces for denial. Although denial strategies involve plans to use nuclear weapons in much the same way as conventional weapons, mutual nuclear vulnerability is revolutionary in its implications in that it 'turns established truths about relationships between force and statecraft on their heads' (Jervis, 1989, p. 15). In particular, Robert Jervis points out that, in a conflict between states armed with conventional forces, one state can push the other to total defeat. This would be an excessively dangerous policy against a nuclear state because the state that is 'winning' must rely on the nuclear restraint of the state that is 'losing'. In a non-nuclear context, the security of a state can be unilateral because it can develop a capacity to prevent the destruction of its homeland, but nuclear security can only be mutual in nature. This is because protection from nuclear attack can only ever be afforded by the restraint of the other side. While one's own measures can help to encourage this restraint, unilateral measures cannot guarantee it (Jervis, 1989; Buzan, 1991; Smoke and Kortunov, 1991).

Is deterrence of nuclear attack easy or difficult?

Barry Buzan (1987, pp. 167–96) points out that advocates of MAD see deterrence of nuclear attack as easy, while advocates of warfighting strategies argue that it is hard. The warfighters argue that the best deterrent of nuclear attack is a manifest capability to fight and win a nuclear war should one start. The MAD view is that a secure second strike capability (that is, a capability to inflict unacceptable damage in retaliation to a surprise nuclear attack) is sufficient. Alternatively, some believe that nuclear deterrence is based on what McGeorge Bundy calls 'existential deterrence', that is, restraint based simply on the potential destructiveness of nuclear forces rather than any details of force structure or nuclear strategy (1984; 1988, pp. 593–4).

Deterrence through MAD is difficult if an opponent is unimpressed by the risks of uncontrolled escalation or is very strongly motivated to attack. But this kind of opponent has never existed. Analysts such as Colin S. Gray (1979, 1986) and Richard Pipes (1977, 1982) have argued that it would be dangerous to base deterrence on a capability for MAD because, they maintain, the Soviet Union believed that it could secure military victory in a nuclear war at whatever level it was conducted. For this reason, their argument goes, the West needed to develop a nuclear-warfighting capability in order to deter the Soviet Union. This view of the Soviet attitude to nuclear war has been challenged persuasively (Arnett, 1979; Garthoff, 1978, 1982; MccGwire, 1987). It is true that Soviet leaders before Mikhail Gorbachev did appear to have planned to try to limit damage to the country through counterforce attacks (that is, attacks on nuclear forces), rather than through nuclear restraint to induce US reciprocation should nuclear war occur. In other words, they preferred a doctrine of deterrence by denial rather than deterrence by punishment. However, they had very little confidence that nuclear war could be controlled. As even Pipes (1977, p. 34) admits: 'The Russians certainly accept the *fact* of deterrence.' In the wake of the collapse of the Soviet Union in 1991, there has been no articulation of nuclear strategy so far by the ex-Soviet nuclear states (Russia, Ukraine, Kazakhstan and Belorus), which have been more concerned with making radical reductions in force levels or making commitments to become non-nuclear.

Can nuclear weapons deter conventional attack?

The context of the main debate about the credibility of nuclear deterrence of conventional attack was the North Atlantic Treaty Organization (NATO) concern with what were seen as superior Soviet conventional forces, but it is also relevant for states such as Pakistan which must face Indian conventional superiority. The possibility of uncontrolled escalation to total nuclear destruction means that MAD is compatible with deterrence of conventional attack because '[t]he ability to win a local war cannot be translated into the ability to fight it safely' (Jervis, 1989, p. 81). It may also be possible that nuclear weapons may be able to deter conventional attack or prevent conventional defeat only when *both* sides have nuclear weapons. This idea has not been analysed extensively, but there is supporting evidence in the fact that non-nuclear Egypt and Syria attacked Israel (which then had an undeclared nuclear capability) in October 1973 and pushed it to the brink of conventional defeat. Non-nuclear states may feel themselves to be immune from nuclear attack due to the enormous political costs likely to be inflicted by the international community on any state which breached the nuclear taboo (Herring, 1991, pp. 95–6).

How many nuclear warheads are enough?

The United States and ex-Soviet states are dismantling or mothballing nearly all of their short-range and medium-range nuclear weapons and are planning to cut the number of their long-range nuclear weapons from around 13,000 each to around 5,000 each. Britain, France and China all have hundreds of long-range nuclear weapons and are acquiring more. When the Assured Destruction (AD) criterion was first proposed by US Secretary of Defence Robert S. McNamara primarily as a way of limiting the budgetary demands of the armed services in 1964, the requirement was for a second strike ability to kill between 20 and 33 per cent of the Soviet population and destroy between 50 and 75 per cent of Soviet, industrial capacity. However, unacceptable damage can be well below the original AD criteria. As Bundy (1969–70, p. 10) puts it:

> In the real world of real political leaders – whether here or in the Soviet Union – a decision that would bring even one hydrogen bomb on one city of one's own country would be recognised in advance as a catastrophic blunder; ten bombs on ten cities would be a disaster beyond history; and a hundred bombs on a hundred cities are unthinkable.

The reductions in nuclear forces currently being planned have led many to describe this as a shift to minimum nuclear deterrence (MND). However, there are many different potential versions and degrees of MND. As a result, there is often a great deal of confusion when the term is used. In the West, MND is often used as a synonym for only having a capability for MAD and for abandoning any attempt to develop a warfighting capability. However, in the case of the United States, MND appears mainly to involve only reductions in numbers of warheads and reduced alert levels with retention of a warfighting denial strategy. President Clinton is pressing ahead with modified plans for anti-ballistic missile (ABM) systems as a successor to the Strategic Defence Initiative (SDI) launched by President Ronald Reagan in 1985. SDI is now expected to defend against accidental, unauthorised or 'third country' launches. In 1991 Gorbachev expressed an interest in Soviet participation in the project and, since the collapse of the Soviet Union, Russia's president Boris Yeltsin has also sought to participate, but so far the US response has been cool. Apart from the enormous technical problems involved and the fact that an opponent could simply use aircraft or cruise missiles instead of ballistic missiles, SDI goes against the acceptance of mutual vulnerability required by MAD. However, in an otherwise relatively stable nuclear environment, the residual fear of a ruthless or irrational leader with nuclear weapons will remain and will continue to generate support for ABM systems.

It is often said by Western advocates of MAD that China has a policy of MND, but its strategic posture has many elements of which they would not approve. China has never had a secure second strike capability against either the United States or the Soviet Union, and yet it did not succumb to nuclear blackmail during its border clashes with the Soviet Union in 1969: it ceased its attacks on Soviet forces only once it had achieved its political objectives. Although the question is debated it did not appear to succumb to US nuclear threats during the Korean War and the crisis in the Taiwan Straits during the 1950s when it had no nuclear weapons. It has invested substantially in civil defence measures for damage limitation during nuclear war; it has invested in small numbers of tactical and theatre as well as strategic nuclear weapons; and apparently it has integrated those weapons into a denial strategy (Liu, 1972; Segal, 1991; Lewis and Litai, 1988; Lin, 1988).

Can nuclear war be controlled?

Whereas the United States was more concerned with manipulating nuclear threats for crisis bargaining purposes and the Soviet Union was more concerned with nuclear parity as the key to its superpower status, both tried to develop the ability to fight and win a nuclear war should one occur. The United States eventually took the path of limited options and slow escalation, while the Soviet Union hoped to win with massive use early in a nuclear war. Although such plans reflected in part a desire to enhance crisis bargaining and deterrence (on the grounds that the best way to prevent a war is to show that you can win it), they also reflected a determination to be able to *start* a nuclear war if necessary (Gray, 1979; Scheer, 1983).

Advocates of MAD usually declare that nuclear war is uncontrollable, while advocates of warfighting strategies respond that it is unreasonable to deny even the possibility that a nuclear war could be controlled or won. While it is true that nuclear war might be controllable, the real question is whether or not nuclear war can be sufficiently controllable or winnable for it to be a realistic policy option. If not, then for all practical purposes, nuclear war cannot be fought or won. Neither the United States nor the Soviet Union ever came close to a nuclear warfighting capability. The degree of agreement among leading academic strategists on this point is impressive (Bracken, 1983, p. 233; Kaplan, 1983, p. 391; Kennan, 1982, p. 195; Scheer, 1983, p. 15; Freedman, 1989, p. 433). Initiating nuclear use or responding with further nuclear use in the hope that it would be controllable would be nothing less than the most reckless gamble in human history.

The anti-nuclear perspective

From the anti-nuclear perspective, support for the possession of nuclear weapons is flawed as a general prescription and as a long-term strategy. As a general prescription, the pro-nuclear perspective implies that all states should either seek an ally who will provide extended nuclear deterrence, or else acquire and deploy substantial invulnerable forces of their own in order to ensure stability. In this way it generates permanent incentives and pressures for nuclear proliferation. As a long-term strategy, it assumes that, for the indefinite future, decision-makers will be rational enough to avoid nuclear war, or at least that they will concentrate on war-termination rather than war-winning should nuclear war occur.

Opponents of nuclear weapons argue that, in order to justify threatening such terrible destruction, an ideology of nuclear deterrence has developed in which opponents have to be dehumanised; threats have to be wildly exaggerated; the dangers of loss of control downplayed; and the human and environmental costs of thousands of nuclear tests and dozens of lost and damaged nuclear weapons hidden (Green, 1966; Lifton and Falk, 1982; MccGwire, 1984, 1985–6; Booth, 1987; May, 1989; Smith, 1989; Lifton and Markusen, 1990; Weston, 1991). For these reasons, they argue that it is important to think beyond any reliance upon nuclear weapons, and in particular to explore how the transition can be made to a post-nuclear strategic culture. Jonathan Schell (1982, 1984) has argued that 'weaponless' nuclear deterrence can be present even after all nuclear weapons have been abolished as long as the capability exists to produce them. This stands on its head the argument that nuclear disarmament cannot be achieved because nuclear weapons cannot be disinvented. Ken Booth and Nicholas J. Wheeler

(1992, p. 13) refer to this as 'post-existential' deterrence, and argue that such a view of nuclear weapons is very similar to the policies of the near-nuclear states such as India and Pakistan, even though those countries are now moving closer to producing and deploying nuclear weapons. The main criticism of Schell made by Booth and Wheeler is that he does not appreciate that what is needed is a major transformation in the ways in which states relate to each other before they can agree on the abolition of nuclear weapons, and that, to avoid eventual nuclear disaster, all reliance on nuclear weapons must gradually be ended (see also Booth, 1991).

Conclusion

There are fundamental problems with the language used in thinking about nuclear issues (Kennan, 1982, p. 243; Booth, 1987, pp. 252–4). Phrases such as 'nuclear strategy', 'nuclear weapon' and 'nuclear war' have been employed in this chapter, but they have only been used for the want of anything more convenient. Such phrases are in essence oxymorons. Because of the unmanageable risks involved, nuclear strategy is impossible if we are thinking of strategy in conventional terms. Strategy is normally about linking military means to political ends, and war is normally about the use of force to achieve political ends. In the nuclear context we have what could be called pejoratively nuclear 'strategising' – strategy in a political and practical vacuum (Herring, 1991, p. 105). The language of strategy is being used, but the result is pseudo-strategy because strategic analysts have manifestly failed to overcome nuclear vulnerability and find usable nuclear options, in spite of an intensive search lasting over forty years.

Acknowledgement

I would like to thank Ken Booth, Theo Farrell and Nick Rengger for their valuable comments.

References

Arnett, Robert L. (1979), 'Soviet Attitudes Towards Nuclear War: Do They Really Think They Can Win?', *Journal of Strategic Studies*, Vol. 2, No. 2, pp. 172–91

Baylis, John and Garnett, John C. (eds.) (1991), *The Makers of Nuclear Strategy*, London, Frances Pinter

Betts, Richard K. (1987), *Nuclear Blackmail and Nuclear Balance*, Washington, DC, Brookings Institution

Booth, Ken (1987), 'Nuclear Deterrence and "World War III": How Will History Judge?', in Roman Kolkowicz (ed.), *The Logic of Nuclear Terror*, Boston, Allen and Unwin, pp. 251–82

— (1991), 'Security in Anarchy: Utopian Realism in Theory and Practice', *International*

Affairs, Vol. 67, No. 3, pp. 527–45

Booth, Ken and Wheeler, Nicholas J. (1992), 'Beyond Nuclearism', in Regina Cowen Karp (ed.), *Security Without Nuclear Weapons?*, Oxford University Press/Stockholm International Peace Research Institute, pp. 1–36

Braken, Paul (1983), *The Command and Control of Nuclear Forces*, New Haven, Yale University Press

Brodie, Bernard (1946), *The Absolute Weapon: Atomic Power and World Order*, New York, Harcourt, Brace

Bundy, McGeorge (1969–70), 'To Cap the Volcano', *Foreign Affairs*, Vol. 48, No. 1, pp. 1–20

— (1984), 'Existential Deterrence and its Consequences', in Douglas Maclean (ed.), *The Security Gamble: Deterrence Dilemmas in the Nuclear Age*, Totowa, NJ, Rowman and Allenheld, pp. 3–13

— (1988), *Danger and Survival: Choices about the Bomb in the First Fifty Years*, New York, Random House

Buzan, Barry (1987), *An Introduction to Strategic Studies: Military Technology and International Relations*, London, Macmillan

— (1991), *People, States and Fear: An Agenda for International Security Studies in the Post-Cold War Era*, 2nd edition, London, Harvester Wheatsheaf

Freedman, Lawrence (1989), *The Evolution of Nuclear Strategy*, 2nd edition, New York, St Martin's Press

Garthoff, Raymond L. (1978), 'Mutual Deterrence and Strategic Arms Limitation in Soviet Policy', *International Security*, Vol. 3, No. 1, pp. 112–47

— (1982), 'A Rebuttal by Ambassador Garthoff', *Strategic Review*, Vol. 10, No. 4, pp. 58–63

Glaser, Charles L. (1990), *Analyzing Strategic Nuclear Policy*, Princeton University Press

Gray, Colin S. (1979), 'Nuclear Strategy: A Case for a Theory of Victory', *International Security*, Vol. 4, No. 1, pp. 54–87

— (1986), *Nuclear Strategy and National Style*, Lanham, MD, Hamilton

Herken, Gregg (1987), *Counsels of War*, expanded edition, Oxford University Press

Herring, Eric (1991), 'The Decline of Nuclear Diplomacy', in Ken Booth (ed.), *New Thinking About Strategy and International Security*, London, HarperCollins, pp. 90–109

Jervis, Robert (1984), *The Illogic of American Nuclear Strategy*, Ithaca, NY, Cornell University Press

— (1989), *The Meaning of the Nuclear Revolution: Statecraft and the Prospect of Armageddon*, Ithaca, NY, Cornell University Press

Kaplan, Fred (1983), *The Wizards of Armageddon*, New York, Touchstone

Keeny, Spurgeon M., Jr and Panofsky, Wolfgang K. H. (1981–2), 'MAD vs. NUTS: Can Doctrine or Weaponry Remedy the Mutual Hostage Relationship of the Superpowers?', *Foreign Affairs*, Vol. 60, No. 2, pp. 287–304

Kennan, George F. (1982), *The Nuclear Delusion: Soviet–American Relations in the Atomic Age*, expanded, updated edition, New York, Pantheon

Kull, Steven (1988), *Minds at War: Nuclear Reality and the Inner Conflict of Defense Policymakers*, New York, Basic Books

Lifton, Robert Jay and Falk, Richard (1982), *Indefensible Weapons. The Political and Psychological Cases Against Nuclearism*, New York, Basic Books

Lifton, Robert Jay and Markusen, Eric (1990), *The Genocidal Mentality: Nazi Holocaust and Nuclear Threat*, New York, Basic Books

May, John (1989), *The Greenpeace Book of the Nuclear Age: The Hidden History, the Human Cost*, London, Victor Gollancz

MccGwire, Michael (1984), 'The Dilemmas and Delusions of Deterrence' in Gwyn Prins (ed.), *The Choice: Nuclear Weapons Versus Security*, London, Chatto and Windus, Hogarth, pp. 75–97

— (1985–6), 'Deterrence; The Problem – Not the Solution', *International Affairs*, Vol. 62, No. 1, pp. 55–70

— (1987), *Military Objectives in Soviet Foreign Policy*, Washington, DC, Brookings Institution

Pipes, Richard (1977), 'Why the Soviet Union Thinks It Can Fight and Win a Nuclear War', *Commentary*, Vol. 64, No. 1, pp. 21–34

— (1982), 'Soviet Strategic Doctrine: Another View', *Strategic Review*, Vol. 10, No. 4, pp. 52–8

Scheer, Robert (1983), *With Enough Shovels: Reagan, Bush and Nuclear War*, London, Secker and Warburg

Schell, Jonathan (1982), *The Fate of the Earth*, London; Picador

— (1984), *The Abolition*, London, Picador

Segal, Gerald (1991), 'China', in Regina Cowen Karp (ed.), *Security With Nuclear Weapons? Different Perspectives on National Security*, Oxford University Press/Stockholm International Peace Research Institute, pp. 189–205

Smoke, Richard and Kortunov, Andrei (eds.) (1991), *Mutual Security: A New Approach to Soviet-American Relations*, London, Macmillan

Trachtenberg, Marc (1988), *The Development of American Strategic Thought: Writings on Strategy, 1961–1969, and Retrospectives*, 6 volumes, New York, Garland

Weston, Burns H. (ed.) (1991), *Alternative Security: Living Without Nuclear Deterrence*, Boulder, CO, Westview Press

The North–South divide

The 'third world' and the 'South'

In the period since the Second World War, states in the international system have been separated by two overlapping but distinct divides. One – the East–West divide – reflects the antagonisms and security alliances arising from the Cold War, in which the United States and the Soviet Union were the major protagonists (until external pressure and internal change led to the break-up of the Soviet Union in the early 1990s). The other – the North–South divide – reflects the more enduring division between the advanced capitalist countries on the one hand, and the less developed countries of Africa, Asia, Latin America and the Middle East on the other. In the decades following the Second World War it became common to describe the less developed countries collectively as the 'third world'; the current tendency is to talk of the 'South' instead. This altered usage reflects changes in the reality of global relations between states, and in perceptions about the crucial driving forces behind the international system as a whole. The idea of a third world arose in the context of a bipolar global system, shaped by the hostility between the 'first world' of developed capitalist states, and the 'second world' of socialist states led by the Soviet Union. The large group of states outside these two groupings was seen as constituting a 'third bloc'. It became the object of rivalry between East and West. At the same time, these states were seen as seeking to establish their political and economic independence by finding a 'third way' towards development away from what was almost invariably a common background of colonial rule and economic backwardness. With the disappearance of the second world of established socialist states, it makes less sense to talk of a third world than it once did. And with the apparent global triumph of capitalism, there may seem less likelihood of *any* alternative path of economic development, let alone a third way between capitalist and socialist alternatives.

At the same time, the idea of a global divide between 'North' and 'South' has some difficulties of its own. First, the division between advanced capitalist and less developed economies is not strictly geographical. Second, there are some groups of countries, such as the rich oil states of the Middle East, the East Asian 'tigers', or the former Soviet satellites in Eastern Europe, which do not seem to fit into either category. Third, membership of each group may not be fixed: it may be possible for some countries to move from 'South' to 'North' or even from 'North' to 'South' over time. Fourth, talk of a division between 'North' and 'South' tends to obscure the extent to which the world constitutes one single, integrated economy, and to draw attention away from the dynamic global forces which shape it. If these limits are recognised, the idea of a North–South divide makes a good starting-point for an understanding of a number of key issues in the political economy of the late twentieth century world.

The dimensions of the North–South divide are best grasped by examining the relative fortunes of different states and regions around the world in the last half-century or so – a period dominated in global economic terms by the sustained global economic expansion which ran from around 1950 to the mid-1970s. For much of this period a major aspect of the global picture was the commitment to developmentalism in the South, and the lip-service paid to it as a goal in the North. But as Giovanni Arrighi (1991, p. 40) has recently shown, 'after more than thirty years of developmental efforts of all kinds, the gaps that separate the incomes of the East and of the South from the West/North are today wider than ever before'. Some regions, such as South Asia and Southern and Central Africa, have seen a steady widening of the income gap throughout the last fifty years. Others, such as Western and Eastern Africa, South-East Asia and Latin America, have seen small improvements later lost in sharp reverses. And even in such cases as South Korea, with its 'economic miracle' over recent years, income levels remain only a fraction of those in the developed world. In addition, much ground was lost throughout the South in the disastrous global collapse of the 1980s. On this evidence, the North–South divide is as real today as it ever was; and on balance, it is probably growing wider.

Contested causes and remedies

But if the reality of the North–South divide is not in dispute, there has been considerable disagreement over its causes and possible remedies. At one extreme are the radical 'dependency' theorists, such as A. G. Frank (1969), who have argued that the interests of the developed and the underdeveloped world are diametrically opposed to each other. For Frank, the development of the North *produced* the underdevelopment of the South. At the other extreme are the liberal optimists, whose faith in the market leads them to believe that there is no conflict of interest between North and South. They argue that capitalist production and free trade maximise development throughout the global economy as a whole. This is the dominant position today, endorsed by many governments and inter-national financial institutions in the North, and (for reasons considered further below) by a growing number of governments in the South.

Cutting across the two is the classical Marxist position, which is that capitalism is in some contexts a progressive force, and that its internal dynamics tend to lead to its development on a global scale. B. Warren revived this approach at the height of the dependency debate, arguing that capitalist development *was* taking place in the third world, and bringing about 'significant progress in material welfare and the development of the productive forces' (1980, p. 252). It should be noted that Warren was writing in the closing years of the long post-war boom, and that he did not live to see either the publication of his major work, or the catastrophic global collapse of the 1980s. In recent years these debates have been transformed by close attention to the experience of the East Asian 'tigers', in particular South Korea and Taiwan. Here, again, a major division of opinion has arisen between those who ascribe their success to the magic of the market, and those who attribute it to authoritarian government and pervasive state intervention.

Against this background, one can trace the rise and fall in international politics of a distinctive consciousness and institutional articulation of the interests of the South in the five decades following the Second World War. As we shall see, a radical perspective informed by anti-colonialism and anti-imperialism was influential in the 1950s and 1960s, but it was largely a spent force in the early 1990s despite the severe setbacks to development in the South during the previous decade. An obvious question arises: why have attitudes to the North–South divide changed so dramatically, even in the South itself, despite evidence that it remains as entrenched as ever? To answer it, one needs to examine the development of the global economy and the international system since the Second World War.

National development within a global economy

In the early post-war years, the developing countries of the day – primarily but not exclusively the long-independent states of Latin America, and newly independent India – proved largely unable to influence the character of new international institutions concerned with money, finance and trade. The International Monetary Fund and the World Bank (i.e. International Bank for Reconstruction and Development), the twin products of the Bretton Woods Agreement of 1944, were designed primarily to restore the prosperity and global power of the advanced capitalist countries led by the United States. A proposal for an International Development Board to fund broader efforts to promote economic growth, put forward by John Maynard Keynes, was quickly brushed aside. A projected International Trade Organisation failed to materialise, and the limited scheme for the freeing of trade which appeared in its place, the General Agreement on Trade and Tariffs (GATT), made few concessions to the particular needs of developing countries. As a result, the wave of decolonisation which created the third world from the late 1950s onwards took place in the context of rapid recovery and increased trade between the developed countries, while the developmental concerns of the newly independent states were given short shrift. Partly as a result of specific restraints on exports from the South (e.g. textiles), but largely as a consequence of the in-built bias towards trade and investment between the developed countries themselves, the share of world exports from the South has fallen steadily in the post-war period. Between 1950 and 1960 alone it fell by one-third, from 31.6 per cent to 21.4 per cent, reflecting the way in which the economies of the South were being pushed to the margins of world trade (Spero, 1990, p. 207).

In this situation, nationalism and developmentalism became the watchwords throughout the developing world. New national leaders in the South had been left in no doubt that their concerns had a very low priority in the eyes of the more advanced states, who attached far more importance to their relations with each other than their links with the South. They therefore pursued development at national level, through strategies which often brought them into conflict with domestic opponents, foreign investors, and governments in the West. Despite the confrontations which arose, these strategies were generally moderately reformist, and rarely anti-capitalist in content. There *was* a genuine radical and even internationalist spirit to the anti-colonial movement in particular, reflected for example in the Bandung Conference of non-aligned states (1955). But at the same time, most third world states aspired to the same end state of urban and industrial development and relative prosperity with which they identified the United States and much of Western Europe. Revolutions which rejected the Western model were relatively rare, and mostly associated with armed opposition to colonial rule – as in Indochina and Portuguese Africa. Indigenous socialist revolutions – such as those in Cuba in 1958–9 and in Ethiopia in 1974 – were rare indeed.

It quickly became apparent that the adoption of doctrines of self-reliance or nationalist industrial development was not enough in itself to alter the unequal economic relationships deeply embedded in the international system. One by one the national developmentalist leaders of this early period – such as Juan Perón in Argentina, Abdel Nasser in Egypt, Kwame Nkrumah in Ghana – changed course and sought, though generally with little success, to attract foreign capital in an attempt to rescue faltering development programmes. Many such leaders, these three among them, were themselves replaced by governments far more willing to conform to the limits laid down by the West. The North–South divide had been accentuated by the structure of international institutions and the pattern of global economic growth that took shape in the post-war period. As a result, national developmentalism proved inadequate as a means to shift the balance back in favour of the states of the South.

During the 1960s and more dramatically in the 1970s, tentative efforts by individual nations to bridge the North–South divide gave way to a new approach: an effort to assert the interests of the South, in international institutions and in the global economy, by means of concerted international action. These efforts focused at first on the United Nations, where the countries of the South had a majority in the General Assembly. In 1963, seventy-seven of them sponsored a Joint Declaration of the Developing Countries, calling for reforms to international trade regimes to encourage development. Thereafter, the Group of Seventy-Seven (a name it retained although it came to represent well over a hundred states) became a permanent voice for the interests of the South within the UN system. The outcome was the founding in 1964 of the United Nations Conference on Trade and Development (UNCTAD), and the negotiation in 1965 of a new section of the GATT agreement, dealing with trade and development. However, these and other minor reforms failed to reverse the discrimination against the countries of the South in international trade. As a result, the international campaign of the countries of the South peaked in the 1970s with two related initiatives of a more confrontational nature.

Confrontation or convergence?

The first of these, responding in part to the strategic issues in the Middle East concerning the state of Israel, and in part to falling revenues arising from the devaluation of the dollar against gold, was the joint effort of producers, organised in the Organization of Petroleum Exporting Countries (OPEC), to force up the price of oil. The second was the renewed promotion of an agenda for reform through calls for a New International Economic Order. Despite the enormous upheavals to which the increased price of oil gave rise, and the considerable debate prompted, particularly in liberal circles in the West, over the New International Economic Order, neither initiative succeeded in reversing the existing balance of power. Two successive hikes in the oil price, in 1973 and again in 1979, sharply accentuated a global wave of inflation that was already taking shape. This led to deep recession, falling commodity prices, and a global debt crisis which hit the countries of the South particularly hard. A small number of oil producers did gain considerably, but many others, particularly those such as Mexico and Nigeria with large populations and ambitious plans for industrial development, were thrown into deep economic crisis. Overall, the whole episode confirmed the vulnerability of commodity producers, and the complex interdependence of the global capitalist economy. Meanwhile, the calls for a new and more equitable international order were briefly taken up in such initiatives as the Brandt Report (1980), but very quickly lost support once recession began to bite in the leading economies of the West. In Britain and the United States in particular, newly elected right-wing governments interpreted the events of the 1970s as demonstrating the futility of state intervention, and the need for tight financial discipline. They set out to cut back on state spending in their own economies, and to restore what they saw as the logic of the market.

This new international climate proved extremely hostile to aspirations for development in the South, and the greatly increased burden of global debt made it virtually impossible for developing countries to resist pressure from the North to change course. During the 1980s, therefore, the strategy of national developmentalism was displaced almost everywhere by a quite different approach, often directly imposed from outside. The national sovereignty of states in the South, and their ability to pursue national development strategies through state intervention, were under assault. They were being undermined by international agencies and leading Western governments, intent upon promoting policies of 'structural adjustment' centred on economic liberalisation and the privatisation of production owned or run by the state. Indigenous strategies of economic and political development had gone into apparently irreversible decline. In the 1990s, the economies of the South are tending to conform ever more closely to models of development defined externally.

What this means for individual countries may actually vary from case to case, and the implications for the North–South divide are by no means straightforward. Although change in the international capitalist economy happens slowly, it does happen, and there is no guarantee that the countries dominant today will remain dominant tomorrow. The most significant change over the last half-century has been the rise of Japan, counterbalanced by the decline of Britain, and perhaps the beginning of the end for the dominant post-war economy, the United States. It is significant that the fast-rising economic successes of the South – led by Taiwan and South Korea – have had the unique advantage of being within the economic area dominated by Japan, and at the same time receiving substantial financial backing and other support from the United States because of their sensitive location on the East–West divide. Even if their success should continue, it does not follow that they have a recipe which can easily be copied elsewhere. In addition, their combination of low wages, authoritarian government and heavy reliance on the provision of social support from within the family unit rather than the state makes it questionable that the model *should* be copied. South Korea has followed Japan in having the largest differential in the world between male and female wages. Furthermore, women also bear the burden of providing the bulk of social support, with care for the elderly being a major item.

In the early 1990s, the great majority of states in the South are being pushed towards economic liberalisation by forces which are rendered irresistible by the South's own weaknesses. They are in no better position to control their own destinies than they were in the past, when national development or collective resistance to pressures from the North were the favoured strategies for advancement. The likelihood is, therefore, that the North–South divide will persist, although perhaps in a different form to that which it has taken in earlier decades. Some of the rapidly growing economies of the South look set to make the transition to industrial development and relative prosperity, although it is unlikely that they will adopt the patterns of welfare spending and social support which were the general aspirations of the North in the decades after the Second World War. At the same time, however, the exacerbation of capitalist competition on a global scale, glimpsed by Marx more than a century earlier, is also threatening the social structures and patterns of state provision of many of the historically dominant economies of the North. It remains likely that if the North–South divide is to be bridged, it will be as a consequence of declining levels of income and welfare in some of the weaker economies of the North, rather than as a result of improvements across the South as a whole. While some economies are rapidly heading 'north', others are moving just as precipitately to the 'south'.

References

Arrighi, G. (1991), 'World Income Inequalities and the Future of Socialism', *New Left Review*, No. 189, September/October, pp. 39–65

Brandt, W. (1980), *North–South: A Programme for Survival*, London, Pan

Frank, A. G. (1969), *Capitalism and Underdevelopment in Latin America: Historical Studies of Chile and Brazil*, New York, Monthly Review Press

Spero, J. (1990), *The Politics of International Economic Relations*, 4th edition, London, Unwin Hyman

Warren, B. (1980), *Imperialism: Pioneer of Capitalism*, London, Verso

Further Reading

Harris, N. (1986), *The End of the Third World: Newly Industrializing Countries and the Decline of an Ideology*, Harmondsworth, Penguin

Ravenhill, J. (1985), *Collective Clientelism: The Lomé Conventions and North–South Relations*, New York, Columbia University Press

Zionism

Zionism is the national movement of the Jewish people. Its aim is the creation of a Jewish sovereign entity in Palestine/the Land of Israel, the ancestral homeland of the Jews. The emergence of this movement as a political force in the latter part of the nineteenth century led to the establishment of the State of Israel in May 1948. Zionism has changed fundamentally the course of Jewish history. It has transformed the nature of the relationship of the Jewish people with the Land of Israel and has radically affected the international politics of the Middle East.

Meanings and roots

The term Zionism was first coined publicly by the Viennese Jewish writer Nathan Birnbaum in 1892. But the history of Zionism as a political force is most closely identified with Theodore Herzl (1860-1904), regarded as the father of modern Zionism, and dates from the publication of his book *Der Judenstaat* (The Jewish State) in 1896. After considering the alternatives to the 'Jewish question' and the problematic status of Jews in contemporary society, Herzl concluded that their plight could only be successfully resolved by means of a political solution and that the Jews must leave the lands of their dispersion and be concentrated in a sovereign state of their own. In order to translate his ideas into practice Herzl was instrumental in founding the World Zionist Organization, which held its first congress in Basle in 1897, and in actively seeking the help of the great powers for the realisation of his dream.

Herzl had his forerunners in Russia, Germany and other countries. Their writings also reflected the longing for the ancestral homeland, the precariousness of Jewish life in Eastern and Central Europe and the need to find a solution to the Jewish question. Of particular significance was the founding of the *Hovevei Zion* movement (Lovers of Zion) in 1881, which, in contrast to Herzl's focus on mobilising political support for his ideas, actively promoted the migration (*aliyah*) and settlement of Jews in Palestine. This movement heralded the beginnings of 'practical Zionism'. In the era following Herzl's death in 1904, both the political and practical approaches played an important role in the development of Zionism and the Zionist endeavour in Palestine. This combined approach was called Synthetic Zionism, a phrase associated with Chaim Weizmann who played a pivotal role in securing the Balfour Declaration from Britain in November 1917 and was later to become the first president of the State of Israel (Vital, 1975; Laqueur, 1972).

The root of the term Zionism is, of course, the word Zion which, after the destruction of the First Temple, became not only a synonym for Jerusalem but also represented the yearning of the Jewish people for redemption and a return to their homeland. During the eighteen centuries of exile the link between the Jewish communities in the Diaspora and the Land of Israel always figured strongly in their value system and their religious liturgy. It was central in their self-consciousness not just as a minority but also as a group in exile. Yet the prominence and the strong emotional intensity of this bond did not affect the daily lives of Jewish communities in the Diaspora. In their prayers, Jews would ask for deliverance but aside from the occasional messianic movements which caught the imagination of individuals and a few communities, they did not move to Palestine. Divine will, rather than human action, would determine when and how the Jewish people would return to Zion. Zionism differed from the previous yearnings for a return to Zion in its predominantly secular character. Its leaders and driving forces did not come from the traditional religious background but were products of a European education and were imbued with the ideas of liberalism, nationalism and socialism which were sweeping across the European continent (Hertzberg, 1970).

The emergence of Zionism as a political force at the end of the nineteenth century can only be understood in the context of European and Jewish history since the French Revolution and rise of modern anti-semitism. Political Zionism would not have come into existence, nor could it have flourished, but for the problematic status of Eastern and Central European Jewry during the latter part of the nineteenth century and the fierce growth of anti-semitism in Europe during the first half of this century. The successive waves of suppression and pogroms in Czarist Russia, the appearance of racist theories and anti-semitic movements in Germany, and the Dreyfus affair in France challenged severely the hopes that Jews would acquire equal rights and status in their countries of residence. All served as a warning and reminder that neither the Enlightenment nor the emancipation of the Jews would suffice as a solution to the Jewish question. It was the Dreyfus affair, which Herzl witnessed as a reporter for a Viennese newspaper, and the eruption of virulent anti-semitism that it produced in many sectors of French society, that galvanised his conversion to Zionism. But it would be wrong, however, to conclude that Zionism was solely a response of a people to persecution. It was necessary but not a sufficient ingredient.

A nation in exile

The central and most important tenet which underlies the Zionist idea is that the Jewish people constitute a nation and, like all other nations, they possess the right to self-determination and to a state of their own. In this respect, Zionism's intellectual origins lie in the impact of the ideas and social forces unleashed by the French Revolution. As the aspirations of an undifferentiated universalism of the early Enlightenment faded away so Jews began to change their perception of themselves, as did others of them. Where previously the identity of an individual or a group had been defined in terms of one's religion, so being Jewish was viewed by Jews and non-Jews alike in a religious context. The religious orientated self-perception of society was being replaced by a new identity distinguished by nationality, ethnicity, a common language, culture and a shared common history, real or imagined. Zionism was a product of this new world of nationalism. It defined the Jewish people in national and not purely religious terms. It was grounded in the belief of the existence of a common past and future for the Jewish people and viewed the essence of the Jewish problem as a national not an individual question. The early Zionist thinkers were a part of the multi-ethnic, multinational world of Eastern Europe. They, too, were seeking self-determination, identity and liberation under the new world order of nationalism (Avineri, 1981). Where Zionism differed significantly from other contemporary national movements was that the Jewish people had no territorial concentration and were a landless people.

The conviction that the Jews are a nation lies at the heart of the Zionist idea. Yet even today this claim remains a source of puzzlement and contention. Those who question the legitimacy of Zionism reject the Jewish claim to nationality, arguing that Judaism is a religion and therefore does not constitute any right of self-determination. The issue is further confused by the fact that the majority of Jews in the world do not live in Israel and, to a large degree, are fully integrated in, and identify themselves culturally and politically with, the societies and states in which they reside. The question of Jewish identity in the modern world is complex and any attempt to force it into a neat and simple category is doomed to failure. Zionism maintains that the individual has the right to self-identification and that Jews throughout the world have the personal right to define their own sense of belonging and identity. In this respect, the Law of Return, passed by the Israeli Knesset in 1950, which allows the right of every Jew in the world to immigrate to Israel and automatically confers Israeli citizenship upon him or her, is regarded as an unassailable right around which all Zionists vehemently unite.

From the outset the followers of Zionism have maintained that the continuation of Jewish existence in the Diaspora, under the twin pressures of anti-semitism and assimilation, was increasingly untenable. The extreme version of this 'Negation of Exile' (*Sheilat Ha-Golah*) was 'Catastrophic Zionism', a term associated with Max Nordau (1849–1923). This form of Zionism referred to the belief that unless Jews moved to Palestine, a catastrophe would befall them. The

Nazi Holocaust was a tragic vindication of Catastrophic Zionism. No Zionist leader had ever envisioned a catastrophe on such a scale. It intensified the need for the creation of a refuge for the Jewish people and, in doing so, enhanced the radical appeal of Zionism, based as it was on the central idea of a sovereign Jewish homeland. The belief that Israel should provide a home for all Jews and should commit itself to rescuing Jewish communities in distress arises from the centrality of this principle. The recent wave of mass *aliyah* (immigration) of Jews from the republics of the former Soviet Union and the dramatic airlift of the Ethiopian Jews bears witness to the importance and continuing functionality of this principle.

The Negation of Exile also contained a normative dimension. The aim of Zionism was not just the creation of a territorial base for the Jewish people. What differentiated Zionist thinkers from non-Zionist Jewish thinkers was their belief that the normalisation of the Jewish people and the ending of the historical anomalies of Jewish life could not occur without the creation of a homeland in Palestine. Political sovereignty was seen as a necessary precondition for the transformation of Jewish life. The conditions of 'exile' in the Diaspora did not allow a Jew to realise fully his or her Jewishness. Jewish existence involved more than a matter of religious observance and only by residing in an integral Jewish environment, in a Jewish state, could a Jew live a full Jewish life. The critical question for the founders of Zionism was never how many Jews would live in the Jewish state or what its eventual size and boundaries would be. It centred instead upon the quality of life and the nature of the society that they would be creating. For many, Zionism was not seen as a continuation of Jewish history but as a break from its past. The pioneers who went to Palestine in the first two decades of this century were enthused with the belief that through their actions they were creating a new Jewish experience which would replace the misery and alienation of the Diaspora. Many adhered to some version of a socialist Zionist faith which was best represented by the communal lifestyle of the Kibbutz. This group was eventually to become the dominant element among the founders of the State of Israel. Even though this messianic aspect was not unique to Zionism as a nationalist movement, and although this ideological zeal has waned with time, its importance as a driving force cannot be overestimated. It is an ever-present undercurrent in the on-going debates on the nature and the future course of Israeli society (Bar-On, 1993).

Homeland, statehood and expansion

One of the main controversies in the Zionist movement in the 1920s and 1930s revolved around whether the establishment of a Jewish state should be defined as one of the clear goals of the movement, in place of the vaguer options of homeland, homestead or national home. But this in essence was more a question of tactics and timing. Although a small minority advocated the establishment of a bi-national state in Palestine as a solution to the competing claims of the Jews and Arabs, for the majority the aspiration to statehood was their starting-point of departure. While statehood was the aim, there was no clear conception of how this would be achieved, or what the area of a future state would be. In the early years of the movement a debate raged around whether terrritories other than Palestine could be considered as potential options. This issue was eventually resolved at the Seventh Zionist Congress in 1905 when the proposal to establish a Jewish state in the British territory of East Africa (the Uganda Plan) was overwhelmingly rejected. In 1937, following the publication of the Peel Commission Report (Cmd 5479), which advocated the division of Palestine into three geographic entities: an Arab state, a Jewish one and a large enclave including Jerusalem to be governed by the British, the Zionist movement had to confront the question of whether to consider the establishment of a state in only part of Palestine. After heated debates, the Zionist movement agreed reluctantly to consider the report although the recommendations fell way short of their hopes. In the face of Arab opposition the British shelved the Commission's proposals. A decade later, in November 1947, the United Nations returned to the idea of partition and the creation of two states as a solution to the conflicting claims of the Jews and the Arabs in Palestine. Again the majority of the Zionist movement agreed to the establishment of a Jewish state in only part of Palestine. Until the Six Day War of June 1967 the territorial issue was mute and did not stir any serious controversy within the Zionist movement. Israel was essentially committed to the territorial status quo arising from the 1948 War of Independence. The capture of the West Bank of Jordan in 1967 revived forcefully the entire debate. The dream of the Greater Land of Israel (*Eretz Yisrael Hashlema*) had suddenly become a reality. The question of the permanent boundaries of the Israeli state acquired a renewed relevance and intensity. The settlement of the West Bank was regarded by the right wing in Israel as not only essential for the securing of those territories but was also seen as a natural continuation of the Zionist endeavour. But it is inaccurate to maintain that Zionism means the further settlement and retention of the West Bank and to regard those who advocate withdrawal from those territories as not true Zionists, since it is precisely this issue that bitterly divides one type of Zionist from another. The future of the West Bank and the Gaza Strip has become the most divisive bone of contention in Israel today, cutting right across the heart of the nation as well as Jewish communities in the Diaspora (Bar-On, 1993).

Israel

What has been the impact of Zionism and what role, if any, does it still play at the end of the twentieth century? The basic aim of the Zionist movement was to rebuild the Jewish national homeland in Palestine. This was viewed as an essential step for the normalisation of the Jewish people and for the solution to the Jewish question. Zionism started out as a minority phenomenon among Jews. Few Jews regarded the aims of the movement as feasible or as an answer to their concerns and aspirations. Of the three million Jews who fled from persecution in Czarist Russia from 1882 to 1914, only a small minority chose to build a new home and society in Palestine. The majority adopted the traditional response to the perils of exile and migrated primarily to the United States, Canada and South America. The majority of the Jewish world placed their hopes in democracy and liberalism as the solution to the Jewish question. Others saw their salvation in the advent of international socialism. Zionism was the refuge of dreamers and idealists. Yet within fifty years of the First Zionist Congress, Zionism emerged as the dominant force in contemporary Jewish life and the new State of Israel had been admitted into the community of nations.

The Arab world has never accepted Zionism as a legitimate movement. Seen from the Arab point of view. Zionism was a colonialist aggressive force which would result in their displacement (Said, 1980). Zionism has not just been opposed on the battlefield. The Arab world, backed by the Soviet Union and the Eastern bloc, sought to isolate Israel on the international stage. The watershed in the development of the anti-Zionist crusade came in 1975 with the passing of the United Nations resolution which branded Zionism as a form of racism and racial discrimination. The 'Zionism is Racism' resolution, passed by the automatic anti-Israel voting majority, was fundamental in conferring upon Israel the status of a pariah state and ensuring its international isolation. It was not until the collapse of the Cold War that this resolution was repealed, by an overwhelming majority, in the General Assembly. The start of the Arab-Israeli peace process following the Gulf War of 1991 has witnessed the thawing of relations between Israel and the Arab world. This process has led to the mutual recognition of Israel and the Palestine Liberation Organisation (PLO) and to the signing, in September 1993, of a Declaration of Principles leading to Palestinian autonomy and self-rule in the Gaza Strip and the West Bank. This historic breakthrough has paved the way for the ending of a hundred years of conflict and the integration of Israel within the Middle East.

The creation of the State of Israel saw the fulfilment of the prime goal of the Zionist movement. There were many who argued that Zionism and the Zionist movement had served its purpose and questioned whether it still possessed any future role. The outstanding task was the consolidation of the new state and the securing of its international recognition. Despite the attainment of political sovereignty, the majority of Jews in the world have chosen not to live in Israel. This has resulted in a confusion and a lack of clarity in trying to define the relationship between Zionism and Jewish communities in the Diaspora. Is a Zionist someone who supports the State of Israel or should a tighter and more traditional definition, namely someone who intends to live in Israel, apply? The distinction is, to a large degree, an artificial one and the debate surrounding it continues to revolve more around semantics than substance. Regardless of their personal commitment, Israel is of central significance to all Jewish people. It continues to play a prominent role in the mainstream of contemporary Jewish life. Concern for the welfare, preservation and public fate of Israel unites Jewish communities throughout the world. The centrality of the State of Israel has become an important element in the collective identity of Jews in the modern world. This support should not be confused, nor should it be equated, with either the approval or disapproval of specific policies of the Israeli government. The relationship between Jews in the Diaspora and the State of Israel is dynamic and, in the long run, is dependent on the future content and nature of Israeli society. In the foreseeable future, however, Zionism will remain a dominant force in Jewish life. At the end of the twentieth century the aims and purpose of Zionism still possess an ongoing relevance and functionality for the Jewish people.

References

Avineri, Shlomo (1981), *The Making of Modern Zionism*, London, Weidenfeld and Nicolson.

Bar-On, Mordechai (1993), 'Zionism into its Second Century: A Stock-Taking', in Keith Kyle and Joel Peters (eds.), *Whither Israel: The Domestic Challenges*, London, I. B. Tauris/Royal Institute of International Affairs

Hertzberg, Arthur (1970), *The Zionist Idea*, Westport, Conn., Greenwood Press

Herzl, T. (1988), *The Jewish State* (First published 1896), New York, Dover

Laqueur, Walter (1972), *A History of Zionism*, London, Weidenfeld and Nicolson

Palestine Commission Report (1937), Cmd 5479, London, HMSO

Said, Edward (1980), *The Question of Palestine*, London, Routledge and Kegan Paul

Vital, David (1975), *The Origins of Zionism*, Oxford, Clarendon Press

Further Reading

Vital, David (1982), *Zionism: The Formative Years*, Oxford, Clarendon Press

— (1987), *Zionism: The Crucial Phase*, Oxford, Clarendon Press

Pan-Arabism

Although having several intellectual and political precursors in the nineteenth century, Pan-Arabism is basically a twentieth century doctrine that developed in conjunction with the breakdown of the Ottoman Empire and the encroachment of Western colonialism.[1]

As with many other nationalist movements, Arabism emerged among a small circle of the intelligentsia and was mainly concerned with cultural matters, especially the revival and renovation of the Arabic language and its literature. Several of the pioneering contributions in this respect came from Christian teachers and writers in Syria/Lebanon.

Linguistic nationalism and the dynastic order

Although the linguistic conception of nationalism has remained the most dominant of all Pan-Arabist ideas, it has always acquired additional shades from one thinker to another. Some analysts regard the Syrian 'Abd al-Rahman al-Kawakibi (1849–1902) as 'the first true intellectual precursor of modern secular Pan-Arabism' (Haim, 1974, pp. 27ff.). He was the earliest to declare himself unreservedly a champion of the Arabs against the Turks. He also called for a caliphate limited to the spiritual sphere, even though he still adhered to the conventional goal of an Islamic renaissance (Nassar, 1986, pp. 58ff.).

For some, Arabism was a basically linguistic concept but one mixed with an ethnic, often anti-Turkish, slant, such as, for example, in the writings of Najib 'Azuri (d. 1916), 'Abd al-Ghani al-'Arisi (1889–1916), Salah al-Din al-Qasimi (1887–1916), or 'Umar Fakhuri (1859–1946) (for a detailed anthology see Haim, 1974). Not unexpectedly, such writers were influenced by the European ideas of nationalism circulating at the time, particularly those of the French Gustav Lebon and the German Theodor Mommsen.

The 'cultural nationalism' of the intellectuals could not, however, link up with any ascending social class (e.g. a bourgeoisie) that would have championed its cause. In spite of the reforms of Muhammad 'Ali and his son Ibrahim between 1831 and 1940 and the *Tanzimat* reforms that followed, 'Syria was by no means a bourgeois society. It was more a semi-feudal one with some incipient bourgeois features' (Tibi, 1981, p. 88). As Tibi explains (1981, pp. 80–90), the undeveloped bourgeoisie and the petty-bourgeois writers were unable to lead a revolt against the Ottoman Empire by themselves. They allied themselves with the 'feudal' masters of the Arabian peninsula at the time, the Hashimite dynasty, and entrusted them with leading the 'Arab revolt'. Sharif Husain of Mecca, the head of the dynasty, agreed to lead the movement under assurances from his close allies, the British, that they would support it and guarantee the 'liberation of the Arabs' of Asia within an independent Arab kingdom under Husain's headship. This promise proved to be a tactical manoeuvre, since Britain and France had, with the connivance of Russia, already concluded the Sykes-Picot Agreement in 1916. In this, they had agreed to distribute amongst themselves whatever Arab territories might be liberated from the Turks in the First World War. This Western 'betrayal' paved the way for a formal 'colonial' British and French presence (under the title of Mandate) in the Arab East (Mashriq – Egypt, Palestine, Syria, Lebanon, Jordan) and opened the door for Zionist settlements in Palestine (under the Balfour Declaration of 1917).

The transformation of Arab nationalism

It was this colonial encroachment on the Arab East, combined with the accelerating demise of the Ottoman state, which contributed more than anything to the politicisation of Arab nationalist ideas there. The pre-colonial cultural nationalism of the Western-educated intellectuals had usually been liberal in outlook with the intention of emulating Western constitutional and democratic practices. With the spread of colonial domination, the West was now the oppressor, and the increasingly anti-Western nationalism was becoming also less liberal and more authoritarian and even totalitarian in its general outlook. As Bassam Tibi explains:

> Arab nationalism, once Francophile and partly Anglophile, changed with the British and French colonisation of the area and became anti-British and anti-French, and Germanophile ... Furthermore, the Germanophilia was narrow and one-sided. The German ideology absorbed by the Arab intellectuals at this time was confined to a set of nationalist ideas which had gained particular currency during the period of the Napoleonic wars. These ideas carried notions of romantic irrationalism and a hatred of the French to extremes. They excluded from consideration the philosophers influenced by the Enlightenment.
>
> (Tibi, 1981, p. 91)

The main example of such an intellectual transformation was Sati' Al-Husri (1882–1968), the most influential theoretician of Arab nationalism, who gave the predominant linguistic concept of Arabism more of a 'historical' dimension. Of

Syrian origin, he lived during his early formative years, and then worked, in Ottoman Turkey, witnessing the demise of the empire and the rise of Turkish and non-Turkish nationalities within it (see Cleveland, 1971). He worked subsequently in Iraq and Egypt, and allocated a great deal of his efforts to turning the minds and hearts of the Egyptian intelligentsia towards the idea of Arabism. A dominant theme in Al-Husri's writing is that there is little freedom to be enjoyed by the individual outside the nation: 'patriotism and nationalism come before and above all ... even above and before freedom' (quoted in Haim, 1974, p. 90).

Having studied in France, Switzerland and Belgium, Al-Husri seems to have been attracted in his younger days by the ideas of Rousseau and Renan, and by the 'French idea of the Nation', but subsequently he became more influenced by German philosophers such as Herder, Fichte, Schönerer and Arndt, and by the whole idea of the organic nation-state. The main political German thinkers, from Herder to Plessner, have always made a distinction between 'state' and 'nation'. The latter is seen in cultural terms, while the state is seen as a mechanical and legal construction that is external to the nation. Al-Husri praised German Romanticism for having distilled the idea of the nation from that of the state, well before the French or the British. He fused this German concept of the nation with the Arabic concept of 'group solidarity' ('asabiyya) which he derived from Ibn Khaldun, and proceeded to develop his own 'pure' theory of nationalism (Tibi, 1981, pp. 100–15).

Renan's concept of a *nationalité élective* was severely criticised by Al-Husri. The idea of free will that makes the nation 'a daily plebiscite' did not help Al-Husri in his attempt to prove the actual existence of a unitary Arab nation. He wanted to demonstrate that the Arab peoples who lived in a number of separate states were actually one nation that should be united in a single state. Al-Husri drew a historical parallel between the divided Germany before 1871 and the fragmented Arab world extending from the Persian Gulf to the Atlantic Ocean. To him, the Arabs longed for an 'Arab 1871' but, as Bassam Tibi adds: 'How this [was] to be achieved [was] a matter of indifference.' For Al-Husri did not consider in specific terms how to apply the German or the French concept to the concrete Arab situation. He tried simply to adduce a general proof that the German concept was superior (Tibi, 1981, pp. 101, 124–5).

In his obsession to prove the existence of the Arab nation, Al-Husri overlooked the state and its foundations, whether geographic or socio-economic. He insisted that the state could never be a factor in forming the nation and employed many historical examples to prove his point (Nassar, 1986, pp. 276–92). But if, as he kept repeating, the nation is not contingent on the state, if it precedes the state and continues even after it has lost its own statehood or after it has been divided among several states, then why, one wonders, are 'nations' constantly striving to create their own states? Territorial continuity is not important except in so far as it affects linguistic unity in the long run. The formation of the state contributes to the development of the nation only in as much as it unifies the language. Nor are common economic interests particularly pertinent in the formation of a nation.

They unify in some cases and disperse in others but they always vary among different individuals, groups and regions.

> Economics plays a very important role in the life of nations, but its role does not include the 'formation of the nation'. Economics may strengthen the nation but it does not create it. It is no different in this respect from what concerns the state. For the state, as is known to everyone, may strengthen the nation or even take it to the peak of power, but it never creates it.
>
> (Al-Husri, 1984/5, p. 278)

The historico-linguistic concept of Arab nationalism was given political life in two main manifestations, one represented by the emergence of the Ba'th Party in the Arab East (in the 1940s) and the other by the emergence (in the 1950s) of Gamal Abdel Nasser's leadership in Egypt. By emphasising the idea of Arab *unification*, both expressions have implicitly considered the state to be indispensable to the self-realisation of any nation, albeit a linguistically defined nation – although as we shall see this consideration has remained only implicit and devoid of any detailed or practical implications.

The Ba'th Party and other nationalist movements

While it is true that one of the sources of the Ba'th ideology may be found in the metaphysical-linguistic ideas of the Alawite Syrian Zaki al-Arsuzi, there is no doubt that its main ideologue has been Michel 'Aflaq (1910–89). A Damascene Christian, he formed the Arab Ba'th (Rebirth) group in 1943, along with a Muslim colleague Salah al-Bitar and a group of the Syrian intelligentsia who had all studied at the Sorbonne. In 1947 this group joined ranks with Al-Ihya' al-'Arabi (Arab Revival), led by Arsuzi, and were eventually joined by the Arab Socialist Party of Akram al-Hawrani in 1952 to form the organisation known to this day by the name of the Arab Ba'th Socialist Party, now active in most countries of the Mashriq.

'Aflaq's conceptualisation of Arab nationalism remained foggy and distinctively romantic. When once asked by some youngsters to define it he answered:

> Love, young people, comes before anything else; first comes love, then the definition will follow ... A tolerant spirituality that will open its heart and will shade with its wings all those who shared with the Arabs their history, who lived for generations in the atmosphere of their language and culture until they have become Arab in thought and in sentiment.
>
> ('Aflaq, 1970, p. 118)

From this and from other writings of 'Aflaq it becomes clear that it is always language that specifies the sense of Arabness, although other factors may be added here and there. Sometimes it is ethnic origin but only as a remote history – for contemporary Arabism is not racial. Sometimes Islam is a factor which is held in high esteem by 'Aflaq – but basically as a cultural heritage and not as a belief system. And sometimes the factor stressed is common history – although this translates more immediately in the contemporary period into 'a unity of suffering and hopes' and a desire for a unified destiny.

From quite early on 'Aflaq had been sensitive to social issues (which tended to be overlooked by Al-Husri), and came increasingly to use a socialistic idiom in his pronouncements. Like Husri, however, 'Aflaq conceived of the individual only as part of the national community. Within the Arab nation, the individual would be culturally fulfilled and socially prosperous. The Arab nation would foster a distinct 'Arab socialism' which would be as much spiritual as it is socio-economic. Eric Rouleau suggests that in his attempt to blend socialism with nationalism 'Aflaq might have derived the theoretical basis for such a synthesis (during his time in Paris in 1937) from Grosclaude's French translation of Alfred Rosenberg's book on the *Myth of the Twentieth Century*. A colleague of 'Aflaq's who taught at the University of Damascus found him full of admiration for Rosenberg and Hitler. He thought at the time that, in contrast to the communist countries, Germany had been more successful in achieving a synthesis between nationalism and socialism. Furthermore, when power in Iraq was seized by pro-German nationalists in the coup of Rashid 'Ali al-Gilani, 'Aflaq formed a committee which assured the new regime of its full support (Rouleau, 1967, pp. 56–7).

Although the idea of the state is implied in most of 'Aflaq's pronouncements, it is basically the idea of the *party* that takes precedence. Not only is the formation of the Pan-Arabist party a measure of the conscious and effective existence of the Arab nation but the party is, more specifically, the nation in miniature: 'we represent the whole of the nation which is still slumbering in [a state of] self-denial of its own reality, and forgetfulness of its own identity' ('Aflaq, 1970, p. 80).

As a political party the Ba'th has, of course, succeeded more than any other Pan-Arabist party in reaching power – often via alliances with the military in *coups d'état* – and in staying there for relatively long periods of time (e.g. modern Syria and Iraq). To this day, it entertains the theoretical concept of being organised on two levels: one pan-Arab (called 'national') and one territorial (or *qutri* in Arabic; i.e. based on a single country). The Ba'th was also behind the one and only experiment in actual unification among Arab countries in the post-independence period, that of the United Arab Republic between Syria and Egypt from 1958 to 1961, under the charismatic leadership of Nasser.

Another significant, but less influential, Pan-Arabist organisation was Harakat al-Qawmiyyin al-'Arab (Arab Nationalists' Movement – ANM). This time the nucleus was a group of Palestinian youths who were studying at the American University of Beirut (Lebanon) shortly after the Arabs' disastrous defeat in the Palestine War of 1948, which resulted in the creation of the State of Israel. A Christian Arab nationalist, Constantin Zuraiq, immediately wrote an influential monograph describing the event as nothing less than a total catastrophe (*nakba*).

The Arabs had little hope of confronting the more advanced and powerful Zionist state, he reasoned, except by dedicated and well-disciplined political organisation for which the Palestinian issue should act as the catalyst. Zuraiq's appeal fell on receptive ears and a group of his students at the American University of Beirut headed by a medical student, George Habash, responded with zeal to his call and in 1948 began to draw together an organisation of enthusiasts (initially under the name Al-'Urwa). The ANM remains poorly researched (the main source being Kazziha, 1975) but there are two particular aspects that concern us here. First is the way in which it allied itself with Nasser's leadership up to the Six Day War of 1967, which deprived it of a great deal of autonomy, and left it with little leeway within Egypt itself.

Second, there was the devastating impact on the movement of the defeat in the 1967 war. This led simultaneously to its radicalisation in a Marxist direction and to its fracturing into smaller groups. The diagnosis was that there was no longer any hope of achieving the liberation of Palestine through collective action by the Arab states, since these states were dominated either by decadent 'feudal' classes or by hesitant petty bourgeoisie whose interests lay neither in Arab unity nor in the liberation of Palestine. Some of these splinter groups became country-based (thus reducing the Pan-Arabist potential of the movement). The most intellectually significant was the Organisation of Lebanese Socialists in Lebanon; the most politically successful as a ruling government was the National Liberation Front in South Yemen from 1967 to 1990; and the most influential as an opposition movement was the liberal-nationalist group led by Ahmad al-Khatib in Kuwait. Other groups split over ideological matters, the most notable example being the division within the left wing of the Palestinian resistance movement between the more populist wing led by George Habash (known as the Popular Front for the Liberation of Palestine) and the more Marxist-oriented wing (known for short as the Democratic Front for the Liberation of Palestine), led by Nayif Hawatmah.

Nasser

Both the Ba'th Party and the Arab Nationalists sought Egypt's encouragement and Nasser's leadership in their endeavour to achieve Arab unity, but what were in fact the Pan-Arabist credentials of Egypt and of Nasser? Egypt was, of course, the largest and most culturally and strategically influential Arab state. But Egypt had been virtually autonomous from the Ottoman Empire since the early nineteenth century; it had already established a modern-looking state under Muhammad 'Ali; and it had constructed a secularist concept of citizenship revolving in particular around the 1919 revolution and the popular Wafd party. Egypt already had its own concept of nationalism in which the 'nation' (*umma*) was Egyptian, not Arab. Space does not permit any dwelling on the intricacies of this process of intellectual and political transformation, but suffice it to say that during the inter-war period Egypt underwent a process of 'political Arabisation'. As with most of the Arab world, including for the first time the hitherto 'secluded' Maghrib countries (Tunisia, Algeria and Morocco), the most important 'Arabiser' was the military triumph of the Zionist settler project in Palestine and the defeat of the Arab armies in 1948 – except in the case of Egypt where the threat of Israel was, geographically, more immediate.[2]

The Arabist line was to receive political sanction in Egypt when Nasser, the leader of the 1952 revolution, gradually subsumed the concept of Egyptian nationalism into a broader one of Arab nationalism. Prior to 1956, there seemed to have been in his pronouncements two concepts for the nation: one Egyptian and one Arab. The overwhelming support that Egypt received from all over the Arab world in 1956 during the Suez crisis and the tripartite aggression by Britain, France and Israel, was the main catalyst. From then on the terminology used was often that of the 'Arab nation' and the 'Egyptian people', both employed in a political, secularist sense (see Nasr, 1981).

Nasser, of course, was a soldier and politician and not an ideologue, and the conceptual structure of his Arabism was quite simple. Arabism started in his thinking as the most immediate and important 'circle' in which Egypt had to function (in addition to the African and Islamic circles). From the beginning, therefore, Arabism had a political character, but this had both cultural and 'strategic' premises: culturally in terms of a common language and shared history; and strategic in terms of a 'common struggle' against colonialism and for liberation and progress. Nasser's Arabism was also political in the sense that it implied that the real test (the real meaning) for Arab nationalism was in fact Arab unity – i.e. a political unification of the Arab countries. This political unification was relegated, however, following the failure in 1961 of Egypt's union with Syria, to third priority after 'liberation' and 'socialism'. From then on, the existence of the 'nation' was presumed to derive from its linguistic-historic reality, whereas the political unification in one state was made contingent on a number of socio-economic and political requisites that were unlikely to materialise in the immediate future (Nassar, 1986, pp. 326–35).

Arab nationalism and the search for identity

From the start, Pan-Arabism has been a reactive, rather than a proactive doctrine, forever trying to respond to a perceived challenge from the 'Other': first the Turkification policies of the late Ottoman Empire, then the division and domination enforced by the colonial powers, and then the settler-colonisation imposed by the Zionist state in the centre of the 'Arab Fatherland', thus separating its Asian from its African wing. The conceptual tenets and points of emphasis in the doctrine have been frequently adjusted in an attempt to cope with the changing challenges and the perceived threats. However, the doctrine of Pan-Arabism has remained, from its inception to the present time, basically language-centred and rather reluctant to take adequate account of other factors. Although the slogan of 'unity' has been invoked by most Arab nationalists, Arabism remains closer to a concept of a *Kulturnation*, and has not been pushed far enough in the direction of a *Staatsnation*. Arabism forms a cultural community and an emotional bond that can be invoked in the political arena, although it has not been able to modify the practice of state sovereignty in any significant way (the only political union among Arab countries being the League of Arab States, i.e. an organisation of sovereign independent *states*).

Pan-Arabism is an extremely belated doctrine of national unification which confronts serious problems, not the least of which is the general Western and Zionist hostility to what it stands for. Its death warrant has been signed several times, most notably by Fouad Ajami (1981). It is still quite influential, however, among many segments of the intelligentsia in most Arab countries (Ibrahim, 1980), even though in recent years it has had to concede ground to the potentially, though not necessarily, competitive doctrine of 'Islamic fundamentalism'.

The evident failure of Arab nationalism hitherto in realising its objectives cannot simply be attributed to its European derivation, or to its logical inconsistency (Kedourie, 1985), or to the opportunistic inclinations of some of its leading proponents (Davis, 1978). There is little doubt that the 'Theory of Arab Nationalism' itself is not entirely flawless. Even its 'myth of origins' in time, space and ancestry (Smith, 1991, chapters 1 and 2) is not adequately defined.[3] It also remains excessively 'romantic', and it has only recently started to pay adequate attention to the importance of social and economic variables (including the huge wealth disparities among Arab countries), and to the crucial issue of the state (contrast this, for example, with the Zionist ideology, one of whose earliest manifestos was a book on the Jewish *state*). Pan-Arabism continues to be characterised by a kind of 'identity-mania': the eternal question is forever: 'who are we?' and very rarely 'what are we going to do?', and 'how can we do it?' One Moroccan scholar (Bin 'Abd al-'Ali, 1992) has recently expressed this 'mania' most succinctly. The Arab world witnesses, according to him, what amounts to 'a pathological obsession with identity'. What is more, this search for identity is only manifested at a static level of reaction and emotion. It is not the outcome of an actual engagement in a real act of constructing the self through interaction with the other, but is a purely theoretical issue, concerned merely with 'displaying ourselves to the other' in endless, repetitive 'letters of introduction'!

Notes

1. The term 'Pan-Arabism' has no equivalent in the Arabic language. It is normally to be inferred from those who use terms such as *al-umma al-'arabiyya* (the Arab 'nation') *al-qawmiyya al-'arabiyya* (Arab nationalism), and *al-watan al-'arabi* (the Arab fatherland). Such concepts are often contrasted with the concepts of *wataniyya* ('patriotism' – i.e. attachment to one's 'country', *patrie*, rather than to one's 'people', *Volk*) and – more pejoratively – with the adjectives of *iqlimi* and *qutri* (territorial/provincial; country-based).

2.   The *ideology* of Arab nationalism has remained basically a *mashriqi* preserve and has not significantly penetrated political ideas in the Maghrib, where preference seems to be for
the concept of the territorial state. Morocco was never part of the Ottoman Empire and Algeria and Tunisia lost their connections with the Ottomans in 1830 and 1912 respectively. Unlike in the Mashriq (and Egypt), where the presence of sizeable native Christian minorities had imposed the secular-nationalist issue on the political agenda at an early stage, the main divide in the Maghrib was that between the 'Arabs' and the 'Berbers', and Islam (not Arabism) was more convenient as a unifying national bond. The French annexation of Algeria and attempts at cultural assimilation in Tunisia and Morocco encouraged that orientation by normally categorising Algerians (and other North Africans) simply as Muslims – since their nationality was meant, of course, to be French, not Arab. The help received by the Algerian revolution from Egypt and Syria in the 1950s and 1960s, and the relocation of the headquarters of the League of Arab States to Tunisia in the 1970s, have, among other things, helped in the 'political Arabisation' of the Maghrib. The exceptionally strong popular support for Iraq and condemnation for the Western 'role' in the Gulf crisis of 1990/1 provided ample proof that at least Pan-Arabist sentiments are alive and well in the Maghrib.

3.   The point of reference is sometimes *jahili* (i.e. pre-Islamic Arabian), sometimes Islamic – on the grounds that it was Islam that unified Arabia and initiated the large and civilised Arab-Islamic state; and sometimes 'Semitic' as manifested in attempts at classifying several ancient Near Eastern civilisations (Chaldean, Assyrian, Akkadian, Phoenician, etc.) as being 'Arab'.

References

'Aflaq, Michel (1970), *Fi sabil al-Ba'th* (In the Cause of the Rebirth), 4th edition, Beirut, Darl al-Tali'a

Ajami, Fouad (1981), *The Arab Predicament: Arab Political Thought and Practice since 1967*, Cambridge University Press

Amin, Samir (1978), *The Arab Nation*, London, Zed

Bin 'Abd Al-'Ali, 'Abd al-Salam (1992), 'Hawas al-hawiyya' (Identity-Mania), *Al-Hayat*, 23 November

Cleveland, William L. (1971), *The Making of an Arab Nationalist: Ottomanism and Arabism in the Life and Thought of Sati 'al-Husri*, Princeton University Press

Davis, Eric (1978), 'Theory and Method in the Study of Arab Nationalism', in *Review of Middle East Studies*, No. 3, London, Ithaca Press

Haim, Sylvia (1974), *Arab Nationalism: An Anthology*, Berkeley, University of California Press

Al-Husri, Sati' (1984/5), *Al-A'mal al-quawmiyya: Abhath Mukhtara* (The Nationalist Oeuvres: Selected Investigations), Beirut, CAUS

Ibrahim, Sa'd al-Din (1980), *Ittijahat al-Ma'y al-'am al-'arabi nahwa mas'alat al-Wahda* (Attitudes of the Arab Public Opinion Towards the Issue of Unity: An Empirical Study), Beirut, CAUS

Kazziha, Walid (1975), *Revolutionary Transformation in the Arab World: Habash and his Comrades from Nationalism to Marxism*, London, Charles Knight

Kedourie, Elie (ed.) (1985), *Nationalism*, rev. edition, London, Hutchinson

Nasr, Marlène (1981), *Al-Tasawwur al-qawmi al-ʿarabi fi fikr Jamal ʿAbd al-Nasir* (The Arab Nationalist Perception in the Thought of Nasser), Beirut, CAUS

Nassar, Nasif (1986), *Tasawwurat al-umma al-muʿasira* ... (Perceptions of the Contemporary Nation in Modern Arabic Thought), Kuwait, Muʾassasat al-Taqaddum al-ʿIlmi

Rouleau, Eric (1967), 'The Syrian Enigma: What is the Baʿth?', *New Left Review*, No. 45

Smith, Anthony D. (1991), *National Identity*, Harmondsworth, Penguin

Tibi, Bassam (1981), *Arab Nationalism: A Critical Enquiry*, trans., London, Macmillan

Ethnic consciousness

'Are the Cornish an ethnic minority?' asked *The Times* in 1992 (quoted in *Cornish Banner*, 1992, No. 70, p. 10). The note of incredulity in the question was soon tempered by a more perceptive analysis, in which the Commission for Racial Equality's current concern for the 'special characteristics' of contemporary Cornwall was discussed. This assessment reported not only the persistence of a Cornish identity, but also a heightening of ethnic consciousness in response to rapid socio-economic change in post-war Cornwall. In the Commission's words, the renewed sense of Cornishness was epitomised by the 'substantial number of indigenous Cornish people who felt disadvantaged compared with "incomers" in relation to class, income, housing, [and] employment' (*Cornish Banner*, 1992). *The Times*, in searching for an understanding of modern Cornwall, had however surprisingly stumbled across not merely a fragment, but in certain respects a microcosm, of a much wider global phenomenon – i.e. the growing assertion of ethnic consciousness in the modern world, as a result of wide-ranging social, economic and political change.

Ethnicity and modernity

In the 1950s and 1960s most political scientists considered that an essential feature of the process of 'modernisation' was the inevitable dilution of ethnic distinctiveness. The powerful assimilatory and homogenising agencies of mass-communication, social and geographic mobility, universal education, political participation, and institutional centralisation facilitated the erosion of diversity in the 'civic culture' of 'modern' societies. As late as 1972 a major textbook on political sociology could all but ignore the issue of ethnicity. It merely acknowledged that some 'subcultures may be politically consequential' (Dowse and Hughes, 1972, p. 226) and that notions of 'race' might inform the ideologies of nationalist movements. Historians, too, were in agreement, with the traditional Whig explanation that emphasised the inevitable and even desirable decline of ethnic diversity in any movement towards liberal-democratic modernity. At the other end of the spectrum, Marxist interpretations insisted that ethnicity was merely a 'false consciousness' which would surely disappear as the historical dialectic worked itself out.

Such collective confidence was misplaced. A closer examination of the evidence would have revealed that surveys in the United States since as early as 1914 had pointed to the persistence of ethnic pluralism. Ethnic diversity and consciousness survived stubbornly in the face of determined efforts by the state at integration and assimilation. The American 'melting-pot' was really a myth. Immigrant communities in the United States clung tenaciously to their sense of identity, which is the central characteristic of ethnic consciousness: the shared but separate common origin, value-set, culture, religion, race, nationality, territory, region, or historical experience with which a community or individual chooses to associate and affirm. Here perception is more important than reality, and in the United States the immigration experience often served to further elaborate myths of ethnic identity. Migration was inextricably interwoven into the fabric of Irish nationalism, while Zionism became in part an expression of the American-Jewish experience.

Nonetheless, whilst conventional wisdom could overlook this American dimension, it was unable to ignore the upsurge in ethnic consciousness that developed after the Second World War. Even as social scientists articulated their 'end of ethnicity' and 'homogeneous state' theories (e.g. Almond and Verba, 1963; Blondel, 1963), events were unfolding in modern Western states which would lead shortly to a fundamental reassessment (see Krejci and Velimsky, 1981; Rokkan and Urwin, 1982; Meny and Wright, 1985; Keating, 1988). There was, as Michael Keating wrote (1988, p. 1), a 'wave of "peripheral nationalist" movements which, confounding most orthodox wisdom, swept through advanced western countries in the 1960s and 1970s'. They challenged the territorial integrity, and even the *raison d'être* of states. They pointed not to homogeneity but to diversity. Scholars were now forced to adopt a new orthodoxy which stressed the importance of ethnic and territorial diversity.

The rise of nationalism in Scotland and Wales (together with the onset of renewed ethnic conflict in Northern Ireland), in the 1960s and 1970s, led observers systematically to dismantle the 'homogeneous Britain' paradigm and usher in a new perspective in which the United Kingdom had become a 'multi-national state' (Rose, 1970). In Spain, Castilian cultural and political hegemony was successfully challenged in the new democratic order that emerged after Franco. This involved the creation of a radically redefined, but often uneasy, state structure in which historic territories with developed levels of ethnic consciousness (such as the Basque Country, Catalonia, and Galicia) achieved significant measures of self-government. In France, the 1960s and 1970s also witnessed the emergence of various nationalist and regionalist groups, often with an ethnic identity as their ideological base. With the exception of Corsica, these groups did not seriously confront the integrity of the French state. Nevertheless it introduced a new element of diversity in what had been a highly centralised structure.

Ethnicity emerged as a political issue in other parts of Western Europe. In Belgium it led to a *de facto* division of the state into its Flemish and Walloon components, while in Italy the rise of separatist sentiment first in Sardinia and later in Lombardy and elsewhere on the mainland reminded observers that the Italian state was a relatively recent and possibly fragile construct. Friesians in the Netherlands and Lapps in Finland also re-emerged on the ethnic map of Western Europe, as did a host of other smaller ethnic minorities. Across the Atlantic in Canada, similar events were observable, with the assertion of a separate Quebeçois identity leading by the early 1990s to a constitutional impasse, in which the future shape, or even survival, of the Canadian state was in question.

Factors in the ethnic revival

Having acknowledged the existence and significance of ethnic diversity within modern Western states, scholars were now at pains to seek explanations for this apparent upsurge in ethnic consciousness since 1945. In marked contrast to the earlier orthodoxy, it became fashionable to argue that ethnicity had a primordial quality, with enduring ties of kinship, territory, language and religion that cut across class or other political variables. It was said to possess a dynamic of its own which could lead in certain circumstances to increased ethnic assertion and a heightening of ethnic consciousness. Stein Rokkan and Derek Urwin, however, have warned against too simplistic or mono-causal an explanation of diversity. They argued for 'a broader approach which stresses the dichotomy between centre and periphery, seeking to place ethnic variations in a general framework of geopolitical location, economic strength and access to the loci of decision-making' (1982, p. 2). Here the emphasis was on the historical processes of state-formation in Western Europe, especially the construction of symbiotic 'centre–periphery' relationships, with the 'peripheries' in general representing the territorial homes of ethnic minorities. Ethnic consciousness was to a considerable degree a function of this relationship. The extent of such consciousness is dependent in part upon the success of the 'centre' in securing the political, economic and cultural 'accommodation' of the periphery. This model, it was claimed, helps to explain the differing levels of ethnic assertion and constitutional response in the various Western European states since 1945. Bavaria, which enjoyed a considerable degree of accommodation, has been content within the federal West German state. Scotland, with its less generous accommodation in the United Kingdom, has been restive, while Catalonia has broken free from the 'accommodation'-denying policy of the old Franco regime and opted for a considerable measure of self-government.

Urwin has further argued that the centre-periphery relationship is itself dynamic in quality so that over time, levels of ethnic consciousness and assertion might be expected to vary within a particular state. This echoes Sidney Tarrow's (1977) analysis, which postulates periods or phases of peripherality, identifying not only a pre-modern 'Older Peripheralism' of territorial and cultural isolation, but also – in the era of Western European industrialisation – a 'Second Peripheralism' in which peripheries experienced economic and social marginalisation. To this has been added Payton's 'Third Peripheralism' (1992), which refers to a post-1945 movement in the centre-periphery relationship, in which the paralysis of economic and social marginalisation has been disturbed by new forces of rapid socio-economic change. In Wales, Cornwall, and similar peripheries elsewhere in Western Europe, heightened ethnic consciousness has been one result of this 'Third Peripheralism', seeking not only to maintain ethnic identity in the face of socio-economic change but also to furnish critiques of those policies that had facilitated change and to demand renewed constitutional 'accommodation' to ensure future protection from such policies. Thus, for example, Welsh activists sought to defend the Welsh language, to expose those policies that had allowed (even encouraged) widespread inward-migration from England, and to argue for a Welsh Assembly so that Wales might create and control its own socio-economic policy.

The emphasis in this analysis on ethnic assertion in the West in response to post-1945 socio-economic change is echoed in the work of Nathan Glazer and Daniel Moynihan (1975) and others, who argue that this upsurge in ethnic consciousness has in fact been a carefully calculated political act, indicative not of some primordial ethnic instinct but in fact of a pragmatic, voluntary and strategic group response to socio-economic needs. Ethnicity was not after all a core attachment but merely a factor that could be mobilised as desired by a particular territorial or other group in pursuit of economic or political goals. Inevitably, rapid socio-economic change provoked responses from threatened interest groups, and thus ethnic conflict was no more than interest group conflict, with ethnic consciousness being mobilised deliberately as an ideological device. From this perspective, ethnic consciousness was a post-1945 political idea *par excellence*, a strategy for marshalling threads of common interest in response to movements in socio-economic conditions. For others, ethnicity was busy transforming itself into a 'post-modernist' social category of increasing relevance, with Walker Connor (1977), pp. 19-45, concluding that ethnicity was likely to be enhanced rather than diluted by the onset of 'modernity'.

Anthony Smith reminds observers that this process of 'ethnic revival' is not confined to the regions of Western Europe that have latterly occupied academic attention. It is to be encountered elsewhere in both the developed and developing worlds. He cautions that 'the notion of ethnic revival implies . . . the pre-existence of ethnic ties' (1981, p. 70). He infers that purely functional, interest-related explanations of ethnic assertions should be treated circumspectly, but he also acknowledges that the post-war upsurge in ethnic consciousness has been a genuine transformation and not merely a restoration of earlier roles.

Certainly in the years after 1945 ethnic consciousness began to play an increasing role in American politics, not only through the perpetuation of the familiar Irish or Jewish lobbies, but in the emergence of an increasingly confident black consciousness movement, which led amongst other things to the civil rights crises of the 1960s. By the 1980s an important Hispanic lobby had also emerged, while in the 1970s Dee Brown's moving (1971) history of the American West assisted the rehabilitation and renewed accommodation of Red Indians as 'Native Americans' (their counterparts in Central and South America were less lucky). Similarly, a remarkable upsurge in Maori consciousness prompted a wide ranging reassessment of the nature of New Zealand, while in Australia there was a limited settlement of Aboriginal rights. Extensive immigration after the war from Southern and Eastern Europe and, more recently, from Asia also forced Australia to abandon notions of Anglo-Celtic homogeneity. This prompted the development of an official policy of 'multi-culturalism'[1] in which the expression of ethnic diversity has been actively encouraged. Interestingly, this Australian experience helped inform Britain's attempts to come to terms with the ethnic aspirations of its own immigrant communities, principally Afro-Caribbean and Asian, with a policy moving from benign assimilationism to a more proactive accommodation of diversity.

Ethnic consciousness in non-Western states

Notwithstanding the violence of Northern Ireland or the Basque Country, or the extreme disabilities suffered by communities such as the Indians in America or Aborigines in Australia, or indeed the extreme reluctance of institutions in states such as the United Kingdom to react to a heightening of ethnic consciousness, there was in the liberal-democratic structures of Western states an opportunity for a constitutional and peaceful resolution of ethnic issues and for the 'accommodation' of ethnic minorities. Unfortunately, this was rarely the case in so-called third world states. Even in democratic India, ethno-religious conflict in Kashmir, the Punjab and elsewhere was often characterised by widespread bloodshed. A major feature of the post-1945 upsurge in ethnic consciousness was the propensity for ethnic conflict in newly independent African and Asian states. Ironically, ethnic consciousness was often mobilised as an ideological weapon by nationalist elites in the anti-colonial struggle. The very names of new states such as Ghana and Mali are evocative of ethnic history and territoriality and provide evidence of strenuous attempts at nation-building.

It is true that a great many of these new states were 'artificial' in that their territorial extent and boundaries had been devised by imperial powers, without any consideration of ethnic make-up. For example, although the Ibo elite had played a major role in the 'Nigerianisation' of Nigeria in the period before British withdrawal, once independence had been achieved their aspiration shifted (in vain) to the creation of a separate Ibo state, Biafra. Similarly, the successful attainment of independence in the Belgian Congo was followed by the bloody attempt at secession by Katanga. In Sri Lanka, nearly forty years after the granting of independence, growing resentment felt by the politically eclipsed Tamil community (i.e. the former colonial elite) boiled over into civil war. In countries such as Uganda and Somalia, the collapse of coherent civil administration heralded widespread conflict as ethnic rivalries filled the political vacuum – ethnicity often being mobilised as a means of organising factions in the pursuit of scarce and dwindling resources. In many of these instances, political exclusion and/or economic inequality were powerful precipitators of ethnic consciousness; as in South Africa where the apparatus of apartheid systematically denied non-whites access to the political and economic fruits of an exclusive white-dominated state. But although Western liberal opinion approved of the consequent heightening of black consciousness, it has been shocked by the propensity for ethnic rivalry between elements of the non-white community just when black access to power seemed to be within reach.

Ironically, one territorial entity (Palestine) that might in its extent have corresponded, more or less, to an ethnic aspiration has instead been contested by two competing and virtually mutually exclusive ethnic groups, namely the Jews (Israelis) – motivated by the powerful ideology of Zionism – and the Palestinian Arabs who for the past forty years have increasingly integrated their identity within the broader assumptions of Arab ethnicity. Elsewhere in the Middle East, Arab states were for the most part the 'artificial' creation of British and French imperialism, producing a variety of territorial and other anomalies. Saddam Hussein, for example, was quick to exploit this point in his attempted annexation of Kuwait in 1990. The synthetic nature of Arab states has prompted a Pan-Arab ethnic consciousness which holds that all Arabs belong to a wider Arab nation, and that this fact should be reflected in political institutions. The Arab League was one such institution. Various attempts to create similar unities were mostly doomed to failure, because states such as Egypt, Syria, Iraq and even Libya have all vied for the leadership of the Pan-Arab ideal. Additionally, Arab states themselves are often not ethnically homogeneous (e.g. the existence of Kurdish communities in Iraq and Syria). Moreover, the ethno-religious sentiment of Pan-Islam, especially with its focus increasingly in revolutionary and non-Arab Iran, has ofen been a competing rather than complementary ideology to Pan-Arabism. The re-emergence of Pan-Turkism in the region during the 1980s, much of it associated with the disintegration of the Soviet Union, has been a further complicating factor.

Indeed, the collapse of the external, and then internal, Soviet empires in the late 1980s and early 1990s provides perhaps the most startling demonstrations of the political significance of ethnic consciousness in the post-war world.[2] Again, this experience caught many academic observers by surprise, earlier assumptions of homogeneity in the West matched by a similar set which considered that the impact of Marxist-Leninist ideology, the effect of one-party totalitarian rule, and the consequences of Soviet domination and economic/military integration, had created a similar homogeneity in Eastern Europe and the Soviet Union. However, as the era of *glasnost* and *perestroika* unfolded, with the attendant 'Sinatra doctrine' (in which the Soviet Union allowed its satellite states to 'do it their way'), the opposite proved to be the case. Not only did long-standing ethnic and attendant territorial issues (fossilised and unresolved in the communist era, despite the alleged succcess of 'federalism' in the Soviet Union) appear prominently in the range of newly released ambitions and expectations, but the frustration and intense difficulties in realising the economic and democratic dimensions of those aspirations were further cause for the disappointed and disillusioned to turn to the panacea of ethnic rivalry.

The remarkable speed with which German unification was achieved caused some alarm in Poland and elsewhere, raising the spectre of German nationalism, as concerns over the Oder-Neisse line re-emerged and as hitherto invisible ethnic German communities in Poland, Romania, the Ukraine and elsewhere resurfaced with demands of their own. Latvia, Lithuania and Estonia (which had been independent states within living memory) extricated themselves completely, but most components of the Soviet Union decided to participate in the transformation to the Commonwealth of Independent States – which itself proved a rather grudging confederation, with differences over economic, military and territorial issues continuing to fuel ethnic suspicion.

Although the division in 1993 of Czechoslovakia into its two constituent parts was achieved in a relatively amicable manner, elsewhere in the former Soviet empire the lack of appropriate political mechanisms to achieve satisfactory levels of 'accommodation' meant that ethnic disputes often led to large-scale bloodshed. Most notable was the war between Armenia and Azerbaijan, but in Moldavia there were extended clashes between the indigenous Romanian-speakers and post-1945 Russian settlers. Paradoxically, the most dangerous ethnic warfare to break out in the wake of the Soviet collapse was that in the former Yugoslavia. When the Soviet threat that had so motivated Titoism disappeared, the shaky *raison d'être* of Yugoslavia also vanished. Slovenia gained its independence with relative ease. Croatia seceded at the price of a civil war with Serbia which was the dominant ethnic-territorial element of the old state. It fought not only to contain ethnic aspirations amongst Hungarians and Albanians within its own borders, but also to annex neighbouring Serbian-settled districts. In the complex ethnic mosaic of Bosnia-Hercegovina, this drive for Greater Serbia had led by 1992 to the unscrupulous practice of 'ethnic cleansing', shocking the wider international community but also prompting other Balkan states such as Bulgaria, Albania and Greece (each with its own ethnic-territorial concern) to look on with increasing unease.

New world order?

The pattern that had emerged by the early 1990s, then, was one of pronounced ethnic consciousness. Despite all earlier predictions, ethnic consciousness remained an integral part of global politics and one whose contemporary significance was rising rather than in decline. In the West, states had generally weathered the ethnic assaults of the previous decades. Many had furnished new mechanisms of accommodation to meet ethnic demands. The growth of the European Community, for example, provided a forum for the expression and consideration of a variety of ethnic-regional issues. In stark contrast, however, the absence of such structures in the East, combined with the security vacuum left by the demise of the Warsaw Pact, did not augur well for the management of ethnic disputes. Elsewhere in the world the prospects for peaceful resolution were also slim. The new-found diplomatic authority and military credibility of the United Nations in the 'New World Order' could allow the UN to point to some success, but the likelihood of that organisation containing, let alone resolving, the multiplicity of ethnic crises seemed remote.

Notes

1. For an exhaustive discussion of 'multi-culturalism', see James Jupp (ed.), *The Australian People*, Sydney, Angus and Robertson, 1988.
2. A concise analysis of this process is contained in Victoria Syme and Philip Payton, 'Eastern Europe: Economic Transition and Ethnic Tension', in Michael C. Pugh (ed.), *European Security: Towards 2000*, Manchester University Press, 1992.

References

Almond, Gabriel A. and Verba, Sidney (1963), *The Civic Culture: Political Attitudes and Democracy in Five Nations*, Princeton University Press

Blondel, Jean (1963), *Voters, Parties and Leaders: The Social Fabric of British Politics*, Harmondsworth, Penguin

Brown, Dee (1971), *Bury My Heart at Wounded Knee: An Indian History of the American West*, London, Barrie and Jenkins

Connor, Walker (1977), 'Ethnonationalism in the First World', in M. J. Esman (ed.), *Ethnic Conflict in the Western World*, Cornell University Press, pp. 19–45

Dowse, Robert E. and Hughes, John A. (1972), *Political Sociology*, London, John Wiley and Sons

Glazer, N. and Moynihan, D. (1975), *Ethnicity: Theory and Experience*, Cambridge, MA, Harvard University Press

Keating, Michael (1988), *State and Regional Nationalism: Territorial Politics and the European State*, London, Harvester Wheatsheaf

Krejci, Jaroslav and Velimsky, Vitezslav (1981), *Ethnic and Political Nations in Europe*, London, Croom Helm

Meny, Yves and Wright, Vincent (eds.) (1985), *Centre-Periphery Relations in Western Europe*, London, Croom Helm

Payton, Philip (1992), *The Making of Modern Cornwall: Historical Experience and the Persistence of 'Difference'*, Redruth, Dyllansow Truran

Rokkan, Stein and Urwin, Derek W. (1982), *The Politics of Territorial Identity: Studies in European Regionalism*, London, Sage Publications

Rose, Richard (1970), *The United Kingdom as a Multi-national State*, Glasgow, University of Strathclyde Survey Research Occasional Paper No. 6
Smith, Anthony D. (1981), *Ethnic Revival in the Modern World*, Cambridge University Press
Tarrow, Sidney (1977), *Between Centre and Periphery: Grassroots Politicians in Italy and France*, New Haven, Yale University Press

Further Reading

Birch, Anthony H. (1989), *Nationalism and National Integration*, London, Unwin Hyman
Brass, P. (1985), *Ethnic Groups and the State*, London, Croom Helm
Rex, J. (1986), *Race and Ethnicity*, Oxford University Press
Williams, C. H. and Kofman, E. (1989), *Community Conflict, Partition and Nationalism*, London, Routledge

Glasnost and *perestroika*

Between them the two concepts of *glasnost* and *perestroika* encompass almost everything that Mikhail Gorbachev tried to accomplish in the years of reform between 1985–1990; and in some ways also everything that he failed to achieve. They acquired enormous symbolic significance not only within the USSR but outside it, particularly so in the case of *glasnost*. And they became objects of intense political struggle between the different social forces that emerged within Soviet society after 1987–8. In some respects they were never ideas at all in themselves but symbols that came to stand for a whole series of interrelated and very complex processes. Unravelling their meaning and significance in a limited space is not, therefore, an easy task.

Perestroika

Perestroika was the over-arching name given to a whole series of economic and political reforms, including *glasnost*, all of which were intended to serve the same underlying purpose, namely, the modernisation of the Soviet system rather than its transformation.

Perestroika has been consistently translated as 'reconstruction' or 'restructuring'. Even in the Russian context, however, this meant very little in itself. Joseph Stalin used the term *perestroika* on occasion to describe his transformation of Soviet society during the 1930s. But it is also translated in dictionaries in a more limited way as 'reorganisation' or 'reorientation' – of work patterns, institutions and so on. The term therefore needed considerable amplification if it was to have any significant effect on social action, and much therefore depended on how it was actually fleshed out in practical terms.

Perestroika did not represent a new philosophy, but rather a series of pragmatic solutions to the USSR's problems. This was reflected in Gorbachev's own use of the word which was always rather ambiguous. He originally used it in early 1985 to refer narrowly to the reform of the Soviet economic mechanism. It retained this as its essential core but by mid-1986 had also acquired a much broader meaning. From then on Gorbachev consistently equated *perestroika* with 'a genuine revolution in the minds and hearts of people', which was to encompass 'not only the economy but all other sides of society's life: social relations, the political system, the spiritual and ideological sphere, the style and work methods of the party' (quoted in Melville and Lapidus, 1990, p. 20). This call to 'revolution' captured the popular imagination but it was never quite clear to anyone what it was actually supposed to achieve or what, precisely, it represented. This is because the policies that were implemented in its name, and the explanations that accompanied them, appeared to be deeply contradictory.

On the one hand, they did very little to change the basic structures of Soviet society. Economic *perestroika* retained the basic principle of central planning on which the Soviet economic system had been built, although considerable efforts were made to streamline the enormous party-state bureaucracy that ran it and to introduce elements of autonomy and democracy into the system at lower levels. Political *perestroika*, referred to more usually as *demokratizatsiya* (democratisation), retained the Communist Party in its old position as the dominant force in the political system – known as the 'leading role of the party'. *Perestroika* also assumed that the Soviet federal system would retain its old highly centralised form. On the other hand, certain policies, notably *glasnost* and the multi-candidate elections introduced into the system of government (i.e. the soviets) in 1989 and 1990, set in motion social forces that did indeed revolutionise the Soviet system to the point of destroying it. The process of *perestroika* was, consequently, rather mystifying at the time both for the people who lived through it and for the people who watched it from abroad.

It is possible to understand the contradictory nature of *perestroika*, however, if we look at its underlying purposes which were always more limited than Gorbachev's rhetoric suggested. Put simply, Gorbachev ultimately wanted to create a modern democratic socialist system. He did not want to abandon the basic institutional principles of Soviet socialism (i.e. central planning, the leading role of the party, the soviets as organs of popular representation) which he considered to be the defining characteristics of the socialist system. But he did want a radical transformation of the ways in which these institutions functioned and related to each other. He wished to make them more democratic and more open, with their officials made more accountable and responsive to popular opinion, thereby giving the system as a whole a legitimacy based on genuine popular support. Accordingly, his reforms were concerned not so much with altering institutional structures as with changing the behaviour of the people who worked in them. In this respect Gorbachev's description of *perestroika* as primarily a revolution in hearts and minds was to be taken quite literally. He wanted to change people's consciousness and consequently their behaviour within the system, rather than the system itself.

Gorbachev believed it possible to do this because his analysis of the system's failings located their origins in what he called its Stalinist 'deformations' (Sakwa,

1990, p. 123). He grew increasingly critical of Stalinist practices. He argued that it was Stalinism, rather than the principle of central planning itself, that had been responsible for transforming the economy into an over-centralised, extraordinarily bureaucratic 'administrative command system' (White, 1991, p. 26), in which party-state officials were able, in principle at least, to dictate what should happen at almost every stage in the processes of wealth creation and distribution. And that it was also Stalinism, rather than the principle of one party rule *per se*, that had been responsible first for the creation of a repressive political system that excluded almost all public dissent, criticism and debate; and second for the transformation of the Communist Party into a bureaucratic mechanism concerned only with the perpetuation of its own dictatorial power. The result, in his view, had been the development of a grotesquely inefficient system which was almost totally insensitive to people's needs and in which party-state officials were able to wield enormous power without any public accountability whatsoever.

Gorbachev anticipated that the removal of these Stalinist deformations through the partial decentralisation of the economic and political system, the introduction of *glasnost* and limited democracy and the establishment of the rule of law would enable the advantages of Soviet socialism to be exploited to their full. The central planning system would be streamlined and combined with industrial democracy, quasi-market mechanisms like profit and loss accounting, and limited private enterprise where this could be of most benefit (notably in the service sectors). These changes would enable the rational allocation of resources by the planners at the top without stifling innovation, creativity and initiative at the bottom, as had always been the case in the past. Equally, increasing the flow of information in the system, and forcing party and state officials to subject themselves to proper elections and to the rule of law, would improve the policy process. It would open the process up to public scrutiny, sensitise it to popular needs and make officials publicly accountable for their decisions. At the same time, it would maintain their exclusive right to determine the overall direction of social development on a rational, scientific basis. In short, Gorbachev hoped to find a third way between the Stalinist version of socialism and the exploitation and inequalities of the capitalist system. He proposed combining the best of both worlds: overall political and economic guidance by the party and the central planners which would ensure the rational allocation of resources and the equitable distribution of wealth with elements of Western democratic and economic practice which would ensure that the central decision-makers could not abuse their power and would genuinely rule in society's best interests on the basis of a meaningful popular mandate.

In some ways it was an immensely idealistic vision. It was, however, impossible to implement because it rested on unworkable assumptions. For example, Gorbachev (somewhat naively) assumed that the Soviet population would not challenge the continued rights of the party once given the opportunity to do so. He also failed to grasp that there is a strong correlation between the principles on which institutions are founded and the ways in which the individuals who work in them behave. Whatever people may think in private, if they do not conform to the rules, the procedures and the cultures of the institutions for which they work, then those institutions cannot maintain their organisational integrity and would cease to function or turn into something else entirely. This is effectively what happened to Soviet institutions as a consequence of *perestroika*. Soviet citizens were able to speak out, to vote and, thereby, to challenge the behaviour of their rulers and force party officials, in particular, to be responsive to them. In this way, *perestroika* not only transformed the behaviour of individuals at all levels in the system, but in doing so, inevitably, and fatally, disorganised the institutions that held the system together and made it what it was. This applied, above all, to the Communist Party itself. *Perestroika*, therefore, achieved the opposite of what Gorbachev intended. Instead of providing the party, and through it the Soviet system, with a genuinely popular mandate, it simply revealed for all to see that a democratic one-party state is a contradiction in terms. *Glasnost* was instrumental in this process.

Glasnost

The word *glasnost* is not as easy to translate as *perestroika*. It has most commonly been translated as 'openness', but also variously as 'publicity', 'public disclosure', 'criticism'. One of the most authoritative Russian dictionaries defines its adjectival form *glasnyi* as 'that which is known or evident to all, not concealed, everywhere made public' (quoted in Melville and Lapidus, 1990, p. 28). The word *glasnost* is also associated in Russian with 'voice' and 'eye' and therefore with sight, enlightenment and the speaking out of truth (*ibid.*). *Glasnost* was not, therefore, Gorbachev's invention. Nor was he solely responsible for giving it its reformist overtones. It first appeared in a reformist context in 1861 when it was used to describe the slight lifting of state censorship that accompanied the great reforms of Tsar Alexander II. It was also used by party reformers in the 1970s to refer to the need for greater information flows both within the party and within local government (i.e. the soviets). By the time Gorbachev came to use it, therefore, it already had a considerable historical lineage. Its implications for practical politics, however, were somewhat ambiguous. On the one hand, *glasnost* had the potential to be extremely subversive of established institutions. Ordinary people were able to become active participants in the speaking out of truth, constraints were lifted from the media, and so on. On the other hand, it could also be understood as a process of controlled 'public disclosure' in which the authorities still made the essential decisions about what could be 'publicised' and, therefore, publicly discussed, and what could not – while retaining both the right and, more importantly, the *means* to silence those voices of which they disapproved. Much depended on how the policy of *glasnost* was actually fleshed out and implemented. In the event, Gorbachev's understanding of *glasnost* tried, unsuccessfully, to combine elements from both interpretations. He sought to retain the Communist Party's right, and in particular his own right as party leader, to determine the outer limits of what could be said in public. At the same time, he sought to encourage active popular participation in the discussion of the system's problems through the development of what he called a 'socialist pluralism of opinions' (Sakwa, 1990, pp. 229–30). This generated an enormous amount of conflict between those who wanted *glasnost*, and *perestroika* as a whole, to become genuine revolutions and those who wanted to retain them within limits. It also penetrated to the heart of the Soviet structure of power.

The coercive nature of the party's rule was not just the product of Stalinism, but reflected the party's basic principles of organisation. From its foundation at the beginning of the century, the Communist Party had justified its rule on firm ideological grounds. First, it asserted that it was the only genuine representative of the real interests of all working people, and as such there was no need for other political parties. Second, it claimed that it was the sole possessor of accurate, scientific knowledge, in the form of Marxism–Leninism, about the direction that social development should take. The practice that followed from these principles was inevitably dictatorial and coercive. Since the party knew what was in society's best interests, it followed that it had both the right and the obligation to dictate the direction, and oversee the implementation, of economic, political and social policy down to the very smallest details. Moreover, since party officials claimed to know everything and were always right by definition, they were not obliged to listen to specialist advice unless they chose to; they could not be challenged or called to account for their actions (except by their party superiors); and they could not be opposed when they intervened in matters about which they actually knew next to nothing. Finally, since the party was the sole repository of truth, it had the duty to eliminate or repress any individual or group that tried, publicly at least, to argue otherwise. Such opponents were designated 'anti-Soviet' and 'anti-Marxist' by definition.

Glasnost exploded these myths. In order to get Soviet citizens to speak out at all, Gorbachev had to remove not just censorship but the coercion and fear that had kept society in public subjection to the party for most of Soviet history. *Glasnost*, therefore, went hand in hand with Gorbachev's calls for the establishment of the rule of law and of a law-based state which would for the first time subject party members to civil law and protect citizens from the arbitrary abuse of official power. It was also given added impetus by the introduction of multi-candidate elections both within the party and in the country's legislatures (the soviets). Party candidates now had to listen to their constituents because for the first time Soviet voters were able to exercise some real choice about who would represent them. The reform drive was further encouraged by Gorbachev's own increasingly savage critiques of the party's Stalinist past and its Stalinist methods in the contemporary USSR. These indictments were highly significant because, beginning with Stalin, the General Secretary of the Communist Party of the Soviet Union (CPSU) became the final source of 'revealed truth' within the system.

By the same token, simply by enabling Soviet citizens, including party members, to speak their minds, to discuss the system's faults and enquire honestly into their causes, *glasnost* led to the rapid emergence of a diversity of opinions and interests, some of them vehemently anti-socialist. It also led to an orgy of truth-telling about the past and the present which revealed that the party did not know best, was not genuinely representative of any interests except its own, and that party rule had led directly to the colossal mess in which the country now found itself. *Glasnost* not only removed the essential basis of the party's power and control, but undermined the legitimacy of the system as a whole. The party could no longer silence dissident voices, nor prevent the emergence of a pluralism of, often highly critical, views about the system's failings. Consequently, party officials, Gorbachev included, could no longer convincingly maintain that only they knew what was in society's best interests. Their continued attempts to do so after the introduction of democratisation in 1988 simply served to increase popular radicalism and heighten public contempt for the party and all its works. It is no accident that *glasnost* and democratisation very quickly led to public demands (as early as 1988) for the abolition of the party's leading role, a demand that was finally conceded in March 1990, at which point *perestroika* as a party-led process of reform finally came to an end. In short, once unleashed, *glasnost*'s subversive potential could not be contained.

Glasnost was not, of course, solely responsible for destroying the Soviet system. Nonetheless, it might have been less disruptive had it not been for the multicandidate elections to the Soviet Congress of People's Deputies in 1989 and, more importantly, to the republican and local soviets in 1990. Where *glasnost* had given people the opportunity to speak out, the elections gave them the chance to act through the ballot box. It forced them to organise politically, in order to promote their candidates against the superior organisation of the CPSU. The result was the emergence of an embryonic political pluralism that the CPSU could not handle, and the election (particularly during 1990) of anti-party representatives. In some cases it led to anti-party republican governments (e.g. in Lithuania), which were able to challenge the party leadership from positions of real political power to the extent that they had a genuinely popular mandate. The electoral process destroyed the organisational integrity of the CPSU as a nationwide executive institution. In order to stand any chance of election, local party officials had to submit to local demands which frequently meant disobeying, and even disassociating themselves from, the central party leadership. And it created a situation in which the governments of the fifteen Union-republics which made up the Soviet federation were successfully able to challenge the demands of the Soviet centre in the cause of republican autonomy and independence. The revolutionary consequence was the chaotic, but remarkably bloodless, disintegration of the USSR from 1989 onwards and the subsequent emergence in late 1991 of fifteen newly independent states into the international arena.

Glasnost and *perestroika*: ramifications

The revolutionary effects of *perestroika* and *glasnost* were not restricted to the USSR alone and are still continuing to reverberate around the world even now.

At the global level, the Soviet bloc rejected extreme coercion and force as instruments of conflict resolution. The ideas of democratic restructuring, openness and fundamental human co-operation which is what, in part, these two concepts came to represent internationally (in the guise of Gorbachev's foreign policy of 'New Thinking') led to the ending of the Cold War and the reunification of Europe, symbolically at least. On the negative side, it has to be said that the disappearance of the Soviet superpower has led to a drastic destabilisation of international relations with which the world is still coming to terms.

Glasnost and *perestroika* captured the international imagination in other ways. Both terms, but particularly *glasnost*, entered the English language as symbolic antonyms for bureaucracy, secrecy and the power of big government. Their introduction in the USSR coincided with debates in the capitalist democracies about the nature of the state, the role of government, and the scale of individual rights and freedoms. The increased usage of these two terms heightened the perception that the Western democracies had become sclerotic, over-bureaucratised and over-secretive. It could be said that *glasnost* and *perestroika* threw into high relief the growing alienation of Western voters from politics. Their general thrust in favour of reducing the size and power of the state and enlarging the realm of individual freedoms coincided, at least superficially, with the political programmes of conservative governments then in power. For example, the Thatcher administration in Britain was particularly swift to make political capital out of this apparent convergence in order to promote its own ideological preferences.

Glasnost and *perestroika* also coincided with popular demands in a number of countries for greater democracy, greater freedom and greater self-determination for small nations. Although there is no way of proving it, it is difficult to avoid the conclusion that the dissolution of the USSR (partly as the result of the 'revolution from below' that *perestroika* encouraged) and the peaceful transfer of power in countries like Czechoslovakia has had an enormous and widespread influence on events. In Italy the state has been shaken to its core by judicial and popular protest against political corruption. In South Africa one cannot help feeling that former President De Klerk modelled himself on Mikhail Gorbachev. And in the former Yugoslavia, the struggle for national self-determination, fuelled at least in part by the successful struggles of nationalists in the USSR and the international community's willingness to legitimise those struggles, has reaped its most brutal harvest.

In short, *glasnost* and *perestroika* appeared to challenge old power structures in commonsense ways that people outside the USSR could readily understand and even identify with. In doing so, however, they have caused problems and raised issues without providing solutions. Gorbachev's search for a third way between

Stalinism and capitalism was not underpinned by a philosophy that enabled communist parties in the rest of the world to come to terms with the rapid loss of identity that beset them with the collapse of the USSR. Only the Chinese Communist Party, with its own version of communism and reform and with the enormous coercive resources at its disposal, has successfully withstood the process of disintegration. Smaller countries like Cuba and Vietnam, however, are presently under siege as are non-ruling communist parties elsewhere.

The problems which communism sought to end – poverty, inequality, exploitation and general human misery – have not gone away. Instead, they are getting worse and statist solutions to them have now been discredited. In some respects, socialism is having to return to its Christian roots in the search for alternatives. By the same token, democratic theory in the capitalist states has not been greatly enhanced by *perestroika*. The latter borrowed from this body of theory rather than adding to it. *Glasnost* and *perestroika* highlighted both some of the weaknesses and some of the strengths of Western democratic practices, but they did not provide new philosophical or theoretical means for commenting on them. They did, however, serve to demonstrate just how dangerous a process of genuine democratisation can be for established institutions and power structures. *Glasnost* and *perestroika* as concepts may subsequently fade into history. However, the democratic impulse which has driven political change for the last two centuries, and which is helping to drive change in Russia now, will undoubtedly outlast them, not least because *perestroika* gave it added impetus.

References

Melville, Andrei and Lapidus, Gail W. (eds.) (1990), *The Glasnost Papers: Voices on Reform from Moscow*, Boulder, CO, Westview Press

Sakwa, Richard (1990), *Gorbachev and his Reforms, 1985–1990*, London, Philip Allen

White, Stephen (1991), *Gorbachev and After*, Cambridge University Press

Further Reading

Morrison, John (1991), *Boris Yeltsin: From Bolshevik to Democrat*, Harmondsworth, Penguin

Sobchak, Anatoly (1992), *For A New Russia: The Mayor of St Petersburg's own Story of the Struggle for Justice and Democracy*, London, HarperCollins

Urban, Michael E. (1990), *More Power to the Soviets: The Democratic Revolution in the USSR*, Aldershot, Edward Elgar Publishing

Walker, Rachel (1993), *Six Years that Shook the World: Perestroika – the Impossible Project*, Manchester University Press

White, Stephen (1993), *After Gorbachev*, Cambridge University Press

Terrorism

The concept

The concept of terrorism is often totally misused, as when it is employed as a synonym for political violence in general or when it is used as a pejorative for any insurgent campaign of which we disapprove. It is also frequently used loosely and inconsistently. In this respect it shares the same problem of other key strategic political concepts, such as 'revolution', 'imperialism', and 'democracy'. None of these concepts lends itself to universally agreed one-sentence definition yet all of them are indispensable for political discourse, and there is a sufficiently widely shared acceptance of the core meaning of such concepts for them to play a central role in international political and social scientific debate.

Alex Schmid and Albert Jongman have produced impressive evidence of the extent to which a minimum consensus definition of terrorism has become accepted among the international community of social scientists who study conflict (1988, pp. 1–32). Equally significant is the development of a whole body of international resolutions, conventions, and agreements dealing with aspects of the prevention, suppression, and punishment of acts of terrorism,[1] in which there is near-universal acceptance of the terminology used to describe the form of behaviour to be condemned or prohibited. Contemporary international academic, diplomatic, and juridical debates on terrorism no longer become bogged down in days of definitional debate. The major disputes that arise concern culpability for specific attacks or for sponsoring or directing them, and over the kind of international measures that should be taken in response.

Terrorism is neither a political philosophy nor a movement, nor is it a synonym for political violence in general. It is a special means or method of conflict which has been employed by a wide variety of factions and regimes. It is premeditated and systematic, and aims to create a climate of extreme fear or terror. The modern words *terror* and *terrorism* are derived from the Latin verbs *terrere*, to cause to tremble, and *deterre*, to frighten from. *Terrorism* and *terrorist* did not come into use until the period of the French Revolution in the 1790s. The term was used by Edmund Burke in his polemic against the French Revolution, and came to be used to denote those revolutionaries who sought to use terror systematically either to further their views or to govern, whether in France or elsewhere.

A key feature of terrorism is that it is directed at a wider audience or target than the immediate victims. It is one of the earliest forms of psychological warfare. The ancient Chinese strategist, Sun Tzu, conveyed the essence of the method when he wrote 'kill one, frighten ten thousand'. An inevitable corollary is that terrorism entails attacks on random and symbolic targets, including civilians, in order to create a climate of extreme fear among the wider group. Terrorists often claim to be carefully selective and discriminating in their choice of targets, but to the community that experiences a terrorist campaign the attacks are bound to seem arbitrary and indiscriminate. In order to create the widespread sense of fear he seeks, the terrorist deliberately uses the weapons of surprise and disproportionate violence in order to create a sense of outrage and general insecurity. As Raymond Aron (1966, p. 170) observes: 'An action of violence is labelled "terrorist" when its psychological effects are out of all proportion to its purely physical result . . . The lack of discrimination helps to spread fear, for if no one in particular is a target, no one can be safe.' It is this characteristic which differentiates terrorism from tyrannicide and individual political assassination.

As Hannah Arendt has observed (1973, pp. 141ff.), the belief that one could change a whole political system by assassinating the major figure has clearly been rendered obsolete by the transition from the age of absolutist rulers to an age of governmental bureaucracy. In all but a handful of regimes today real power is wielded by a bureaucratic elite of anonymous or faceless officials. Arendt provides a powerful explanation for the fact that the age of bureaucracy has coincided with the burgeoning of political terrorism. Terrorism has become for its perpetrators, supporters and sponsors, the most attractive low-cost, low-risk but potentially high-yield method of attacking a regime or a rival faction. The bomb plot against Hitler, had it succeeded, would have been an act of tyrannicide, not of terrorism. Who can deny that Hitler was the linchpin of the Nazi system? Is it possible to find analogous cases today where the removal of an all-powerful dictator would dramatically change the system? Some have argued that Saddam Hussein is one such case, but others suggest that if he were to be assassinated he would be succeeded by a powerful Ba'thist general of comparable brutality.

The concept of terrorism used in the contemporary academic literature is essentially political. What about the use of terrorist methods in the name of a religious cause? Or for the pursuit of criminal gain? It is true that militant religious fundamentalists have often throughout history waged holy terror as part of a holy war, and there is much concern about the rise of contemporary fanatical Islamic fundamentalist groups such as Hizbollah, Hamas, and Al-Gama'a Al-Islamiyya. But the major reason why moderate Muslim leaders and secular movements see these particular fundamentalist groups as such a threat is precisely because their revolutionary Islamic agenda aims not merely at the purifying of religious practice but at the overthrow of existing governments and their replacement by fundamental theocracies. Hence these movements are inherently religious *and* political. The worrying trend whereby powerful criminal gangs, such as the Italian Mafia (Jamieson, 1989) and the Latin American narco-barons (Clutterbuck, 1990, pp. 89–114), have adopted some of the tactics and weapons of terrorist groups, does pose grave problems for the relevant law-enforcement authorities. But it does not detract from the value of the core concept of political terrorism. In reality the overwhelming majority of perpetrators of contemporary terrorism use the weapon to influence political behaviour.

Typology

It is important to note that the above defining criteria of political terrorism are broad enough to encompass states' use of terror as well as that performed by groups. Typologically it is useful to distinguish *state* from *factional* terror. Normally, in the literature, a state's use of terror is referred to as terror, while sub-state terror is referred to as terrorism. This distinction is employed through-out this chapter. Historically, states have conducted terror on a far more massive and lethal scale than groups. They have employed terror as a weapon of tyranny and repression and as an instrument of war. Another important distinction can be made between *international* and *domestic* terrorism: the former is terrorist violence involving the citizens of more than one country, while the latter is confined within the borders of one country, sometimes within a particular locality in the country. This distinction is useful for analytical and statistical purposes. However, in reality, it is hard to find an example of any significant terrorist campaign that remains purely domestic: any serious terrorist campaign actively seeks political support, weapons, financial assistance and safe haven beyond its own borders.

Once we move beyond these very broad categories it is useful to employ a basic typology of contemporary perpetrators of terrorism based on their underlying cause or political motivation.

Nationalist terrorists

These are groups seeking political self-determination. They may wage their struggle entirely in the territory they seek to liberate, or they may be active both in their home area and abroad. In some cases they may be forced by police or military action or by threat of capture, imprisonment or execution to operate entirely from their places of exile. Nationalist groups tend to be more capable of sustaining protracted campaigns and mobilising substantial support than ideological groups. Even those nationalist groups that can only claim the support of a minority of their ethnic constituency (e.g. IRA (Irish Republican Army), ETA (Basque Homeland and Liberty)) can gain political resonance because of their deep roots in the national culture for which they claim to be the authentic voice.

Ideological terrorists
These terrorists seek to change the entire political social and economic system either to an extreme left or extreme right model. In the 1970s and 1980s studies of ideological terrorism focused on the extreme left, because of the pre-occupation with groups such as the Red Army Faction in Germany and the Red Brigades in Italy. Yet, as Walter Laqueur (1977) observes in his magisterial general history of terrorism, the dominant ideological orientation of European terrorism between the world wars was fascist. And it is neo-Nazi and neo-fascist groups which are behind so much of the racist and anti-immigrant violence in present-day Germany and other European countries. The Red Army groups so active in the 1970s and 1980s have now largely faded away, the victims of their own internal splits, determined law enforcement by their respective police and judicial authorities, and changing political attitudes among young people in the post-Cold War era.

Religio-political terrorists
The most frequently cited examples of this type of terrorism are groups such as Hizbollah and Hamas. But it is important to bear in mind that militant funda-mentalist factions of major religions other than Islam have also frequently spawned their own violent extremist groups. Striking examples can be found among Sikhs, Hindus, and Jews, and there is a well documented link between certain Christian fundamentalist groups and extreme right-wing terrorism in North and Central America.

Single-issue terrorists
These groups are obsessed with the desire to change a specific policy or practice within the target society, rather than with the aim of political revolution. Examples include the violent animal rights and anti-abortion groups.

State-sponsored and state-supported terrorists
States use this type of terrorism both as a tool of domestic and foreign policy. For example, when the Iranian regime sends hit-squads to murder leading dissidents and exiled political leaders they are doing so for domestic reasons, to intimidate and eradicate opposition to the regime. However, when North Korea sent its agents to mount a bomb attack on the South Korean government delegation on its visit to Rangoon, the communist regime was engaging in an act of covert warfare against its perceived 'enemy' government in the South, an act designed to further their foreign policy aim of undermining the Republic of South Korea. State sponsors may use their own directly recruited and controlled terror squads, or choose to act through client groups and proxies. They almost invariably go to some lengths to disguise their involvement, in order to sustain plausible deniability. The ending of the Cold War and the overthrow of the Eastern European communist one-party regimes and the former Soviet Union certainly removed in one fell swoop the Warsaw Pact's substantial network of sponsorship

and support for a whole variety of terrorist groups. But this does not mean that state sponsorship has ceased to be a factor in the international terrorist scene. Countries such as Iraq, Iran, Syria, Libya, North Korea, and Sudan are still heavily involved.

Effectiveness and motivation

How effective has terrorism been as a weapon for attaining political objectives since 1945? History shows that terrorism has been more effective as an auxiliary weapon in revolutionary and national liberation struggles. Most of the key modern theorists and leaders of revolutionary insurgency, such as Mao Tse Tung and Che Guevara, have recognised the dangers of depending on terrorism and have come down against giving it the major role in the struggle for revolution. The few cases where terrorism played a major part in bringing about sweeping political change arose in a limited number of colonial independence struggles against foreign rule. Included in this group would be the circumstances surrounding the end of the Palestine Mandate after the terrorist campaigns of Irgun (National Military Organisation) and Stern (Fighters for the Freedom of Israel) and the British decision to withdraw from the Suez Canal zone base together with the campaigns which led the British to withdraw from Cyprus and Aden, and the French to withdraw from Algeria. In all these cases special conditions existed which made terrorism a more potent weapon: (i) due to humanitarian and judicial restraints the occupying power was unwilling to carry through draconian measures to wipe out the terrorist organisations; (ii) in each case there were inter-communal power struggles within the colony which rendered a peaceful diplomatic settlement and withdrawal difficult if not nigh impossible; (iii) the terrorists who succeeded in these conditions (as in Aden up until 1968) enjoyed massive if not solid support from their own ethnic groups, and this created an almost impenetrable barrier for the intelligence branches on which the government security forces depended for success, and a vast reservoir of active and tacit collaboration and support for the terrorist operatives. Even taking into account the influence of terrorism as an auxiliary tactic in revolutionary and independence struggles, and in the rise of fascism between the First and Second World Wars, the overall track record of terrorism in attaining major political objectives is abysmal.

But if this historical assessment is correct we are left with the thorny problem of explaining why, in the 1990s, political terrorism remains such a popular weapon among such a wide range of groups around the world. There are at least four hypotheses that may help provide an answer to this question. They are by no means mutually exclusive: (i) some terrorists may be poor students of history and may continue to believe that they can repeat the success of groups such as EOKA (National Organisation of Cypriot Fighters) in Cyprus and the FLN (National Liberation Front) in Algeria, not realising that their own situations are not truly colonial in this sense, and therefore not comparable; (ii) some may fully recognise the severe limitations of terrorism as a means of attaining strategic goals, but may see sufficient tangible short-term rewards from terrorism, such as huge publicity, the gaining of ransoms, securing the release of fellow terrorists from gaol etc., to make it worthwhile in their view to continue to use it as an auxiliary weapon; (iii) some may be motivated by the *expressive* value of terrorist activity rather than by its *instrumental/operational* value, and may wish to continue the terrorist campaign primarily because it is a relatively quick and easy way to express their hatred of their opponents and their belief in the justice of their cause; and (iv) some may become addicted to the business of terrorist operations and material gain from extortion and racketeering by the group and may be unable to kick the habit. Politically motivated terrorism is generally justified by its perpetrators on one or more of the following grounds: (i) any means are justified to realise an allegedly transcendental end (in Weber's terms, 'value-rational' grounds); (ii) closely linked to (i) is the claim that extreme violence is an intrinsically beneficial, regenerative, cathartic and enabling deed regardless of other consequences; (iii) terrorism can be shown to have 'worked' in the past, and is held to be either the 'sole remaining' or 'best available' method of achieving success (in Weber's terms 'instrumental-rational' grounds); (iv) the morality of the just vengeance or 'an eye for an eye and a tooth for a tooth'; and (v) the theory of 'the lesser evil' which assumes that greater evils will befall us or our nation if we do not adopt terror against our enemies.

Problems of democratic response

Unless we wish to live in an anarchic world of unrestrained egoism the individual terrorist cannot be allowed to exert the petty tyranny of the bomb and the gun. Any society which enjoys democratic government under the rule of law must, as a matter of basic principle, do its best to protect the life, property, and well-being of all its citizens: it must endeavour to prevent any violations of their basic human rights. Terrorism poses other significant risks and dangers in a democratic society. If it takes hold it may help to encourage or inspire a wider rebellion, which could gravely damage or undermine the democratic government. Prolonged and intensive terrorist campaigns can also do serious harm to the electoral system and the processes of inter-party debate and collaboration. Through intimidation and terror it can polarise relations between communities and destroy the middle ground of political bargaining and compromise. Nor should we underestimate terrorism's capacity to inflict economic damage, by destroying and scaring away investment, disrupting trade and poisoning labour relations. Nor should we overlook the destructive long-term effects of protracted and intensive terrorist campaigns on community relations. When whole generations grow up in a climate of violence, inter-communal hostility and suspicion, whole communities tend to develop the mentality of beleaguered ghettos, and it becomes an impossible task to reconstruct the inter-communal trust and co-operation which is the basis of a civil society. In particularly grave circumstances of escalating terrorism the situation can rapidly develop into full-scale inter-ethnic or inter-religious civil war.

The challenges of severe domestic terrorism pose major dilemmas for democratic policy-makers and institutions. The government and its security advisers and criminal justice system cannot simply do nothing in the face of increasing terrorism. They have a clear duty to protect the life and property of citizens and to uphold the law. Their central dilemma is that by taking harsh measures to deal with the emergency they may destroy the very fabric of freedom under the law which they have a duty to defend.

Democratic governments and societies attempting to respond to severe domestic terrorism face a number of acute dilemmas. If they commit the military in support of the civil power because the situation is beyond the capabilities of the police, there are inevitable dangers of military overreaction. The army may well be seen as the last line of defence, but soldiers are trained for an external defence role, not for peacekeeping in support of the police. Soldiers do not find it easy to cope with the frustrations of this role over long periods, being forced to operate at mid-levels of coerciveness while presenting a constant target for terrorists familiar with the local terrain. There is also the danger that once the police and the public become used to the deployment of troops in support of the civil war it becomes politically almost impossible for the government to withdraw them.

In their attempts to strike the right balance in their response to severe domestic terrorism democratic governments also confront a number of dilemmas concerning civil liberties. For example, intensive intelligence gathering and surveillance by the security authorities has led to the development of vast computerised data banks of personal information covering vast numbers of citizens, and experience has shown that good intelligence can save lives and is the key to defeating terrorism in an open society. But how can one avoid the intelligence system intruding on the ordinary citizen's right to privacy? Is the development of fine-grained computers for security purposes, computerised identity cards for access control and increasingly ubiquitous security camera surveillance bringing us ineluctably to a Big Brother state?

Yet it would also be a grave mistake to overlook the dilemmas of underreaction and the violations of the most basic rights suffered by the victims of terrorism. If the police and the judicial authorities lack the necessary legal powers, procedures, witness collaboration and witness protection to secure the conviction of terrorists, and those who direct terrorist organisations, how can the innocent be protected? And how can citizens have any confidence in the legal system and the government as a whole? In such circumstances vigilante groups and private armies proliferate, virtual 'no go' areas spring up and law and order are undermined. Every terrorist situation is different and the tightrope between underreaction and overreaction is pitched at a different height and angle. It would be foolish to pretend that there is any universal formula that can be applied. The key underlying principles that must be followed are: first, that all measures taken to prevent and combat terrorism must be compatible with the maintenance of a fully operative democracy and rule of law, and second, that emergency laws should be appropriate and proportionate in the light of the level of violence and must be frequently reviewed by parliament and rescinded when no longer necessary.

The dilemmas faced by democratic states confronting attacks on their citizens by foreign terrorists can, under certain circumstances, pose even more daunting problems to policy-makers. For example, when the US diplomatic staff were taken hostage in Teheran in 1979 the situation developed into a major national security issue. Following the failure of the hostage rescue mission in April 1980, President Carter's administration became increasingly the target of domestic political criticism for its alleged weakness in handling the crisis. It became an election issue, exploited to full effect by the Republican candidate, Ronald Reagan, and the White House became locked into a desperate search for a way of gaining the freedom of the hostages that was compatible with national security and national honour. However, in due course President Reagan's administration was to suffer its worst, and entirely self-inflicted, political disaster over its handling of the crisis concerning the US hostages held by pro-Iranian terrorists in Lebanon (Draper, 1991). The Iranian arms-for-hostages affair marked some of the highest figures in the government and almost undermined the president himself. By a secret conspiracy to obtain the hostages' freedom by supplying weapons to Iran and then ploughing the profits of the arms deal into the Contra campaign in Nicaragua, the Reagan administration was simultaneously flouting the policy of Congress regarding Nicaragua and its own declaratory policy of no ransoms and no deals for terrorists.

The US government and other Western policy-makers have also attempted to grapple with the problem of finding an appropriate response to state-sponsored terrorist attacks against their own citizens. One form of response attempted has been economic sanctions. In a very limited form these were in summer 1993 being applied against Libya because of Colonel Gaddafi's failure to hand over suspects indicted for their alleged role in the Pan Am 103 bombing over Lockerbie in 1988. In practice it is impossible to make sanctions work effectively without the full co-operation of the major industrial countries. The reality is that some countries are unwilling to sacrifice what they see as important economic interests for the sake of international action against terrorism which did not directly involve their own nationals in any case. Faced with this dilemma many countries are unwilling to place the collective security interest in suppressing state-sponsored terrorism before their national economic self-interest.

It was partly their wish to avoid the frustrations of ineffective international economic measures, and partly a desire by US presidents to prove to their public that they can act decisively against terrorist states, that led President Reagan to bomb Libya in 1986. Similar considerations led President Clinton to bomb Iraq in 1993, following the discovery of an alleged plot by Iraqi agents to assassinate former President George Bush during his visit to Kuwait. There is no evidence that military reprisals of this kind cause state sponsors to abandon terrorism. The Gaddafi regime certainly does not appear to have abandoned the weapon after April 1986. Since the ending of the Cold War and the dismantling of the Soviet Union the main pressure on state sponsors has been the changed global strategic environment. When there is no rival superpower to go to for support and assistance, a state such as Syria finds it in its interest to avoid confrontation with the United States. And even the Iranian regime may be prepared to modify its international behaviour in order to improve its prospects of freeing frozen assets, and obtaining access to technology, arms, markets, and credits.

In retrospect the international problems caused by spectacular incidents of terrorism of the 1970s and 1980s, such as the Munich Olympics massacre, the Teheran hostage crisis of 1979–81, the suicide truck bombings against US and French troops in 1983, and Lockerbie in 1988, are likely to pale in significance in comparison to the mass terror of 'ethnic cleansing' (genocide) and the atrocities of the savage ethnic and ethno-religious wars of Bosnia, the Armenian–Azerbaijani conflict, Sri Lanka, Kashmir, Sudan and Angola.

The major paradox of the post-Cold War era is that the demise of the communist systems of state terror in Eastern Europe and the former Soviet Union did not bring an end to terror and political violence. National independence, economic freedom and democratisation have provided the citizens of these countries with the opportunities of peaceful co-operation and genuine political freedom. But as we see in Bosnia and elsewhere, some ethnic groups have taken advantage of their new found freedom to strike out at their neighbour's territory, using military aggression and terror against civilians to change the demographic map. As Barry Posen (1993) has perceptively observed, the security dilemma conventionally applied by the realists solely to relations between states applies with equal force to the rivalries between ethnic groups. In Bosnia and elsewhere we have seen the re-emergence in Europe of mass terror used as a weapon of 'ethnic cleansing' or genocide on a scale not seen since the regimes of Hitler and Stalin.

It is tragic that the major European powers, the European Community and the United Nations have proved unable to intervene effectively to stop the atrocities. At the time of writing (August 1993) it appears that the main aggressors in Bosnia, the Serbs, are about to have their project of a Greater Serbia legitimated by yet another 'peace plan'. Yet international appeasement will only encourage other would-be ethnic expansionists to try the policy of mass terror to achieve 'ethnic cleansing'.

The central lesson from the twentieth century experience of the relationship between terror, terrorism and freedom is that terror is the child of tyrannies, of hatred, of ideological dogmatism.[2] Strong and vigorous liberal, open societies are the best protection against terrorist challenges to democratic politics. The best antidote towards terrorism and terror and other major violations of human rights is therefore greatly to strengthen the forces of democracy and the international machinery for peacekeeping and peacemaking. In the light of recent international history there is certainly no guarantee that progress towards greater democracy, peace, harmony, and stability will continue.

Notes
1. A useful collection of the texts of these international measures, together with an authoritative commentary, is provided in Robert Friedlander, *Terrorism: Documents of International and Local Control*, vols. 1–4, Oceana Publications Inc., Dobbs Ferry, 1970–84.
2. For a discussion of the relationship between terrorism and freedom see Paul Wilkinson, 'Observations on the Relationship of Terrorism and Freedom', in Lawrence Howard (ed.), *Terrorism: Roots, Impact, Responses*, Praeger, New York, 1992, pp. 135–66.

References
Arendt, Hannah (1973), 'On Violence', in *Crises of the Republic*, Harmondsworth, Penguin
Aron, Raymond (1966), *Peace and War*, London, Weidenfeld and Nicholson
Clutterbuck, Richard (1990), *Terrorism and Guerrilla Warfare*, London, Routledge
Draper, Theodore (1991), *A Very Thin Line: The Iran Contra Affair*, New York, Simon and Schuster
Jamieson, Alison (1989), *The Modern Mafia*, Conflict Studies, No. 224, Research Institute for the Study of Conflict and Terrorism, London
Laqueur, Walter (1977), *Terrorism*, London, Weidenfeld and Nicholson
Posen, Barry (1993), 'The Security Dilemma and Ethnic Conflict', *Survival*, Vol. 35, No. 1 (spring), pp. 27–47
Schmid, Alex P. and Jongman, Albert J. *et al.* (eds.) (1988), *Political Terrorism: A New Guide to Actors, Authors, Concepts, Data Bases, Theories, and Literature*, 2nd edition, Amsterdam, North Holland Publishing Co., pp. 1–32. This volume also contains an invaluable bibliography.

Further Reading
Laqueur, Walter (1987), *The Age of Terrorism*, London, Weidenfeld and Nicholson
O'Sullivan, Noel (ed.) (1986), *Terrorism, Ideology and Revolution: The Origins of Modern Political Violence*, Brighton, Wheatsheaf
Wilkinson, Paul (1994), *Terrorism and the Liberal State*, 3rd edition, Basingstoke, Macmillan

Democratic renewal

Crisis of democracy

Throughout the Western democratic world, political systems and establishment politics are under pressure. Popular respect for politicians and democratic institutions is everywhere in decline. Politicians are seen to be either out of touch or on the make, indifferent or incompetent – but above all, failing the people they purport to serve. A crisis of demands and expectations is developing as politicians appear unable to deliver what their people have come to expect. And a crisis of democracy is developing as people have less and less confidence in the ability of their politicians or democratic institutions to provide answers and solutions to the problems they face.

The 'end of history' brigade should note the irony. At just the moment when Western liberal democracy in concert with liberal market capitalism became triumphant over authoritarian command societies, our present nineteenth century model of parliamentary democracy seems itself to be reaching the limits of its own utility and effectiveness. As democracy takes root in countries around the world previously dominated by one-party rule and dictatorship, parliamentary democracy seems more ineffective than at any time since the Second World War.

The political contract and the political challenge in Britain

Politics in advanced democracies has been founded in this half century on an implicit 'contract' between the politician and the voter. The voter gives the politician power and the politician in return provides – at best for the whole nation, at worst for their own supporters – security (through national defence, law and order, employment, health and social security assistance) and the economic growth to provide a rising standard of living. The gap that is opening up between politicians and people is a gap that has emerged as this old political 'contract' has broken down.

Over the decades, the costs of welfare, health care, and other public provision have risen dramatically but, fuelled by the promises of politicians, so have expectations. The effects have been exacerbated by a culture of decision-making in Britain that is secretive rather than open, concentrated rather than dispersed, and exclusive rather than inclusive. Since people are the passive recipients of decisions made for them, not the masters of those decisions, there is no sense of ownership of policy decisions, or of responsibility for the consequences. Moreover, the strains on our political system are not going to lessen – they are going to grow. Our future is a future of challenges: the challenge of resourcing the welfare state in the face of demographic change and rising social costs; the challenge of competing effectively in a total global economy; the challenge of altering radically our lifestyle in order to save our environment; the challenge of maintaining peace in an increasingly fractured but interdependent world. And as we are forced to make the difficult decisions necessary to confront these challenges, it is profoundly dangerous that our political system is held in such low esteem and appears so ineffective.

Take the future of Beveridge's post-1945 welfare state. The resource implications of an ageing population, shrinking tax-base, increasing demand and rising social costs are presenting some unpalatable choices. Under pressure of public expectations and under-resourcing, our welfare state is visibly creaking under the strains. The public resent the cuts in services, the tightening of benefits, the rationing (through waiting lists) of health care in the National Health Service – not least because they have been led to believe that these services and benefits were being protected. Yet while costs are rising enormously, 'lower taxation' appears to have become the number one national political priority. At the same time politicians find it harder and harder to deliver what they have led people to expect. All they leave in the wake of paltry political debate is diminishing respect for politicians and disillusionment with the political system.

In the NHS, where the consequences of demographic change and increasing demands are compounded by the spiralling costs of medical technology, there is no rational debate about resource implications, or about how to prioritise health care demands on the public purse. In its absence, the health debate rages around emotive case-studies and claim and counter-claim about cuts. The people politicians are meant to serve are shielded from the real problems and challenges in health care provision, and left disillusioned with both the service and the politicians.

Similarly, in the debate about employment: the combination of demographic changes, shifting employment patterns, and new technology is having an ever-greater impact on all sectors of employment. Yet the debate on the issue remains little more than a matter of headline reactions to monthly employment statistics. There is no wide-ranging, rational and open assessment of how we redefine the traditional notion of 'full employment' and manage broader changes to ensure work, reward and opportunity for all.

Instead of candour about the problems we face, and co-operation in addressing them, our national political debate has become a sterile combination of confrontation and point-scoring and the public know it. Yet never has such candid debate been more desperately needed. Global economic trends make highly unlikely the levels of economic growth in the next ten years that will be needed to meet these challenges in traditional ways. The growing inter-dependence of the global economy is progressively diminishing the control of national politicians over their own economies. Indeed, as Robert Reich (1993, p. 3) has argued, in an emerging economy of 'global enterprise webs' – in which the generation of 'national wealth' will depend solely upon how much value each nation's citizens can add to the global economy – there will no longer be national economies as we have come to understand the concept. Even within this global economy, the broad shift of economic might away from the old powers of the Atlantic shore to emerging forces of the Pacific Rim is likely to render Western European countries much less able than South-East Asian competitors to achieve dramatic levels of economic growth. The weakening of national political power internationally over the last forty years, in the wake of European integration and the globalisation of the world economy, is mirrored at home by a substantial decline in the authority of the state in the wake of dramatic changes in the nature of society. British society today is characterised more by a market-driven egalitarianism than by deference and rigid hierarchy, more by diversity and choice than by broad conformity. It is more uncertain, less rule-bound, more heterogeneous. Although politicians resolutely refuse to acknowledge it, the state no longer holds the same nodal position it once did.

These seismic shifts in our society, and the economic context in which they are taking place, pose huge challenges – to established thinking and institutions of the post-war welfare state; to entrenched attitudes about Britain's place in the world; to traditional assumptions about what it is the state's duty to provide; and about the entitlements and responsibilities of citizens. And yet politicians con-tinue to pretend that nothing has changed. They continue to pretend that our political institutions, and especially Westminster, have supreme control over the nation's affairs, when more and more events are determined by forces beyond our national control – decisions which are taken in the European Community, in multinational boardrooms, or in the currency markets well beyond the influence of Westminster.

But if political leaders appear increasingly paralysed by the rising tide of internal problems like crime, or external challenges like Bosnia, individual citizens themselves appear to have correspondingly less control over the institu-tions and people making decisions and exercising power in Britain. More and more decision-making is passing into the hands of unaccountable appointees on unelected boards, trusts, and quangos. And a growing section of society, excluded from the benefits of Galbraith's 'culture of contentment' (1992), are losing all sense of a stake in the cohesive bonds which hold that society together. Powerlessness leads to alienation. Alienation to hopelessness. Hopelessness to vulnerability to extremist and anti-establishment ideas and groups.

So we see, throughout Western democracies, people rejecting establishment politics. It was seen in the referendum votes on the Maastricht Treaty in Denmark and France. It has been seen in the collapse of the traditional party structure in Italy and in the emergence of far right groups in Eastern Europe. It is seen in the steadily increasing proportion of people who consistently do not vote for one of the two largest political parties in Britain. And it was seen in the support for Ross Perot in the 1992 US presidential election – a candidate whose potency lay in his role as the little boy who dared to say that the emperor had no clothes. Unfortunately that little boy will return again under different names and under increasingly unpleasant guises – it is, after all, in re-emergent nationalism, increasing xenophobia and ugly extremism that the rejection of establishment politics is manifested more potently than anywhere else.

As all these strands intertwine, we are left with a growing crisis of democracy that is becoming apparent in most Western democratic societies. The traditional political contract is breaking down under the strains of massive shifts in social, economic and global realities. Yet politicians appear trapped by the language and illusions of old terms – despite the changes that render them less and less able to deliver what they promise.

Changing the system

In Britain, we are particularly ill-equipped to deal with the challenges ahead, for resistance to reform has left our political institutions stagnating in an unhealthy, moribund state. After centuries of gradualist, pragmatic constitutional change, Britain has arrived at the end of the twentieth century, relatively bloodlessly, a constitutional monarchy. This is the problem. Without the effective constitutional safeguards provided by a written constitution, the distribution of power between state and individual, government and parliament, and centre and locality, has become dangerously out of balance for an effective modern democracy.

All power, exercised in the name of the 'absolute sovereignty of Crown in Parliament', is concentrated at the top of an over-centralised, over-secretive state. The monarchy's medieval prerogative powers have ended up in the hands of an overmighty, unrepresentative 'elective dictatorship' that draws untrammelled executive power from parliamentary majorities elected on minorities of the popular vote. Parliament itself has insufficient power to act as an effective check on government or the civil service, to scrutinise and hold ministers to account, or even to deal effectively with legislation. The local communities, regions and nations of the kingdom have no independent constitutional status or powers, or protection against the centralising tendencies of Westminster or Whitehall. Individual citizens have no entrenched civil rights. And thus we approach the twenty-first century!

If people in Britain have yet to identify the systematic flaws which are a central cause of Britain's problems, they know only too well the policy failures that are its outcome. This political system has produced, in Professor Norman Lewis's words, 'a crop of policy failures in recent times that, in all probability, cannot be matched' – and these policy failures are increasingly coming to be *recognised* as failures of the system. 'That system has failed to meet the functional and democratic demands of the second half of the twentieth century; unreformed, it is clearly inadequate if Britain is to tackle effectively the challenges to our society and democracy in the years ahead' (1993, p. 11).

There must be two fundamental shifts in constitutional attitudes from which practical reform can flow. First, there must be a conscious transformation of the notion of 'sovereignty of parliament' to a concept of 'sovereignty of the people' – in which all power is recognised as being rooted in the citizen. Only then will parliament be constitutionally at ease in the sharing of sovereignty – handing power to the judiciary to protect individual rights and to protect minorities against the tyranny of the majority; pooling sovereignty with other nations in emerging international institutions like the European Community and the United Nations; and dispersing power within Britain itself. Secondly, we must aim to transform the passive subjecthood of the British people into an active citizenship. This objective must flow through every element of the institution-building that is the first step to democratic renewal.

Dispersing power

With this in mind, it is essential that any programme of institutional renewal in Britain is based on a radical dispersal of power. The challenge is to recreate a vibrant, decentralised, pluralist political culture in Britain. This is vital for the effective working of a modern democracy – to broaden involvement in decision-making; to give people greater control over their lives; to foster experimentation and innovation through diversity; and to provide checks and balances to an overmighty central power.

The democratic corollary of the assumption that the state does not know best how to run business is the recognition that the state does not know best how to run our lives, either. The democratic corollary of the belief that competition increases choice and improves quality and consumer power is the understanding that political pluralism encourages innovation and experimentation, widens par-ticipation, and improves the responsiveness of government to different needs and interests. The democratic corollary of the acceptance of the importance to a strong economy of thriving small businesses is a recognition of the importance to a strong democracy of strong communities and powerful local government. This power must be protected against the centralising tendencies of Westminster and Whitehall – and the only way to do that is to build effective constitutional safeguards into a written constitution. Within such a constitution we would then be able to guarantee basic civil liberties in a Bill of Rights, and guarantee access to information (the key to individual empowerment) through statutory Freedom of Information provision. The working of parliament must also be reformed. In particular the powers of committees and individual MPs to challenge the executive need to be increased. For all the public service charters, the British system of govenment remains shrouded in secrecy. Opening up the workings of government to public scrutiny is the first step to improving democratic accountability – and by so doing, improving the quality of government. As the cornerstone on which this whole new institutional structure is built, we must introduce an electoral system that really enhances democratic choice, increases accountability, ensures governments that reflect the popular will of the people, and which itself enhances the pluralism of the democratic system.

Democratic renewal

This root-and-branch reform of Britain's outdated political institutions is now essential if we are to create an open, plural, participatory democracy in Britain. But purely constitutional reform of this sort, though necessary, will not be sufficient by itself to bridge the gap opening up between politicians and people in our society. For this problem is rooted, at least in part, in a crisis of social demands and expectations. As the old political contract – based on what former Conservative Minister John Biffen (1993) recently called the 'politics of growth and easy distribution' – breaks down in the face of lower growth and rising social costs, the task before politicians is, as he put it, 'to adjust expectations'. This will only be achieved by involving people more in confronting these challenges. It is more than unfortunate, of course, that at just the moment when popular involvement and control is needed more than ever, decision-making is passing progressively into the hands of democratically unaccountable appointees on central government quangos.

Rebuilding confidence in the political process will require more than purely institutional changes of the sort outlined earlier. Unless we can find ways of involving people in confronting the difficult decisions ahead; unless we can enable them to feel a shared responsibility in the choices that have to be made; and unless we can bind them more firmly into the actions that have to be taken, then we risk disillusionment growing and alienation festering and endangering the democratic process itself.

The extension of participation is vital if we are to open up an active dialogue between politicians and people about how we respond to the realities of Britain today. It is a task politicians have too readily turned away from. This is true not just of government politicians, who constantly claim that things are better than the people palpably know they are. It is also true that too many opposition politicians are all too ready to raise expectations of spending on the basis of levels of economic growth which they know are beyond their capacity to deliver. Both contribute to an unhealthy disillusionment with politicians. Nor does this simply apply to economic questions. Take the process of European integration, driven forward by politicians and civil servants who have conspired to exclude people from this crucial decision about their own future. As Anthony Sampson writes in *The Essential Anatomy of Britain*:

> the public had little chance to adjust; for governments remained fearful of a popular backlash, and did not try to educate them. Britain joined Europe not in a fit of absence of mind, as she was said to have acquired her Empire, but by a process of deliberate deception. Twenty years later the public is beginning to realise some of the consequences; but will face many more shocks in the future.
>
> (1992, pp. 156–7)

The question of a referendum and the extent to which, in a modern democracy, we are prepared to permit instruments of direct democracy, has been raised by the Maastricht Treaty, and will not go away. It is probably in this area that we are going to have to contemplate the most substantial step away from our nineteenth century model of democracy towards a new democratic settlement, in which individual citizens have more direct control over certain areas of governance.

Around the world there is a growing bank of experience in successful direct democracy. If in Britain we can bring ourselves to accept the concept of the sovereignty of the people rather than the sovereignty of parliament, and the concept of active citizenship rather than passive subjecthood, there are exciting new possibilities for democratic renewal in our society. Local authorities in Britain provide fertile soil for experimentation. The combination of cuts in central government grant and capping of independently raised revenues has put immense strain on public services under local authority control. More far-sighted councils understand that actively involving people in confronting the difficult choices enforced as a result – and binding them into the political decisions it entails (and therefore into the responsibility for those decisions) – is vital, not only to prevent a growing disillusionment with politicians that is destructive, but also actively to revitalise democracy in a way that is constructive. That is why more progressive councils are opening up council meetings – not just to public observation, but to public question and answer sessions; carrying out polling research to find out, between elections, popular attitudes to different policy proposals and spending options; and carrying out local consultative referenda to give people a direct say in levels of local tax and spending.

Central government must follow this lead. Fostering a new political culture has to involve experimentation, at every level of government, into mechanisms for widening participation in decision-making. Nowhere is this more essential than in taxation. For it is tax that lies at the heart of the 'contract' between politicians and people. And it is tax that lies at the heart of the dilemma for progressive politicians who recognise the need for investment for future prosperity and success, but who seem to have lost the ability to win the positive arguments for tax. People are angry about cuts in the NHS, angry about the state of our schools, angry about the condition of public transport, but they seem extremely reluctant to pay the tax needed to improve these services. As Geoff Mulgan and Robin Murray have written in their (1993) pamphlet:

> On the one hand there is resistance to tax, on the other a continuing demand for expenditure. Electorates say they want better public services, particularly health and education, yet they consistently vote against the means of delivering it.

The unwillingness of people to trust their politicians not to waste their money – which is at least part of the reason for this situation – is clearly linked to the breakdown of the established political 'contract' between politicians and people. In the same way, finding ways to recreate a sense of value-for-taxation must be a central element in rebuilding confidence in, and reconnecting people with, the political process. In terms of tax this means finding ways to reconnect money raised with money spent; explaining to people how their taxes will be used by the state for their benefit. As a first step, government must make greater efforts to explain taxation. There is no reason why the government should not, on its tax demands, follow the directive it has given to town halls to set out where individual taxpayers' money goes. There are some who argue that we should go further; that public spending generally needs to aspire to the clarity and symmetry of a road toll – a simple charge levied on the individual to maintain a particular facility used by that person. The theory is that although some taxes have such an earmarked or 'hypothecated' character, most tax disappears into the Treasury pool, reappearing, aggregated with money from other sources, in vast blocs of public spending.

These are interesting ideas which need to be explored. The government has already accepted the case for 'ring-fencing' some areas of expenditure. Meanwhile the new moves towards environmental taxation could open up possibilities for further earmarked taxation. A 'revenue neutral' tax on pollution and energy consumption, for example, could logically be directed towards energy efficiency and environmentally friendly projects. The virtue of increasing tax transparency is that it builds a sense of community. It is like providing solid accounts for a shareholder. The result is that citizens – the nation's shareholders – are required to come to a consensus decision, not on how much money to contribute to a pool from which random sums are later drawn, but on whether to set aside particular sums for clearly defined processes. As tax policy becomes more transparent, democratic debate becomes clearer with it.

Conclusion

The task for politicians now is to provide the structures and mechanisms that will enable individuals and communities to take control of their own lives. It will only emerge in a political system that disperses power. It will only occur within a political culture geared to widening participation. But it is only through this process that we will succeed in renewing our creaking political structure. That is what is needed if our society is to meet effectively the new challenges bearing down on it.

The state must be moulded into an enabling institution that puts real power into the hands of individual citizens and their communities; one that opens up opportunities for eveyone in society, throughout their lives, to make the most of their lives; one that unleashes the power of our communities. For ultimately, it is only by empowering individual citizens with the *responsibility* that comes from greater involvement in, and control over, decision-making that we will have a chance of containing the crisis of democracy within our society.

References
Biffen, John, Parliamentary Debates (Hansard), House of Commons, Vol. 226, 9 June 1993, col. 312

Galbraith, John Kenneth (1992), *The Culture of Contentment*, London, Sinclair-Stevenson

Lewis, Norman (1993), *How to Reinvent British Government*, London, European Policy Forum

Mulgan, Geoff and Murray, Robin (1993), *Reconnecting Taxation*, London, Demos

Reich, Robert (1993), *The Work of Nations; Preparing Ourselves for Twenty-First Century Capitalism*, Hemel Hempstead, Simon and Schuster

Sampson, Anthony (1992), *The Essential Anatomy of Britain*, London, Hodder and Stoughton

Further Reading
Ashdown, Paddy (1989), *Citizens' Britain*, London, Fourth Estate

Home, Richard and Elliot, Michael (eds.) (1988), *Time for a New Constitution*, London, Macmillan

Marquand, David (1988), *The Unprincipled Society*, Jonathan Cape

Mount, Ferdinand (1992), *The British Constitution Now*, London, Heinemann

Progress

When observing those ideas that structure experience, shape attitudes and prompt action, there can be little doubt that progress ranks as one of the most significant over the past two hundred years. Although its extensive pedigree always runs the risk of undermining its *raison d'être*, it nevertheless remains at the forefront of the West's contribution to social thought and popular perspectives. The theme of progress continues to possess a compulsive quality that conditions the economic suppositions, the political aspirations and the historical conscious-ness of a wide range of different cultures. Progress not only implies modernity, but defines it in terms of its own restless precepts of necessary advance.

The notion of change fused with benevolence has become a central pre-supposition of contemporary political discourse. Progress pervades the identification of problems, the shaping of solutions, the choice of options and the language and legitimacy of decisions. Progress has permeated other values and principles to such an extent that the term has become a conventional summation of the Western tradition. In his seminal work on the idea of progress in history, Robert Nisbet concludes that:

> No single idea has been more important than, perhaps as important as, the idea of progress in Western civilization ... Other ideas will come to mind, properly: liberty, justice, equality, community, and so forth ... [T]hroughout most of Western history, the substratum of even these ideas has been a philosophy of history, that lends past, present, and future to their importance. Nothing gives greater importance or credibility to a moral or political value than belief ... that is an essential element of historical movement from past through present to future. Such a value can be transposed from the merely desirable to the historically necessary.
>
> (1980, p. 4)

Progressive suppositions

At its most basic, progress denotes a series of cumulative suppositions concerning the relationship between the passage of time and the development of human society. First is the assumption that societies do not and cannot remain static because they are essentially dynamic in nature and are, therefore, in continual motion. The second assumption is that beneath the myriad changes which society experiences over time, there exists a discernible order to them. Multiple changes can be reduced and rationalised through a uni-linear development that integrates change and gives it a direction. With direction comes a third assumption – i.e. that history has a purposive end. In such a context, history is no longer a succession of events or part of a divine drama, so much as an autonomous temporal process moving towards a projected outcome. Just as the present is determined by the past, so the future is necessarily and ineluctably inherent in contemporary conditions and arrangements. History, therefore, moves society in a continuous cumulative advance, irrespective of conscious will or human agency. Progress as an idea depends upon the extend to which it is treated as a fact. Like 'providence or personal immortality, [it] is true or it is false, and like them it cannot be proved either true or false. Belief in it is an act of faith' (Bury, 1955, p. 4).

The willingness to accept such an apparently fateful progress is linked to a fourth supposition. This is the attachment of prescriptive value to the empirical dynamics of social direction. Advance and improvement become interchangeable entities. They support and verify one another in respect of belief and principle. Progress is to be welcomed rather than merely received. Far from describing the blind consequence of a blank process, progress is substantiated into an ethos of irreversible betterment, indefinite improvement and enriched optimism. Its synthesis of past, present and future is repeatedly corroborated by demonstrable advances in knowledge, technology, opportunity, prosperity, health, education and living standards. The logic of progress, and the belief system it supports, not only fosters the acceptance of all four assumptions, but establishes a faith in the timelessness and universality of progress as both a fact and a value.

Origins and forward development

The origin of this progressive conception of history are many and varied but three themes in particular provide the main roots. The notion of movement was first introduced in classical Greek thought. Even though 'speculative Greek minds never hit on the idea of progress' (Bury, 1955, p. 19), the Greeks did believe in a lost 'golden age'. This not only provided an idealised perspective of social possibilities, but confirmed the present to be a form of corruption and degeneration. Improvement was possible, but only by a regeneration of a previous condition. Later, the Greeks schematised their sense of incessant movement into a perspective of history as a series of cycles moving from recovery to degeneration and back to improvement.

The second root was provided by the Judeo-Christian tradition which also looked back to an idyllic past – albeit in the prehistory of the Garden of Eden – but which, unlike the Greeks, offered an escape from the interminable repetition of cycles through the millennium and thence to salvation. While the Jewish faith limited this cosmic climax to 'the chosen people', the Christian tradition made the concept of the fulfilment of all historical processes into a universal opportunity of salvation. The golden age was translated from an earthly past to a heavenly future. Pessimism concerning human destiny was replaced by the optimistic prospect of eternal life.

The third root came with the secular challenge to the church's religious doctrine, its social standing and its political authority. The seventeenth century witnessed the rise of secular governments, the expansion of industry and commerce, an increased contact with other cultures, and the onset of an educated, prosperous and abrasive middle class which was intolerant of ecclesiastical power and privileges and critical of the restrictive incorporation of church and state. In the same way that the traditional wealth from landed estates began to be superseded by the novelty and scale of wealth from manufacturing and commercial activities, the established authority of the church was progressively supplanted by new sources of knowledge and explanation.

Empirical science, in particular, opened up alternative constructions of the universe and nature. As the corpus of scientific knowledge was increased, as the magnitude of its explanatory power grew, and as the material benefits that could be derived from science became more evident, the concepts of nature changed accordingly. It was transformed from a realm of ineffable essences, animated objects and unpredictable phenomena to a unified calculus of physical cause and effect, whose uniformities were intelligible through observation and measurement. According to Isaac Newton's celebrated dictum, nature was simple and conformable to itself. It adhered to, and could be explained through, its own physical properties and universal laws.

> Laws formulating regular concomitances of phenomena – the observed order and conjunctions of things and events – were sufficient to . . . describe all that is describable, and predict all that is predictable, in the universe. Space, time, mass, force, momentum, rest – the terms of mechanics – [were] to take the place of final causes, substantial forms, divine purpose, and other metaphysical notions. Indeed the apparatus of medieval ontology and theology were to be altogether abandoned.
>
> (Berlin, 1962, p. 8)

Intellectual liberation brought with it the promise of human emancipation. The utility of the Enlightenment's scientific advances provided successive improvements in material benefits and technological provision. The eighteenth century was 'perhaps the last period in the history of Western Europe when human omniscience was thought to be an attainable goal' (Berlin, 1962, p. 6). Natural revelation outstripped divine revelation so much that there appeared to be no limit to the extent to which nature would yield up its secrets and, therefore, no limit upon future material and human improvement.

This modern idea of progress did not dispense with the Christian tradition of salvation. It transformed it into a secular faith in which human salvation would be secured through and within itself – not God's nature so much as nature's God. The use of conscious reason to elicit the reason of nature's laws made progress towards an earthly salvation wholly plausible. In fact, such was the Enlightenment's confidence in the record and prospect of successive linear advance, it was widely believed that humanity had not only equalled the previously incomparable standards of Greece and Rome, but had actually exceeded them.

The Enlightenment's sense of advance brought with it the rationalist confidence to explain contemporary conditions as the fulfilment of time's potential. A. R. J. Turgot typified the absorption in cultural transformation that was common amongst the *philosophes* at the time. He was the first to give sustained emphasis to the material forces of progress in human history, as opposed to the spiritual properties of providence. These forces had propelled humanity from a hunting and pastoral existence to a settled agricultural condition and, thenceforth, to a commercial and urban basis of life. Every major institution and medium of communication passed through a parallel three-stage form of development. While many of his contemporaries sought to relate cultural diversity to variations in natural causes (e.g. Montesquieu), Turgot was the first to reduce all such variation to points on an underlying continuum of historical development oriented towards economic progress, intellectual emancipation and individual liberty.

If it was Turgot who postulated the existence of progressive historical development, it was the Marquis de Condorcet who sought to systematise the idea into an altogether more rigorous construct based consistently upon a clear social philosophy and drawn from the Enlightenment's attachment to discernible laws of nature. Turgot alluded to a philosophy of history supporting progress. But it was Condorcet who not only transformed the concept of historical development into an iron law, but regarded progress as something to be actively pursued with enthusiasm and confidence. To Condorcet, it was the scientific study of history which established the facts of progress and which provided humanity with the knowledge to fulfil the possibilities of its own inherent future. Historical interpretation had a contemporary utility to human development:

> In the past progress had been fitful, blind, and accidental; but in the future it was to
> be consciously and deliberately guided according to certain principles. And these
> principles could be discovered only through the study of history.
>
> (Schapiro, 1934, p. 243)

The law of progress was not merely analogous to scientific laws of nature, it was to Condorcet a genuine natural law in its own right. 'The law of progress was essential in Condorcet's social machine as was the law of gravitation in Newton's world machine' (Schapiro, 1934, p. 259).

After nine epochs of history, humanity was about to enter the tenth and final stage in which the errors and backwardness of traditional authority – cultural superstition, religious intolerance, political inequality, feudal anachronism, royal despotism – would give way to an equality between nations and individuals and to an unlimited perfectability of mankind. Enough evidence already existed for Condorcet to look forward to a secure, cosmopolitan, peaceful and humanitarian social order, in which increased knowledge would coincide with increased virtue and moral advance. History provided the technique, the motivation and the assurance of a forward march into perfection.

The Enlightenment's conception of progress was based upon an appreciation of science and an affection for scientific analogies with regard to social order and development. Although the modern idea of progress was established in the eighteenth century, its operational dynamics had never really been demon-strated. Progress was assumed to be a fundamental law of nature, but the ways in which it could be ranked as a natural phenomenon were by no means clear. Exactly how one stage of human history developed from its predecessor was not explained. It was left to the system builders of the nineteenth century (e.g. Herbert Spencer, Karl Marx) to raise progress to a position where it could more readily satisfy the contemporary criteria of a science. Just as progress had advanced the course of science, so now scientific rigour, which the idea of progress had done so much to encourage, was turned on progress itself.

> After the middle of the century natural science invested the doctrine of progress with a more materialistic implication. Progress was still regarded as the result of a force external to man; but the force was to be found not above but inherent in the phenomenal world.
>
> (Becker, 1934, pp. 497–8)

Progress was pushed ever further away from providence and ever nearer to an autonomous process of culmination, independent of conscious motivation and deliberative guidance.

Herbert Spencer, for example, placed his theory of progress within a framework of cosmic cause and effect (1954). Social advance was merely one part of a truly universal set of dynamics based upon the principles of physics. The story of the universe had been one of successive transformations from unstable homogeneous entities to complex heterogeneous arrangements. The physical, the organic and the social realms all provided demonstrable proof of the existence of such a natural law of successive and linear development. Social progress was characterised by a movement away from monolithic, static and oppressive arrangements towards plural, dynamic and freely adaptive organisations. The former were destined to decay, while the latter were assured of the same natural pre-eminence which had been acquired by the heterogeneous entities in the physical and biological fields. To Spencer, the state was not the climax of social organisation but a restrictive and regressive anachronism that obstructed progress by diminishing the effect of natural and spontaneous forces towards heterogeneity that would assure advance. Spencer had no doubt that only perversions of nature could, and would, fall under the necessity of all forms of life and culture to reduce deficiencies and unfitness, in favour of an adaptive evolution to the conditions of existence.

For Karl Marx, the propulsion of history was not physics or biology, but the internal properties of society itself. Social progress was contingent upon the inherent dynamics of productive relations. The dialetical nature of economic class conflict not only determined the course of human history, but pre-determined a future in which the abundance of economic progress would coincide with a social and moral progress to provide a classless and stateless utopia. History was enclosed within a framework of economic materialism. Progress, therefore, was assured but it was not an open-minded and graduated form of improvement, so much as a predefined condition – secured as a climactic finality to a necessary history of crises, conflicts, convulsions and revolutions.

Herbert Spencer rationalised the disruption and disorientation of accelerated industrialisation by characterising change as orderly progress. He gave the flux of the nineteenth century a secular and metaphysical foundation through organic analogies and biological references. Society evolved through competitive struggle, 'natural values' and the accumulation of acquired characteristics. In such a liberal system, an ultimate mutuality of interests was always assumed. Conflict could, and would, be resolved as society evolved to a higher condition of moral improvement. Marx also believed in evolution and especially in the 'economic formation of society . . . as a process of natural history' (Marx, 1954, p. 21). But unlike Spencer, he thought that progress would entail class struggle and intractable conflict leading to a complete metamorphosis of society. 'No antago-nism, no progress. This is the law that civilisation has followed up to our days' (Marx quoted in Sanderson, 1969, p. 27). It would continue to be so in the future and succeed in subverting the present to produce a qualitatively different social order, where most of humanity would be emancipated from the contemporary alienation from itself.

Spencer and Marx typified the nineteenth century's attachment to the idea of progress. So prevalent was the conception of historical process and purposeful evolution that progress became firmly established by the close of the century both as an empirical condition and a normative value. The triumphant advance of modern civilisation seemed capable not just of liberating humanity at last from original sin or the state of nature, but of finally superseding the golden age of classical antiquity. While despotisms crumbled, commercial riches accumulated and literacy rates rose to reach the masses, science and technology promised a limitless domain over nature. Such was the magnitude of knowledge methodically elicited from nature and deployed for the benefit of human society, that modern civilisation was widely assumed to have decisively surpassed the wisdom and achievements of the ancients. The intellectual emancipation of reason had produced a social emancipation through reason. The golden age was

transformed from the models of the past to the prospect of the future. With the prospect of an ever increasing mastery of the environment and a belief in the infinite capacity of the mind to acquire usable knowledge, humanity's passage to successive and irreversible progress seemed assured.

There would be no turning back to any repetition of the Dark Ages. The faith that Edward Gibbon had invested in progress during the late eighteenth century had become commonplace by the late nineteenth century. To Gibbon, the few barbarians that were left in Europe could only become militarily effective by losing their primitiveness and taking their 'place among the polished nations' (1898, p. 167). This general movement towards civility, combined with the comforting fact that once the useful arts and sciences had been discovered they could never be lost, was cause for an optimistic outlook upon a world assured of continuous improvement. It was just such an outlook that became one of the distinguishing hallmarks of the nineteenth century.

Advanced disillusion

It is often said that the nineteenth century's faith in progress was shattered by the First World War. In that conflict, science, technology and social organisation which had been the handmaidens of progress were transformed into instruments of mass carnage (Pick, 1993). The unprecedented scale of the slaughter inflicted by such advanced methods led not only to a disgust of modern warfare but, more significantly, to a generalised apostasy concerning man's psychological and social potential for progress. In spite of the progressive advances being made in scientific innovation and industrial invention, the conflict was thought to betray an altogether deeper and primal compulsion towards aggression and destruction.

The hope and innocence of the nineteenth century were seen to be crushed by the mechanical application of death and injury. In Erich Remarque's *All Quiet on the Western Front* (1963), the narrator condemns the older generation for failing to reconcile old temperaments with new realities. The myopic optimism of the nineteenth century was typified by the schoolteacher Kantonek who had dragooned his class into volunteering for the German armed forces. Before the war, men like Kantonek had been trusted for their insight and humane wisdom. But in the trenches, the young soldiers believed that they had been badly let down by such people.

> For us lads of eighteen they ought to have been mediators and guides to the world of maturity, the world of work, of duty, of culture, of progress – to the future.
>
> (Remarque, 1963, p. 14)

The horrors of the battlefields shattered the authority of this older generation who had not foreseen the abyss.

> The first bombardment showed us our mistake, and under it the world as they had taught it to us broke in pieces . . . we distinguished the false from the true, we had

suddenly learned to see. And we saw that there was nothing of their world left. We
were all at once terribly alone.

(Remarque, 1963, p. 14)

It was difficult to maintain the nineteenth century's faith in progress in such
brutally regressive conditions where humanity had to confront the evident existence of its brutal instincts. This was a far cry from Edward Gibbon's serene
confidence in the necessary historical advances of knowledge, wealth and happiness, and in the commensurate decline in the prospects of a new dark age. 'It may
safely be presumed that no people, unless the face of nature is changed, will
relapse into their original barbarism . . . We may therefore acquiesce in the
pleasing conclusion that every age of the world has increased, and still increases,
the real wealth, the happiness, the knowledge, and perhaps the virtue, of the
human race' (Gibbon, 1898, pp. 167–8, 169). Gibbon had no conception of the
barbarities of progress nor any grasp of the extent to which states might use such
techniques against their own societies. After the First World War, it was no
longer possible to be blind to the frailties and corruption of progress.

Fascist states deployed the most advanced technologies to carry out purges and
mass executions, to impose censorship and conformity, and to maintain order by
intimidation and terror. Populations were displaced or eliminated to satisfy the
precepts of racial hierarchies intent upon using Darwinian analogies of progressive evolution to justify their brutality towards competitors for power. Even
states explicitly committed to the enlightened pursuit of progress through
rational planning and concerted social reorganisation lapsed into a totalitarian
syndrome of political coercion, repression, fear, and, ultimately, backwardness.
Devastation and disillusionment occasioned by the First World War and its long
aftermath was so intense that it led to an intellectual revival in the classical
conception of natural cycles of periodic growth and decay (see the works of
Oswald Spengler and Arnold Toynbee). Progress was widely seen to be a broken
and empty dogma that had been quite unable to withstand the rigours of the
twentieth century. As such, notions of substantive progress were increasingly
replaced by the more cautious, neutral and purposeless conception of social
change.

Looking at the idea and history of progress from the perspective of the last decade
of the twentieth century, two themes stand out as highly significant and worthy of
extended examination.

Problematic progress

The first is that the concept of progress suffers, and has always suffered, from a
variety of logical and analytical problems which makes it highly susceptible to
ambiguity, disillusionment and abuse. The idea of progress, for example, is
inherently tautological. Progress implies not merely movement but a sense of

direction and even a goal. What translates movement into progress is an implicit value judgement both on the end point and on the relation of any movement towards it. Progress, therefore, is uneasy hybrid of fact and value in which each is defined in terms of the other. This can lead to every development being couched as progress simply on grounds of movement towards an objective that is assumed to exist by the very presence of movement itself. This form of inertia can also lead to the abuse of progress and even to its corruption as reaction disguised as advance.

Other problems confuse the clarity of progress even further. Actual progress, for example, can destroy the very historical foundation on which the original perception of progress was based, and by which progress can be gauged as progressive. In another context, progress is clearly an idea dependent upon time, but also one which cannot be wholly determined by the passage of time without becoming meaningless. Time is a necessary but not a sufficient condition. Progress is often confused with time. It certainly requires time but time is not a generative and purposive process in its own right. Differences also exist between the concept of progress that simply extrapolates change into a projected future state, and the more substantive and deductive view of progress that conceives of a desirable end and then relates and assesses the present directly in terms of such a conscious purpose. Further confusion exists in the way progress is used in political argument. Sometimes progress is regarded as the end that is served by new developments, while on other occasions it is taken to be the process or agency of change itself.

Another source of imprecision that has plagued the history of progress is the question of whether it should be conceived as a spontaneous and autonomous process, or as a condition that can be rationally planned and acquired through organised social effort. A further conundrum is provided by the fact that there always exists a state of tension between progress and its premises. Progress implies a final condition for without a sense of an ultimate objective all movement would be random and purposeless. But such a state flies in the face of progress as dynamic change in a continuously restless universe. Progress, therefore, relies on an end condition and a foreclosed future for its meaning, but depends equally upon not reaching it in order for its identity with change and development to be sustained.

In many respects, the notion of progress has always suffered from the same paradoxes that were first experienced with the advances in scientific knowledge during the Enlightenment. In the first place the dramatic revelation of nature's laws provided a wealth of precisely descriptive and usable information, but from this profusion of fact no ethic concerning what was desirable, or ought to be, could be derived. The hopes of some *philosophes* that nature could provide an objective moral science were never fulfilled. Progress, in knowledge, therefore, resulted in proportionately less guidance over what direction to take it or which uses should be served by it. Such a disjunction was not always recognised, even a century later. For example, it was 'only because of the belief in the inevitability of progress that Marx thought it possible to dispense with ethical considerations. If socialism was coming, it must be an improvement' (Russell, 1946, p. 816).

The other major Enlightenment paradox rested upon the idea that progress in natural sciences entailed a search for an increasingly determinate and predictive universe. At the same time, when the laws of nature were applied to man they were assumed to be inherently emancipatory in effect. A disjunction developed between the sovereign laws of nature that determined the physical world and the laws of nature that apparently set man free (i.e. man was separate from scientific progress in the laws of nature). The alternative disjunction was even more unsatisfactory – namely that man was an integral part of a determinate universe and, as a consequence, possessed no real freedom at all. Science in this sense promised no emancipation, only a more advanced understanding of humanity's own enslavement (i.e. man was inseparable from nature's laws of cause and effect). In this light, scientific progress meant the revelation of humanity's denial of progress. According to the rational calculations of Thomas Malthus, for example, mankind was doomed to famine and wretchedness because of the disparity between the population's geometric growth and the merely arithmetic growth in food supply (Malthus, 1982).

Well before the First World War, therefore, progress was recognised as a highly contestable, and even contradictory, concept. It was also acknowledged to be an inherently plural idea in which intellectual, aesthetic, material and social progress could all be differentiated from each other. Furthermore, they could all conflict with one another. Industrialisation, urbanisation, rationalism, secularism and mass democracy might be construed as the integral features of a progressive age. But they might equally be regarded as leading to social disintegration, impersonal complexity and individual isolation, and, in turn, to the 'morbid conclusion of man's alienation from man, from values, and from self', in other words, 'an inversion of progress' (Nisbet, 1970, pp. 7, 6). Progress could also be plural in another and similarly divisive sense. The progress of a society may incorporate progress in one section of society but at the expense of progress in another. In the words of Roy Porter:

> The shibboleth of progress carried ambiguous messages equivalent to those that 'development' and 'modernisation' today foist upon the 'underdeveloped' world. In the name of 'no alternative' iron laws of competition, it could legitimate exploitative change, the erosion of popular rights and customs. It could rationalise austerity today by offering a better tomorrow which too often proved a mirage. Hence, and *prima facie* paradoxically, the politics of progress were as conservative as they were progressive.
>
> (1990)

These ambiguities and inconsistencies smouldered throughout the heyday of progress in the eighteenth and nineteenth centuries. The First World War may have been the catalyst to the conscious disenchantment with progress, but it was not the root cause of the disillusionment. Doubts over the natural autonomy of social improvement had been multiplying as part of a larger and more generalised scepticism over modernity. It was only after the First World War that the notion of assured progress was subjected to the full force of widespread critical analysis. The ever rising tide of explicit scepticism surrounding progress – even in the midst of so many palpable signs of progress – has since become a distinguishing feature of this century. So much so in fact that according to Robert Nisbet there is 'good ground for supposing that when the identity of our century is eventually fixed by historians, not faith but abandonment of faith in the idea of progress will be one of the major attributes' (1980, p. 317).

Critical progress

The second theme that emerges from the experience of progress throughout the twentieth century is one of constant and cumulative complaint. The indictment of both the present actuality and the future possibility of progress has been a running feature of the century. A jaundiced view of modernity has become increasingly conventional as the century has progressed. In the final decade of the century, doubts over the benefits of technological mastery, anxieties about scientific knowledge, speculation about the limits and wisdom of economic growth, and concern over the state of moral order amidst affluence have all been assimilated as part of a conventional agenda of scepticism regarding progress. Movement is discerned, but there is no consensus over whether or not it ranks as improvement, i.e. whether it constitutes a progression towards a valued end.

What is especially noteworthy is that the arguments against progress have remained fundamentally the same throughout the century. In the 1990s, technological advances allow us to be better informed than ever before. Computer enhancement can provide high resolution pictures of environmental devastation. Likewise, satellite television can convey famine, war, disease and death in shameful realism. An ostensibly modern European country like Yugoslavia is shown to be as susceptible to the destructive forces of ancient enmities and savage compulsion as any less 'developed' country. After fifty years, the genocide of the Nazi holocaust had begun to be rationalised as an historical aberration. But Bosnia suddenly revealed 'ethnic cleansing' and mass slaughter by modern weaponry to be no more than a recurrent condition and an instinctive response to the exigencies of war.

If the furtherance of knowledge can still not extricate humanity from the regressive aspects of its nature, there is little evidence of an escape from the Enlightenment's other great problem of a mismatch between acquired information and available ethics. Modern advances in medicine, for example, have generated a profusion of severe ethical problems which cannot be resolved simply by further technical development.

No innovation demonstrates the confidence and doubts of progress in this field more clearly than the Human Genome Project (Wilkie, 1993a). In one respect, this $3 billion plan to provide a precise map of humanity's genetic composition is a triumph of international scientific research and collaboration. It offers the prospect of precisely locating and sequencing all 100,000 human genes within our 23 pairs of chromosomes and, thereby, providing a complete data base of what genetically constitutes a human being. Since there are over 4,000 known single gene defects that afflict humanity, it is possible that the Human Genome Project will be able not only to provide tests for such illnesses, but also cures through genetic engineering. Observers are confident that the project will 'transform human life more profoundly than all the hi-tech inventions of the space age' (Wilkie, 1993b).

And yet, the project also has the most profound ethical and even political implications. Research into the perfect blueprint of human inheritance threatens to overwhelm our moral and philosophical sensibilities over how such information could and should be used. It can conjure up a nightmare world of mass screening, gene therapy, invasions of privacy, discrimination and even a eugenic quest for the perfection of humanity. At the very least, it threatens people with knowledge about themselves, but provides no guidance as to what to do with such knowledge.

The recent disclosure that homosexuality may originate in a particular gene, for example, immediately caused a sense of 'moral bewilderment' (Parris, 1993) concerning the implications of such a proposition. Screening foetuses for the 'gay gene' might easily lead to a disposition to abort in the same way that Down's syndrome foetuses are sometimes terminated today. Such a practice would raise moral dilemmas and confront rival claims of civil liberties which science would not be able to resolve.

> A woman's right to abortion on her own chosen grounds would have to be weighed against the potential right of a foetus to develop in its own way and, by implication, the right of other adults to live in the way that they prefer without stigma.
>
> *(Times,* 1993)

As for gays already living in the community, they would be absolved of personal responsibility for their orientation but at the price of being positively identified as genetically abnormal, with all the potential for restrictive discrimination that would entail.

It may also be pointed out that furtherance of knowledge into human life can have the effect of challenging its moral worth. In the seventeenth century, the advances in scientific rationalism filled Blaise Pascal with a grave sense of desolation. Mathematics and mechanics increasingly revealed the universe to be devoid of human scale and discernible purpose.

> The eternal silence of infinite spaces fills me with dread ... [W]hen I survey the whole universe in its dumbness and man left to himself with no light, as though lost in this corner of the universe, without knowing who put him there, what he has come to do, I am moved to terror, like a man transported in his sleep to some terrifying desert island who wakes up quite lost and with no means of escape.
>
> (1966, pp. 95, 88)

Science's revelation of the universe's absence of human centrality has continued apace, leaving mankind with a progressive decline in its own identity and distinctiveness. The strides in knowledge may be a tribute to human reason, but they also demonstrate mankind's dependence upon evolutionary processes and human development. Our increasing integration into nature, and into the inconceivable distances in time, has progressively subverted our special relationship with anything transcending nature or lying beyond the earth. A great deal of research has been dedicated to showing that even life itself could have been brought into being spontaneously by the normal interactions of physical and chemical processes.

Other research has calculated that the genetic difference between us and other apes is tiny. In the case of chimpanzees, the similarity reaches a level of 98.4 per cent; arguably leaving 1.6 per cent to embrace the stuff of humanity. Already a group of biologists, anthropologists, psychologists and philosophers have proposed that full human rights should be extended to chimpanzees, gorillas and orang-utans, and that those presently held in captivity should be returned to special reserves and independent territories in their original habitat (Cavalieri and Singer, 1993). Against such a background, it becomes increasingly difficult to sustain the proposition that human life and society are unique and, therefore, uniquely capable of pursuing progress. Progress amongst such 'living fossils' (Jones, 1993) becomes reduced to a self-deceiving artifice – albeit peculiar to man – to disguise the consequences of sociobiology's amoral imperatives.

Throughout the twentieth century, there has also arisen an increased realisation of the logical pitfalls and contradictory pluralities implied by progress. It has now become painfully self-evident that material progress does not necessarily bring social progress in its wake. By the same token, advances in science and technology do not assure aesthetic improvements in the quality of life. With the rise of an ever more interdependent world economy, 'Western progress' is increasingly revealed to be progress acquired at the direct expense of impoverishment and debt in the third world – i.e. that the defining form of progress is by implication culpable for a variety of regression elsewhere. War, for example, has largely become a thing of the past in the developed world. It is regarded as irrational, wasteful, futile and prohibitively expensive (Mueller, 1989). Nevertheless, these self-same nations compete with one another to underwrite wars, with supplies of the advanced armaments, in those areas of the world that can least afford them.

Although it is the West's material lead over other regions that defines its sense of progress, it is precisely that lead which casts moral doubt on the actuality of Western progress. Furthermore, given that it is neither feasible nor even desirable for the rest of the world to imitate the West's use of global resources, it is increasingly difficult to sustain the West either as a model of progess or as a definitive condition of progress. In the view of Paul Kennedy, the much postponed Malthusian nightmare is already present in the developing world. The nineteenth century innovations that saved much of Europe from Malthus's catastrophe (i.e. agricultural improvements and the industrial revolution) have not only run their course but consigned the less developed countries to ever increasing destitution. To Kennedy, the industrial revolution enabled countries like Britain to sustain their rising populations by increasing production and export. But when the developing nations with steeply rising populations attempt the same progressive course of action today, they find that the global markets are already replete with goods from the industrialised nations (Kennedy, 1993). As the escape from neo-colonialism and the Malthusian trap is effectively cut off, 'Western progress' is increasingly interpreted as progress for the West.

Many in the ecology movement have sought to introduce an altogether larger dimension to the assessment and evaluation of progress. They have been swift to condemn human progress as positively 'anti-evolutionary' (Goldsmith, 1992) in that it flatly contravenes the holistic teleology of what is a self-sustaining biosphere (Gaia principle). Unrestrained rationalism has produced a paradigm of modernity and science which is couched as objectively progressive, but which in reality is a highly subjective faith. It is a faith which leaves humanity disengaged from nature's own purposeful scheme. New age science reacts against the mechanistic reductionism of the Enlightenment tradition. It seeks to reintegrate nature into an organic whole whose complexity, creativity and 'chaos' require an altogether different epistemology and a reversal of science's fusion of its own progress with that of the progressive atomisation and manipulation of nature. In much the same way, new age ecology reacts against the myopia, waste and destruction of competitive consumption, and presses the twentieth century's indictment of technological development to its culminating point of a failed and fatal prospectus.

The experience of the twentieth century would seem to provide a final and conclusive rebuttal to Condorcet's notion of progress and perfection. It has been stripped bare of its pretensions of objectivity and feasibility. Progress is now generally acknowledged to be highly relative in nature and unattainable in terms of a condition of fulfilment. Like history, progress tends to be defined and used by the victors. For a long period in this century, socialism and communism were widely interpreted as being synonymous with progress. But progress is associated just as much with the past, relieved as it is with the future acquired. As a result, the decline of communism coincided with an alleged 'new enlightenment' of progress associated with liberal values and arrangements. The end of the communist bloc could, therefore, be construed as the 'end of history' (Fukuyama, 1992) and in effect the fulfilment of liberalism's criteria of progress. By the same token, it was just as reasonable to suppose that communism's collapse represented not so much an end to history as a resumption of history, since nearly every society could now be conceived as moving in the same direction supposedly towards some universal end point.

On the other hand, the contemporary coherence of progress has not been helped by the social disarray and economic decline of the world's most advanced liberal capitalist society, the United States (Thurow, 1985; Kennedy, 1987), nor by the libertarian new right whose evident failures have been attributed to a futile revival of the Enlightenment's conviction in the perfectability of human nature and institutions (Grey, 1993). Conservatives have always been suspicious of the future. Today, communists and socialists find little comfort in historical prognosis. Even liberals, who have always placed their trust in the future, are cautious about the content or even the existence of its provision. To John Dunn, this scepticism is remarkable but also understandable.

> If liberals can no longer blindly trust the future, if they can no longer believe in a guaranteed progress, what precisely *can* they believe in? Today we may still hope to avoid regress. We may strive as best we can to improve those parts of the world which lie within our own grasp. But who now, except a complete imbecile, can still *expect a guaranteed* progress?
>
> (1993, pp. 31–2)

Eternal hope

Yet despite the innumerable references to the incoherence and indeterminacy of progress, the idea remains a potent force in contemporary politics. The language of political argument continues to be soaked with allusions to progress. Whether the references are to 'moving forward', 'improvement', 'advance', or simply to 'the future', they are all based upon the central supposition that politics can secure progress. Political parties continue to couch their programmes as instruments of progress. They compete with one another for the most convincing relationship with the prospect of progress. They appeal to the public for the mantle of being progressive, providing proposals, and offering hope in the form of progress.

In a more passive, but nonetheless closely related, sense progress is used habitually in everyday circumstances to refer both to national (e.g. European regulations) and domestic (e.g. planning decisions) changes. The currency of progress remains strong as countless individuals are regularly deprived of their settled existence, their privacy, property and freedom of choice by change exerted coercively upon them in the name of progress. It is quite extraordinary that an idea, whose credibility and veracity has been cast into doubt so incessantly and convincingly for so long, can still arouse so much adherence. A conception of progress continues to be an integral component of contemporary political allegiance. Government and opposition parties promise it. Public opinion expects it. Political debate is informed and structured by it.

It is, of course, possible to claim that the contemporary usage of progress is vacuous. In contrast to the nineteenth century when progress was a motivating faith in movement towards a positive good, progress in the late twentieth century can all too often appear as a form of condoned inertia. In place of conscious purpose and democratic emancipation is merely an empty fate supported by habitual acquiescence in a supposed utility. According to this perspective, progress is no longer an idea so much as a panacea of unthought; a substitute for failed ideologies; a residual, minimal and eclectic construct that affords the rudiments of an ordered relationship between the past, present and future in an increasingly disordered world.

There is some basis to this view, but it is nevertheless too severe a judgement because progress in the end is not merely a device for securing public submission to any set of short term policies. It denotes a substantive and fundamental disposition in the human mind towards believing in, and working for, an improved state of existence. Progress may be more of an instrumental value than it used to be, but the Enlightenment faith in accessible betterment and evolutionary advance continues to make its presence felt in contemporary politics. Sober scepticism is fused with compulsive hope for the future.

It is that irresistible hope in progress, however selective, partial or local in nature, which can still provide the driving force in political movements and the thrust to political change – even radical political change. Innovative ideas quickly become attached to the claims of progress which afford them intellectual respectability, ethical weight and popular appeal. Being progressive in politics, even at the end of the twentieth century, is still looked upon favourably. So much so in fact it is reasonable to conclude that the 'cultural lag', in which technological and material progress was always thought to precede social and political progress, has now to all intents and purposes been inverted. At a time when the cost, unreliability and danger of scientific progress and industrial development are regularly acknowledged, references to political progress have become more prominent and conventional in comparison with other forms of progress. It may only be a lag, postponing the complete decay of political progress into scepticism and disbelief. On the other hand, given its highly variable usage and its conjunction with other political ideas, the concept of progress in politics might equally provide some form of corrective to other discredited dimensions of progress.

References

Becker, C. (1934), 'Progress,' in E. A. Seligman and A. Johnson (eds.), *Encyclopaedia of the Social Sciences*, New York, Macmillan, pp. 495–9

Berlin, I. (1962), 'The Age of the Enlightenment', in *The Great Ages of Western Philosophy, Volume 2*, Boston, Houghton Mifflin, pp. 3–215

Bury, J. B. (1955), *The Idea of Progress: An Inquiry into its Origin and Growth*, New York, Dover

Cavalieri, P. and Singer, P. (eds.) (1993), *The Great Ape Project*, London, Fourth Estate

Dunn, J. (1993), *Western Political Theory in the Face of the Future*, Cambridge, Canto

Fukuyama, F. (1992), *The End of History and the Last Man*, Harmondsworth, Penguin

Gibbon, E. (1898), *The History of the Decline and Fall of the Roman Empire, Volume IV*, London, Methuen

Goldsmith, E. (1992), *The Way: An Ecological World View*, London, Century

Grey, J. (1993), *Beyond the New Right: Markets, Governments and the Common Environment*,

London, Routledge

Jones, S. (1993), *The Language of the Genes: Biology, History and the Evolutionary Future*, London, HarperCollins

Kennedy, P. (1987), *The Rise and Fall of the Great Powers: Economic Change and Military Conflict from 1500 to 2000*, New York, Random House

— (1993), *Preparing for the Twenty-First Century*, London, HarperCollins

Malthus, T. R. (1982), *An Essay on the Principle of Population*, intro. by T. H. Hollingsworth, 7th edition, London, Dent

Marx, K. (1954), *Capital: A Critique of Political Economy, Vol. 1*, London, Lawrence and Wishart

Mueller, J. E. (1989), *Retreat From Doomsday: The Obsolescence of Major War*, New York, Basic

Nisbet, R. A. (1970), *The Sociological Tradition*, London, Heinemann

— (1980), *History of the Idea of Progress*, London, Heinemann

Pascal, B. (1966), *Pensées*, trans. and intro. by A. J. Krailsheimer, Harmondsworth, Penguin

Parris, M. (1993), 'Genetic Genies Won't Go Back Into The Bottle', *The Times*, 17 July 1993

Pick, D. (1993), *War Machine: The Rationalisation of Slaughter in the Modern Age*, New Haven, Yale University Press

Porter, R. (1990), 'Anatomy of Progress', review of D. Spadafora, *The Idea of Progress in 18th Century Britain*, in *New Statesman and Society*, 27 July 1990

Remarque, E. M. (1963), *All Quiet on the Western Front*, London, Mayflower

Russell, B. (1946), *History of Western Philosophy*, London, George Allen and Unwin

Sanderson, (1969), *An Interpretation of the Political Ideas of Marx and Engels*, London, Longman

Schapiro, J. S. (1934), *Condorcet and the Rise of Liberalism*, New York, Harcourt, Brace

Spencer, H. (1954), *Social Statics: The Conditions of Human Happiness Specified, and the First of Them Developed*, New York, Robert Schalkenbach Foundation

Thurow, L. (1985), *The Zero-Sum Solution*, New York, Simon and Schuster

Times (1993), 'Genes and the Man', 17 July 1993

Wilkie, T. (1993a), *Perilous Knowledge: The Human Genome Project and Its Implications*, London, Faber and Faber

— (1993b), 'Holy Grail or Poisoned Chalice?', *The Independent*, 1 June 1993

Index